Breaking Hearts

Other Books by Roy F. Baumeister

Identity: Cultural Change and the Struggle for Self (1986)

Public Self and Private Self (1986) (Edited)

Masochism and the Self (1989)

Meanings of Life (1991)

Escaping the Self: Alcoholism, Spirituality, Masochism, and Other Flights from the Burden of Selfhood (1991)

BREAKING HEARTS
The Two Sides of Unrequited Love

ROY F. BAUMEISTER
SARA R. WOTMAN

The Guilford Press
New York and London

© 1992 The Guilford Press
A Division of Guilford Publications, Inc.
72 Spring Street, New York, NY 10012

Printed in the United States of America

This book is printed on acid-free paper.

Last digit is print number: 9   8   7   6   5   4   3   2   1

Library of Congress Cataloging-in-Publication Data

Baumeister, Roy F.
    Breaking hearts : the two sides of unrequited love / Roy F.
Baumeister, Sara R. Wotman
       p.   cm. — (Emotions and social behavior)
    Includes bibliographical references and index.
    ISBN 0-89862-543-2   ISBN 0-89862-154-2 (pbk.)
    1. Unrequited love.   2. Unrequited love—Case studies.
I. Wotman, Sara R.   II. Title.   III. Series.
    [DNLM: 1. Interpersonal Relations.   2. Love.   3. Rejection
(Psychology)   BF 575.L8 B347b]
BF575.U57B38   1992
152.4'1—dc20
DNLM/DLC
for Library of Congress 92-1418
                                      CIP

*There is hardly any activity, any enterprise, which
is started with such tremendous hopes and expectations and yet which fails so regularly as love.*
—ERICH FROMM

"I'm not obnoxious. I'm just eager to go out with you. That's a big difference."
—JOHNNY (played by Al Pacino in the film *Frankie and Johnny*)

*We are never so defenceless against suffering as
when we love, never so helplessly unhappy as
when we have lost our loved object or its love.*
—SIGMUND FREUD

*I have so much in me, and the feeling for her absorbs it all; I have so much,
and without her it all comes to nothing.*
—GOETHE *(Sorrows of Young Werther)*

*Love seeketh only Self to please,
To bind another to Its delight,
Joys in another's loss of ease,
And builds a Hell in Heaven's despite.*
—WILLIAM BLAKE

"Nothing takes the taste out of peanut butter quite like unrequited love."
—CHARLIE BROWN (Charles Schultz)

*I hold it true, whate'er befall;
I feel it, when I sorrow most
'Tis better to have loved and lost
Than never to have loved at all.*
—ALFRED LORD TENNYSON

*"I'm not saying it didn't happen. But you'd think if it did, I would have
remembered the first four or five hours."*
—WILLIE NELSON (commenting in response to a woman
who claims she performed acrobatic sexual acts with
him for nine hours straight; *Newsweek*, Feb. 25, 1991)

*To love and win is the best thing;
to love and lose the next best.*
—THACKERAY

Emotions and Social Behavior

Series Editor: PETER SALOVEY, *Yale University*

Contents

Breaking Hearts

The Psychology
of Heartbreak

Love is perhaps the supreme and most popular model of fulfillment in our culture. From sexual bliss, to the mother–child bond, to the spiritual link between human beings and God, images of love pervade our culture's attempts to understand the highest forms of happiness that are available to mankind. Romantic, passionate love between a man and a woman is regarded as one of the most important foundations of a happy life.

We all know how romantic love is supposed to proceed. One is overcome with attraction to someone special, feels rushes of emotion and sexual desire, becomes awkward and preoccupied, tries to approach the person. Ideally, the other person soon begins to feel the same way. Some people prefer to imagine love at first sight, while others enjoy the gradual escalation of attraction. The presence of the other brings joy and excitement. The couple spends more and more time together, sharing thoughts and feelings, neglecting other concerns and relationships, and their world feels thoroughly transformed by the discovery of this overriding need and this overpowering happiness. During the peak of this experience, their attention is focused mainly on each other, and they find an intimate rapport that is scarcely imaginable in other relationships. They celebrate their love with sexual union and mutual commitment to each other.

Such is the dream of love, and there is good reason to think that many people in our society do actually have experiences that conform more or less closely to it. Passionate, mutual love probably does make more people feel good, and to a more intense degree, than any other natural or artificial means. Only the most cynical or pathetic individuals would rather have a week spent drinking whiskey, or playing video games, or sunbathing, than a week of passionate love.

Sadly, things do not always go so smoothly. Love is not always a cycle of shared, escalating bliss. When love is not mutual—when the pattern of attraction, desire, and need is felt by one person but not returned by the other—then the outcome is far from satisfactory. It is not love itself that brings fulfillment, but the mutuality of love. To love alone does not cause joy and bliss. Our culture envies and indulges young lovers, but it pities people who love without being loved in return. Love is only desirable if it is reciprocated.

The trauma of unrequited love is a source of unending fascination for our culture. Books, movies, songs, and other arts continue to treat the theme of someone who loves without being loved in return. One of the most famous treatments is Goethe's novel *The Sorrows of Young Werther*, sometimes considered to be the first modern novel. It is the story of a young man who falls in love with a woman who is "as good as" engaged to another man, who happens to be out of town. Werther's love blooms rapidly and he is beginning to think that Charlotte loves him too, when the other man, Albert, returns to claim his bride. Werther finds his world turned upside down. Nothing brings him pleasure or consoles him. He struggles futilely to recover by going away, but he soon returns. Charlotte's husband begins to suggest that Werther is spending too much time with her. She tells Werther to stay away for a few days, and he becomes extremely agitated. He returns to her that same night while her husband is away. They converse and read poetry together, gradually becoming more and more intimate. Finally Werther seizes her and kisses her passionately. She responds at first but then pushes him away and, filled with guilt and uncertainty, tells him never to see her again. He leaves and commits suicide, leaving behind a letter declaring his love for her. This novel, based partly on Goethe's own two unrequited love experiences and one of a friend of his, exerted a powerful impact on the public when it was first published. It is even said to have inspired a wave of copycat suicides among other hapless lovers. All over Europe, young victims of heartbreak dressed themselves in Werther's style and killed themselves, sometimes clutching a copy of the book in their dying hands.

Love can be compared to a strong drug that transports people to extraordinary, ecstatic states, and in the process tends to be habit-forming. But like many powerful drugs, love holds the possibilities of agony and misery. Like an addict deprived of his fix, the would-be lover faces a brutal and painful process of adjusting to deprivation and learning to stop needing something around which his life has revolved. Sometimes, as in the case of Werther, the adjustment cannot be made, and the withdrawal process is fatal.

And what of the reluctant object of these unwanted affections? Our culture has devoted a great deal of time to exploring the feelings and perspectives of lovers, requited and unrequited. But the figure of the rejector remains an enigma. It is often seen mainly through the eyes of the would-be lover, as in Goethe's novel, which tells the story by means of letters written by Werther and thus depicts Charlotte only as he sees her. What is it like to be loved by someone without being able to return those feelings? The stereotypes offer a variety of un-savory images: the aloof, casual heartbreaker; the manipulative teaser; the exploitative egotist; the cunning seducer. Few people, however, regard themselves as fitting those stereotypes. Although unrequited love always involves both a would-be lover and a beloved but rejecting target of those futile affections, only the would-be lover's story is generally told. In other words, there are two sides to unrequited love, but only one of them is familiar. A major goal of this book is to provide a careful hearing to the rejector.

Let us consider one example—and, because fictional portrayals are scarce and misleading, it will be a true story (except for the names, which are altered throughout this book to protect the anonymity of the people involved). Jessica made friends with several other college students early in the year. One of them, Ben, struck her as particularly insecure despite his adamant nonconformist attitudes, which were typical of students at the art institute where he was enrolled. Still, Jessica and Ben became good friends. During the fall semester, her roommate attempted suicide, and Ben helped Jessica get through that difficult period. They became best friends, although Jessica had no romantic feelings for Ben.

Ben, however, wanted to move from best friend to boyfriend. He began telling Jessica that he loved her. She told him not to say that. He would compliment her on her taste, her intelligence, and her beauty. Jessica was flattered and appreciated the way he made her feel about herself, but she was still romantically involved with a man who lived in another state and did not want to reciprocate Ben's feelings. Gradually she began to feel uncomfortable in Ben's presence and to wish he would leave her alone. In contrast to their earlier friendship, "I didn't enjoy his company at all any more," she recalled later.

Ben sensed her increasing withdrawal from him, and this made him frantic. He became more insistent, telling her how much he cared for her and how he loved her. Jessica tried to be gentle with him, on account of their previous friendship, but she was rapidly reaching the end of her patience. She felt that his pursuit of her was intrusive and disturbing, and she later said that his attentions were beginning to interfere with her studies. She thought it insensitive of him not to care about affecting her work, but his own desire and heartbreak were apparently far more compelling to him than her need to get her assignments completed. He began to tell her he was feeling suicidal, which upset her and made her feel somewhat guilty, even though she also saw it as a cheap, manipulative ploy.

Finally she told him clearly and bluntly (as she recalls it) that she did not want to see him any more, that they would not be lovers, and that they could no longer even be friends. He did not take it well but instead cried and cried and begged her to love him. Jessica remained firm. She hoped that that would be sufficient to get rid of him, but it wasn't. If she refused to talk to him, he would consult her friends and ask them for information about her. He seemed irrational, desperate, asking her friends "When will Jessica love me? When will she stop loving [the other boyfriend]?" By this time she had lost all liking for him and even all respect. "The mere thought or sight of him makes me absolutely nauseous," she wrote, describing her feelings toward Ben at the end of this ordeal.

Gradually Ben began to leave her alone, but his own efforts to deal with his heartbreak caused Jessica further annoyance. She recorded how he, being an art student, painted her from memory in a way that caused her acute embarrassment: " . . . He put me in this bizarre painting next to naked men and ladies French-kissing with statues. YUCK!" Many rejectors have found that in one way or another the process of extricating themselves from unwanted attentions was stressful, troublesome, and ultimately disturbing to the way they liked to regard themselves. Recalling these events some months later, Jessica emphatically repeated that the entire episode made her sick. She said she now found it hard to believe she and Ben had ever been friends, for she was so thoroughly disgusted with him. He had gone from being her best friend to being someone whose company she could not stand.

Jessica's experience was not unlike what many people go through when they find themselves the target of unrequited love. At first she was flattered by it, and she struggled to find a way to reject Ben without being cruel. As time wore on, she found his attentions to be more and more of a problem. Ben's love for her intruded on her life and caused her a broad range of emotional distress, and it began to interfere with her other friendships and relationships as well as with her work. By the end she felt only loathing for the man who loved her, and she was desperate to find an effective way to get him to leave her alone. The friendship, the care, the flattery, the gratitude were mostly forgotten, and all she could think of was how to extricate herself from this supremely unpleasant situation.

This book will attempt to depict what the rejector experiences, as well as what the aspiring lover experiences, in unrequited love. Our culture has focused a great deal of attention on the heartbroken lover, but for every broken heart there is a heartbreaker. And it is not simply the case that there exist a handful of beautiful but cruel and callous individuals who are responsible for all the broken hearts. In the research for this book, nearly everyone who was asked was able to describe an experience in which he or she failed to reciprocate someone else's romantic attraction. Just as we have all had our hearts broken at one time or another, we are also all heartbreakers. People may be reluctant to admit this side of themselves, but it does exist. The experience of being a heartbreaker is in some ways a more compelling puzzle than that of the heartbroken.

Definition and Scope

Unrequited love refers to romantic, passionate love that is felt by one person toward another person who feels substantially less attraction toward the lover. It is not necessary that the object of unrequited love be thoroughly indifferent (or be negative and hostile, the way Jessica eventually felt toward Ben), for as we will see many rejectors do feel some friendship and liking for their admirers. But the discrepancy between liking and loving is apparent to all, and people in love typically find it quite inadequate to hear that the other likes them but fails to love them.

We shall also use the term "love" broadly, referring to any strong romantic attraction. As long as there is the desire for some exclusive, physically intimate and affectionate pairing with the person, it falls within our sphere of interest, even though some people might have preferred more stringent criteria for love. Still, love does differ from friendship in several ways, particularly including the wish for physical or sexual contact.

In particular, it is worth noting that our broad definition of love does generally invoke strong emotion, whether or not one calls it "love." Many people in our research did not spontaneously use the word "love" to describe their feelings (although many did use it), but instead they used other terms to indicate feelings of longing and preoccupation. That powerful romantic attraction is the topic of our concern.

For example, consider the case of one young man who never said he loved the woman and indeed knew that a relationship was unlikely, because the woman was romantically involved with a friend of his. He kept his feelings to himself because of her prior involvement, but there was no doubting the powerful effect she had on him. "Jackie was a beautiful girl—my age with long, blonde hair, very intelligent with a radiant smile and a fantastic physique," he wrote of her. "She had danced for years, and she was very gifted athletically."

He gradually became obsessed with sexual thoughts about her. "Jackie told me once that she could pull her foot straight up over her head from a standing position. The thought haunted me, arousing me every time. I fantasized about her putting on a display of her flexibility for me privately . . . " Thus, a casual remark by her formed the basis for his fantasies for many months, during which he had no interest in other women or other relationships. Looking back, he seriously regretted never having declared his feelings for her or made an effort to win her, and he particularly recalled one occasion when he was alone with her, with an opportunity to reveal his feelings, but he had failed to take the initiative. Was this love? Perhaps not in a strict or limited sense of the word, but it is clear that he had strong, exclusive feelings of attraction for her, that he desired a relationship, and that he suffered over the fact that no romance ever bloomed between them. For our purposes, such cases do qualify as unrequited love.

Unrequited love is a relationship that fails to form. One person wants a romantic attachment in the way his or her culture defines it—in our society, that means a high degree of intimacy, physical and sexual expression (although not necessarily involving a full range of sexual activities), and some mutual commitment to reserve certain parts of one's life and one's psyche to be shared only with one's beloved. The other person does not want this. Unrequited love is thus a rejection of an opportunity, an invitation, for romantic attachment.

Unrequited love therefore belongs to the class of relationship failures that includes couples who break up or fail to bond because of family pressures, geographical separation, and religious differences. What sets unrequited love apart from these other relationship failures is that the relationship is prevented, not by external factors, but by the decision and preference of one person in the relationship. The rejector does not desire the relationship.

It is also crucial to realize that unrequited love does not entail that the rejector never felt romantically attracted to the lover. In many cases, people have some mutual attraction and start dating, but then their emotional trajectories diverge. One begins to feel more deeply and to desire a more intimate, exclusive relationship, while the other's feelings fail to develop. These cases may be especially hard for the would-be lovers, for they know that there was some mutual attraction and they felt that a relationship was in the process of building, and then mysteriously the other simply called a halt and departed.

Our effort will be to understand what is involved in unrequited love—to learn about particular problems and conflicts, to form some model of the typical course of events, to find out some of the aftereffects, and above all to contrast the subjective experiences of the rejector and the would-be lover. We shall try to understand what it is like to love someone who does not return that love, and to understand what it is like to be loved in vain.

Why Is Unrequited Love Interesting?

Before leaping into our study, it is worth pausing to consider what one might hope to learn from unrequited love. There are ample reasons for studying unrequited love. First and foremost, of course, is the inherent interest in a powerful and extraordinary phenomenon that most people experience and that may shape their further attitudes about love, intimacy, self-worth, and members of the opposite sex.[1]

The power and impact of the experience of unrequited love is underscored by some of its effects on people. In one of the few previous research studies to deal with unrequited love, Smith and Hoklund (1988) established several links between love and other important variables. When love is successful and reciprocal, people appear to benefit from it. Participants in the study who enjoyed positive, reciprocal love relationships showed good general health (better than people who were not in love), elevated self-confidence, and less activity by natural killer (NK) cells in the immune system, a pattern that is apparently linked to good health. Indeed, people who enjoyed mutual and reciprocal love reported unusually long times since they had last had a sore throat, a cold, or a hangover. Love, it would appear, is good for you—if the love is mutual.

Unrequited love, however, had effects that differed substantially from the effects of reciprocal love. The positive effects of love on health and the immune system were missing among people whose love was not mutual. Moreover, people experiencing unrequited love showed higher levels of depression and tension, and they were significantly more likely to report a recent hangover than other people. Thus, once again, love is only beneficial if it is mutual, and unrequited love seems to be linked to some pathological patterns that are not found with reciprocal love.

The study of close relationships provides one context in which the importance of unrequited love is apparent. Psychologists have devoted considerable effort to learning about how relationships begin (e.g., Berscheid & Walster, 1978; Byrne, 1971; Rosenbaum, 1986; Snyder & Simpson, 1984), are maintained (e.g., Levenson, & Gottman, 1985; Rusbult, 1980, 1983; Tyler & Sears, 1977), and break apart (e.g., Duck, 1982a, 1982b; Hill, Rubin, & Peplau, 1976; Rodin, 1982; Simpson, 1987), along with the factors that differentiate happy from distressed relationships (e.g., Fincham, Beach, & Baucom, 1987; Holtzworth-Munroe & Jacobson, 1985). Unrequited love sheds new light on relationships, for in unrequited love, typically, one person wants a relationship to grow and flourish yet this fails to happen. Unrequited love can be considered a species of relationship failure.

Relationship failure is particularly interesting in the context of attachment theory and other assertions that people fundamentally, basically, crave social relationships with others. If human beings do have a biologically based need for social attachment, why do people reject romantic love? If someone comes to you with an offer of intimacy, why might you refuse that person? We shall examine this paradox in more detail in the next chapter, but it is relevant here as one of the most theoretically interesting features of unrequited love. Refusing love would seem to go against human nature, but people clearly do refuse love.

Unrequited love also calls attention to the interpersonal vulnerability that goes with forming close relationships. The importance of vulnerability in love was shown by Dion and Dion (1975), who showed that people low in defensiveness had more experiences of love than people high in defensiveness. Defensive people are less willing than others to make themselves vulnerable. As a result they may stay relatively safe from the dangers of unrequited love, but they may also miss out on the satisfactions of successful, mutual romantic love.

Thus, to love is to take a risk: One must expose oneself to the chance of being hurt. Unrequited love shows the dimensions of this risk. Often people may be fortunate enough to avoid this painful, disappointing outcome, but along the way most people sooner or later become acquainted with it.

The nature of the risk derives from the interpersonal nature of emotion. Social psychologists have gradually developed a good grasp of some key aspects of emotion. They have recognized that emotion is both a state of action readiness (such as when fear makes the person run away from danger) and of evaluation (such as when joy involves an appraisal of favorable circumstances) (Frijda, 1986; Frijda, Kuipers, & ter Shure, 1989). But, ironically, social psychologists have been slower to appreciate fully the interpersonal dimensions of emotion. Often one person's emotional state depends on the actions and decisions of someone else. Like jealousy, anger, envy, desire for revenge, and others, unrequited love immediately places emotion in an interpersonal context. The series of books to which this volume belongs is aimed at addressing the interpersonal nature of emotion, and it represents an important departure from the long tradition of theorizing about emotion in terms of only the individual psyche.

One further reason for special interest in unrequited love is the broad importance of love in our culture. As noted at the beginning of this chapter, love pervades our culture's ideas about human fulfillment, from the spiritual to the hedonistic and carnal. Love is also one of the most important values that our culture embraces, able to give purpose and meaning to life and to justify a wide variety of actions (Baumeister, 1991). This broad importance of love makes unrequited love especially difficult. The personal disappointment and emotional trauma are augmented by a sense that one has failed in one of life's most important spheres. To fail at love strikes at the core of one's being as a man or woman. Likewise, to refuse love is to turn one's back on something everyone is supposed to want.

How Often Does This Happen?

How common is unrequited love? No single answer can be given, because undoubtedly unrequited love happens to some people more than others. We can, however, suggest some broad outlines. In our research, we chose to focus on a sample of people who seemed likely to have relatively frequent experiences of unrequited love, namely young, unmarried adults who were students at a coeducational university. People at this stage of life are often centrally concerned with forming romantic attachments, and so one could expect a fair number of romantic failures to be found.

We surveyed upper-level students about the frequency of their experiences of unrequited love (see Baumeister, Wotman, & Stillwell, in press). It appears that, by the early 20s, nearly everyone has had at least one experience on each side of unrequited love; only about one person out of every twenty said it had never happened to him or her. It is thus fair to describe unrequited love as something that happens to almost everyone sooner or later.

Not all experiences are powerful, however. According to our survey, the average 21-year-old student has had about one powerful experience of loving someone who did not return that love during the past five years. Along with this one powerful experience, the average person had two moderately strong experiences and three or four casual attractions or passing crushes. Combining these, one may say that a young single adult feels an attraction toward someone who does not return the feelings a little more often than once per year, although the majority of these experiences are of a minor nature.

It was a little trickier to ask about how often people are on the receiving end of unrequited love, because often one may not be certain that someone feels that attraction. We asked people to count separately the episodes about which they were certain and the ones they merely suspected. Within the last five years, the average person had had nearly two powerful experiences in which someone was attracted to him or her but the person did not return those feelings. They also reported about two more experiences of moderate intensity and nearly three passing attractions or casual crushes. Adding in the "merely suspected" cases roughly doubled all these numbers.

When one adds all these numbers together, a somewhat surprising result emerges: People report being loved more than they report loving. That is, people reported fewer experiences of being a would-be lover during the past five years than experiences of being a rejector. Because every episode involves one of each, one would expect the totals to come out approximately equal, but instead there was a surplus of rejector experiences. Part of this difference may be explained as resulting from exaggerating memory to boost one's self-esteem, because people want to think of themselves as lovable and desirable and so may be more willing to remember incidents that proved their desirability than incidents of being rejected and unwanted. A small part of this difference may, however, be due to the fact that our sample contained slightly more women than men. This brings up the touchy issue of sex differences.

We did not set up our study to look for differences between men and women. One might think that men and women would have radically different experiences in love and views about love, but past research has suggested that men and women are more similar than different in regard to romantic love (Hatfield & Sprecher, 1986; Hazan & Shaver, 1987; Maroldo, 1982; Rubin, 1970; Smith & Hoklund, 1988). We did, however, keep an eye open for such differences. Our sample contained both men and women, and by and large they told quite similar stories. Throughout the book we have noted an occasional issue where gender roles seem to make a difference, although for the most part these differences were negligible.

Still, there were some. One difference was in the simple frequency of experiences. Females had more experiences in the rejector role, whereas males had more experiences as would-be lovers. This finding fits previous evidence that females are more likely to refuse an invitation for a date, whereas males are more likely to have been refused (Folkes, 1982). More broadly, Hill, Rubin, and Peplau (1976) suggested that males fall in love more easily than females, and females fall out of love more readily than males. Our findings fit that view, especially if one expands the idea of "falling out of love" to encompass "refusing love."

Methods Used in This Work

Undoubtedly one reason psychologists have so little knowledge about unrequited love is that it is difficult to study. Laboratory methods, the mainstream core of social psychology, are largely useless here, for it is neither practically viable nor ethically acceptable to make laboratory subjects feel the unhappy emotional investment that is the defining feature of unrequited love. Clinical observation is not an effective means for studying unrequited love, because it is not, fundamentally, a clinical phenomenon (that is, unrequited love is not peculiar to clinically abnormal populations but rather is found throughout the normal and healthy population). The methods that have recently been developed for studying close relationships are likewise not helpful, because the two people are rarely to be found as a couple and would not likely want to take part in a study together, unlike married couples.

In view of these obstacles, we proceeded by collecting first-person accounts of experiences of unrequited love. This technique of using autobiographical narratives has proven useful in studying several phenomena that do not lend themselves to laboratory study, such as divorce and romantic breakup (Harvey, Flanary, & Morgan, 1988; Harvey, Weber, Galvin, Huszti, & Garnick, 1986; Vaughan, 1986), sexual masochism (Baumeister, 1988a, 1988b, 1989), marital disagreements (Ross & Holmberg, 1990), guilt (McGraw, 1987; Tangney, 1991), motivational themes in the life course (McAdams, 1985; also Kaufman, 1986), the interpersonal genesis of anger (Baumeister, Stillwell, & Wotman, 1990), and the appeal of criminal lifestyles (Katz, 1988). The advantages and limitations of this technique have received increasing attention in recent years, reflecting its rising importance (see Banaji & Crowder, 1989; Baumeister & Stillwell, 1992; Gergen & Gergen, 1988; Harvey, Weber, & Orbuch, 1990; Ross, 1988).

What we did was to ask people to write a story about an important experience in which they loved someone who did not return their feelings—and to write a story in which someone loved them but whose feelings they did not reciprocate. In that fashion we assembled a first sample of 134 stories that could be broken down into two sets, one consisting of stories told from the point of view of the rejector, the other set from the point of view of the would-be lover. Then we coded the content of these stories for a variety of features. The core of our work involves statistical comparisons between the two sets of stories.

For example, we coded each story for whether it contained any reference to unpleasant emotional states. We then computed the proportion of would-be lovers' stories that mentioned unpleasant emotional states (44%) and the proportion of rejectors' stories that mentioned them (70%). The chi-square technique was used to assess whether the difference between 44% and 70% was significant, that is, reflecting a real difference as opposed to mere chance variation. In this particular analysis, we were able to conclude with 99% confidence that the difference was real—in other words, it does appear quite certain that rejectors were significantly more likely than would-be lovers to refer to unpleasant emotion when describing an experience of unrequited love. (Chapter 3 will cover this finding along with other issues of emotion.) Because this book is intended for a broader audience, the statistics will not be covered in the text, but professionals with an interest in such material can find them in the Appendix.

It is important to note that all our research subjects were asked to contribute one story from each perspective. Thus, when we compare rejectors and would-be lovers, we are not comparing different kinds of people. Our results refer to the same people in different roles. It is the role, not the individual's personality, that sets the patterns that emerge in our results. Thus, the conclusions tell what it is like for *anyone* to be a rejector or a would-be lover.

Using this technique sacrifices several advantages of the experimental method, such as close control over the experience and the ability to screen out other variables. On the other hand, it has several advantages, including realism: These are real experiences from people's actual lives, rather than simulations set up in the laboratory.

We have also conducted a follow-up study with a second sample of stories (see Baumeister, Wotman, & Stillwell, in press). In this, we had people make judgments themselves about their stories, rather than relying on codings. This follow-up study largely confirmed the findings of our main research, although it also added a few new twists and insights.

One area where our method sacrifices some degree of experimental control is in the selection of which experience to relate. Many people have presumably had more than one experience of unrequited love. Ideally, we would have liked to obtain accounts from the two people involved in the same incident. This, unfortunately, is rarely possible. Even in studying issues of divorce it is often not possible for researchers to obtain accounts from people on both sides. Diane Vaughan (1986), for example, interviewed people about their experiences with divorce and romantic breakup, but when she asked them if they would consent to allow her to interview the former spouse, many of them responded with a resounding "No!" Our investigation therefore relied on having people choose an especially important and preferably recent experience with unrequited love. Would-be lovers and rejectors were telling stories about the same kind of episode, but they were not describing exactly the same episodes. One cannot therefore rule out the possibility that some results were affected by which story people chose to tell, especially among people who have had many recent experiences of unrequited love.

One must also consider the issue of *whose* stories to collect. Is unrequited love experienced differently at different ages or by people in different cultural or subcultural groups? We suspect that heartbreak is more similar than different across the span of human experience, but our data do not permit such comparisons. For better or worse, we collected our accounts from a sample of people for whom unrequited love is probably a current and pervasive concern, namely upper-level university students, most of whom were in their early 20s (although some were in their 30s and 40s). Psychology researchers tend to rely heavily on university students as research subjects in general, partly because they are available and willing. With unrequited love, they form a group of particular interest, because unrequited love is probably more common among college students than in any other group, and so they represent a promising source of recent, fresh, and compelling accounts of the phenomenon we wanted to study. College students are typically young, unmarried adults, and as such they may be expected to be having a high frequency of incipient romantic relationships, including unrequited love.

Our selection of this sample probably means that most experiences will tend to have been recent, and it is plausible that when someone recalls heartbreak across several decades the story may have changed in a variety of subtle ways. The need to restore one's self-esteem after being rejected, for example, may be fresh among our sample of young people who are still smarting from the humiliation, but a rejection may cease to threaten one's ego after twenty years full of career success and happy marriage. In our view, this is all the more reason to use students, for whom the experiences are recent, but one should be cautious about generalizing to all memories of heartbreak.

The age of our sample also brings up one issue we touched on earlier in this chapter, namely the stringency of the criteria one uses for love. In our sample, many of the stories clearly referred to powerful and lasting attachments that caused lasting trauma and heartbreak. Others, however, referred to adolescent crushes and might be described by some people as "infatuation" or "puppy love." We asked people to describe their most important and powerful experiences, but beyond that instruction we did nothing to impose our own definition of love on their experiences. In short, our data contain both major passionate love and adolescent crushes, and if future research should reveal that those two phenomena operate on radically different principles, then one would have to be extra careful in drawing conclusions from our data. But if the difference between a futile crush and a hopeless love is merely a matter of degree, then there is no problem, and we have operated with that as a working assumption.

One area where college students may differ from other parts of the population concerns sex roles and differences. The liberal and progressive atmosphere that prevails at many universities undoubtedly operates to place them in the vanguard of trends toward altering and modernizing relations between the sexes. Men and women probably interact on different terms in universities than outside them, to some degree.

For example, one might have expected substantial differences between men and women in how to handle unrequited love. Tradition has assigned men the role of initiating romantic advances and women the role of waiting passively until they are approached. Because of this, men might have had an easier time knowing how to act as aspiring lovers, and women might have been more familiar with the rejector's role. Our sample of modern university students did not conform to this pattern, however. Both men's and women's accounts referred to women taking the romantic initiative, and both referred also to waiting passively for a sign or an approach from the other person. Few, if any, of our subjects seem to have felt prohibited from taking any action on the basis of their romantic feelings. Our results should not therefore be generalized to enforcedly passive populations, including women in the traditional role. It is plausible that older generations, such as today's elderly, would describe experiences of unrequited love in ways quite different from what we found, particularly in regard to women feeling helpless to do anything to bring about the relationship they desire.

Conclusion

One of life's marvels is the capacity of two people to be overcome with passionate longing for each other, a state that is often characterized by bliss, intimacy, physical desire, and mutual fascination. Passionate love has taken its place as one of our culture's supreme ideals of human fulfillment. Often, however, the passionate longing strikes only one member of the pair, while the other is decidedly uninterested in the experience of mutuality so ardently desired by the would-be lover. Such unrequited love has become recognized by our culture as a common cause of great anguish.

This book reports our investigation into unrequited love. We have collected a large number of first-person accounts of personal experiences of heartbreak, and we will proceed by contrasting the experiences of would-be lovers with those of rejectors.

The rejector's experience is of particular interest in this work because it has been shrouded in neglect and mystery. We shall seek to make clear what it is like to be the target of unwanted romantic affections, by relying on people's firsthand accounts of what they did and felt when they found themselves in such a situation.

Note

1. For the sake of stylistic convenience, and consistent with the majority of our data, we have written this work as if each couple contains one member of each sex, but of course many romantic attractions do arise between members of the same sex. As we shall argue, most of our discussion would apply just as well to homosexual as to heterosexual attractions, although there are some additional issues that arise to complicate homosexual attractions.

T·W·O

Perspectives on Unrequited Love

Among the great and important love stories of history, the story of Nicholas and Alexandra is fascinating for several reasons, one of which is its portrayal of unrequited love. Nicholas was the heir to the crown of Russia as the 19th century drew to a close. As was customary, his parents shopped around for a mate for him who would enhance the glory and political situation of Russia. But at age sixteen, in St. Petersburg, he met and fell in love with a beautiful princess from Germany who was living in England at the court of her grandmother, Queen Victoria. Although separated by thousands of miles, huge cultural gaps, and strong family pressures against the union, he was determined to win her heart.

Alexandra was less than captivated by Nicholas. He was a little dull and frivolous, and Moscow was not exactly considered a desirable spot. Her prospects for becoming empress of Russia were appealing in some respects, but Russia was regarded as backward, primitive, and unfashionable. Its climate was harsh and oppressive, and it was far removed from the exciting centers of Europe. Alexandra was also reluctant to convert to the Russian Orthodox church, which as empress would be necessary for her.

A fair amount of time passed with his love unrequited. Things finally came to a head in 1892, when he was 24 and had loved her already for eight years. With his family starting to prod him toward another match, he determined to make another all-out effort to win her. Then catastrophe struck: He received a letter from her saying that she had firmly decided not to marry him and requesting that they break off all contact with each other. It was over.

Nicholas did not give up. He left the Russian capital at once, traveling through rough territory and difficult conditions all the way across Europe to see her. He arrived in London somewhat the worse for wear but with a firm resolve to win the woman he loved. He courted her passionately and persistently. She finally agreed to become his bride. They were married in 1894, shortly after Nicholas's father had died. The young couple became Czar and Czarina of the Russian empire.

At that time, it was not uncommon for royalty to feel distant from their spouses or to regard their spouses with indifference or even dislike. For example, their neighbor, the Emperor Franz Josef of Austria-Hungary rarely saw his wife, for she was most often to be found traveling around Europe and spending money, while he stayed home to run the country. Nicholas and Alexandra, however, were devoted to each other. Their diary entries spoke of unbelievable happiness, of thankfulness for the great blessing of their togetherness, and of the profound depth of their mutual love.

Alexandra bore Nicholas five children and he was never happier than when at home with them. Some historians think that the Russian empire suffered because he preferred spending much of his time with his beloved wife and children rather than attending to affairs of state. When they had to be apart, such as when Nicholas was commanding the armed forces during the Great War, they wrote each other frequently and pined to be reunited. In general, they remained passionately attached to each other and spent as much time together as they possibly could throughout their married life. Despite Alexandra's initial disapproval and rejection of Nicholas, their love was mutual and deep, and they lived together more or less happily ever after—at least until the Russian Revolution, during which they were gradually converted from monarchs to prisoners and eventually were executed. One may, perhaps, regard the manner of their deaths—awakened in the middle of the night by Communist guards, told to dress, taken down to the basement, and, after a hasty announcement, clumsily murdered along with their children, a few servants and friends, and their pet dog—as unromantic, or as merely symbolic of the sad fate of the milieu of princesses and castles in this harsh totalitarian century. But at least it has the romantic touch of allowing the two lovers to die on the same day and in the same fashion, and together.

For our purposes, the important part of the story of Nicholas and Alexandra (here based on Taylor, 1963) is not its end but its beginning. The context for unrequited love is successful, mutual love. Unrequited love is felt as a contrast to what somehow *ought* to be there, which is true mutual romantic passion. Moreover, when love is unrequited, there are strong beliefs and compelling models for one to keep trying. The popularity of stories like Nicholas and Alexandra's is attributable in part to the successful outcome despite the initial rejection and other obstacles. Alexandra had initially felt attracted to him, but she didn't want to marry him and had even written him a letter to say good-bye forever. Despite these firm and clear messages, he persisted, and when he finally won her she came to love him just as strongly as he loved her. Had he given up and taken her at her word, the great love of their two lives would never have arisen.

It will be necessary to keep such models in mind when examining what people experience in connection with unrequited love. What must two people think when they find themselves on opposite sides of an unreciprocated passion? To the would-be lover, it is clear that one must persist and strive despite setbacks. Even if one's beloved is unresponsive, perhaps some great effort—comparable to traveling across an entire continent on short notice in desperation—will finally succeed. One must never allow oneself to be discouraged by the other's unwillingness, lest *both* people be deprived of a supreme love. Meanwhile, the rejector must wonder if he or she will indeed come to love the other in return. For rarely is one loved by someone whom one hates or despises; usually there is some degree of positive feeling toward the other. It is hard for the lover to know whether these unspectacular feelings might someday blossom into a devoted love like Alexandra's.

The story of Nicholas and Alexandra also offers an ominous hint about another problem for the rejector. Just as Nicholas disregarded Alexandra's rejections, so do many aspiring lovers in today's United States disregard the rejections of their intended partners. That is what the culture teaches, that is what the great love stories show, and so aspiring lovers feel quite justified in persisting. The problem is that this pattern leaves the rejector in an almost helpless situation. Alexandra came around to love Nicholas, but many people *don't* end up reciprocating the other's love, and in those cases they find it painfully unpleasant and remarkably difficult to get rid of the other person. The example of Jessica in Chapter 1 is important to keep in mind as a counterweight to such romantic successes as Nicholas and Alexandra's. We may share Alexandra's joy that Nicholas persisted despite her rejection. But when Jessica's admirer persisted despite her rejection, she felt helpless, frantic, and hounded.

In this chapter we will examine a series of theoretical perspectives that will be useful for studying unrequited love. A logical place to start would be with the theories that being loved is the key to human fulfillment or, alternatively, that giving love is the key; unrequited love suggests that perhaps it is the *mutuality* of love that is crucial, and giving or receiving alone is not only inadequate but sometimes very miserable. Second, attachment theory suggests that people are programmed to form and maintain interpersonal relationships, and so the rejector's role goes against human nature. Rejectors must therefore struggle with their own emotional turmoil arising from violating deeply rooted human tendencies—while they are also struggling with their would-be lovers.

Why Does Unrequited Love Occur?

Let us begin with the most basic of questions, namely: How can unrequited love arise? One might think the answer is simple, for love might arise anywhere without being reciprocated. This view is naive, however. Research has confirmed strong tendencies for people to like those who like them (Jones & Wortman, 1973; Kenny & Nasby, 1980). Indeed, upon finding out that someone likes you or thinks very highly of you, it is difficult to avoid feeling a rush of attraction toward that person. Unrequited love thus constitutes an exception to one of the most fundamental processes of attraction, namely that of reciprocity.

It is possible to make a distinction between liking and romantic, sexual attraction, of course. Perhaps sexual attraction does not follow the principle of reciprocation as closely as liking does. Perhaps people simply find themselves sexually drawn to certain partners and not to other partners, and no one knows why and nothing can be done about it. The novelist Somerset Maugham, for example, typically portrayed love in such a fashion, as something that would strike people abruptly and mysteriously and even contrary to their own preferences. His novels treated love almost as if it were a kind of illness or virus that struck randomly. In *Of Human Bondage*, for example, the protagonist wakes up one morning to find himself in love with someone for whom he has little respect or admiration, but he cannot do anything about his predicament. In spite of Philip's dislike of almost everything about Mildred—her thinness, her unhealthy complexion, her vacuous conversation, her odious gentility, and her vulgar little laugh—he lived for the moments when he could be with her. "Philip cursed the fate which chained him to such a woman" (Maugham, 1963, p. 289).

It is plausible that there are mysterious forces that stimulate romantic attractions, if not all-out love. For example, perhaps people are attracted to individuals who remind them of their parents, because of psychophysiological cues (like having a body odor similar to the way Mom smelled) or deep Freudian dynamics (like Oedipal fixations). Naturally such impulses would arise without much guarantee of reciprocation. Still, these processes seem inadequate to provide a broad context for understanding unrequited love.

One important pattern in relationships concerns equity. In an important sense, romantic love is like other relationships in that there is an implicit exchange or bargain involved (Walster, Berscheid, & Walster, 1976). The term "marriage market" accurately conveys some sense of human mating, because people do shop around for a mate, using their own assets such as income and physical attractiveness to attract someone else. The individual assets do not have to match up exactly, but in some sense the total attractiveness has to offer an appealing bargain to each. Thus, for example, elderly celebrities may offer fame and riches in order to attract a partner who is young and physically attractive. Moreover, as a general principle, people tend to be dissatisfied and even distressed if they are in a chronically inequitable relationship (Walster et al., 1976).

As people pair off, fall in love, marry, and settle down, then, there is some process of achieving equity. There is even evidence that within a given dimension, people tend to match up with ones similar to themselves. The tendency for people to marry those similar to themselves in socioeconomic status has been obvious for centuries (e.g., Macfarlane, 1986). Even if one considers only physical attractiveness, people tend to match up with equals. Research confirms that married people tend to be approximately equal to their spouses in attractiveness (Murstein & Christy, 1976), education, and intelligence (Jensen, 1977).

So far, so good. But there is one serious problem. People are not *initially* attracted to those who are simply equal to themselves. In one ambitious early study of equity and matching, researchers assigned a large group of students into randomly matched couples for dates. The researchers predicted that the couples who were most closely matched would enjoy the dates the most, but their predictions and hypotheses were disconfirmed. Instead, they found that people liked the date as a linear function of the partner's attractiveness. The more attractive the partner, the more they liked him or her, and the more they enjoyed the date (Walster, Aronson, Abrahams, & Rottman, 1966). Attraction didn't obey the principles of matching or equity; people simply preferred the most desirable partners.

There is hence a serious discrepancy between romantic attraction and marriage. People feel attracted to and start to fall in love with the most attractive other person they can find, but they end up marrying someone equal to themselves. As a broad generalization it is fair to say that people tend to fall in love with partners equal or superior, but not inferior, to themselves. Consequently, a great many people will become attracted to someone more attractive than themselves, but this more attractive partner is not likely to reciprocate the less attractive one's love. The transition from the pattern of initial attraction to the final, married state will require that some lovers be disappointed along the way.

Thus, we may anticipate that one substantial pattern in unrequited love will involve a mismatch in attractiveness or desirability. The less attractive person may fall in love, but the more attractive person is unlikely to reciprocate these feelings. We shall refer to this path as "falling upward," that is, falling in love with someone who is above oneself in desirability.

To be sure, this perspective suggests that people could spare themselves a fair amount of heartbreak by being realistic and confining their romantic interests to people equal to themselves. This, however, is easier said than done. Romantic love is not known for following the dictates of reasonable choice and rational considerations. Before the modern era, in fact, established wisdom and sound common sense dictated that one should not choose a partner on the basis of romantic love, because love makes it hard to make a rational, appropriate choice of a good mate (Stone, 1977). Being in love was regarded as a kind of aberration or madness, and such a mentally disturbed state is hardly the proper condition for making long-range, important decisions. Even today, many states in the U.S. have laws that prevent people from marrying while intoxicated with alcohol, but they allow and even encourage people to marry while intoxicated by love. The high divorce rate, perhaps, provides a telling judgment on the wisdom and rationality of such decision procedures.

It is possible that the problem does not lie in the ineluctable nature of love itself but rather in the cultural construction of love. Our culture has come to expect rationality and emotionality, head and heart, to be in perennial conflict. At the individual level, many people may believe that suspending rational, realistic calculation is essential to being romantic. But regardless of whether nature or culture is at fault, the result is the same: Love does not obey rational calculation and the dictates of reason, and so the risks of being hurt through love increase.

A second problem with the process of choosing an equally matched mate is that people tend to overrate themselves in many respects (e.g., Taylor & Brown,1988), and so a person may think he or she has a chance whereas the partner (who may also be exaggerating his or her own desirability) sees a wide gap that makes a romantic pairing out of the question. For example, John may be on the whole a little bit less attractive than Mary, but because he tends to overrate his good qualities he may think they are about equal. Mary, in contrast, may see John accurately while exaggerating her own attractiveness, and so she sees John as far inferior to her. Thus, even if both were following the rule of looking for someone equal to themselves, John might still fall into unrequited love.

Western culture has a long tradition of such one-sided, inequitable love. The notion of romantic love has its roots in the medieval traditions of courtly love, and the prototype for such love involved falling upward: Typically, a knight or minor noble would fall in love with a lady of higher status (e.g., de Rougemont, 1956; Tannahill, 1980). As depicted in the songs and poems of the era, this love remained sexually unconsummated (indeed, the ladies in such stories were often already married, although their husbands may have been away on crusade or at war). Some stories went so far as to allow the man to sleep in the same bed with his beloved lady without having sex, because of his high esteem for her and their mutual dedication to chastity and virtue. One suspects that practice may have departed from theory on occasion, of course. (The very existence of chastity belts indicates that departing husbands recognized the possibility that ideals of courtly love might be compromised in the flesh.) What is important, though, is the powerfully appealing image of romantic attraction to someone higher than oneself. In these stories, the male was ennobled by the experience—including the experience of his own suffering. These stories reflect the theme that it is acceptable and even valuable to fall in love with someone of higher status than oneself, even though the ineluctable rules of equity would doom such love to eventual disappointment.

Thus, one path into unrequited love begins with people's tendency to fall in love with people more, but not less, attractive than themselves. The image of falling upward seems to suggest a great danger of a painful crash, and this is apt. When people fall upward, one must expect that the love is unlikely to be reciprocated.

A second path may be through platonic friendship. Perhaps people manage to choose their lovers based on physical attractiveness and manage to find someone roughly equal to themselves, but these same restrictions may not apply to platonic friendship. People will therefore form close friendships with members of the opposite sex who may not be matched in romantic desirability. As the friends spend time together, discuss personal matters and opinions, disclose feelings, and share experiences, they may inevitably begin to develop some degree of intimacy. Intimacy has been called the common core of all love relationships (Sternberg, 1986). Thus, platonic friendship may gradually furnish a foundation for potential romantic love.

The intimacy and mutual liking may encourage one partner to develop romantic feelings for the other. The result may be that one person wants to move to a romantic relationship while the other prefers to remain platonic. Indeed, from reading the stories of unrequited love in our sample, it is clear that many platonic heterosexual friendships do contain a strong undercurrent of romantic attraction, even if only on one side. In the late 1980s, the movie *When Harry Met Sally* sparked debate about whether a man and a woman could maintain a friendship over a long period of time without love or romance or sexuality intruding. The male character in the movie categorically denied that that was possible, although he then proceeded to have an off-and-on friendship with the female character over several years. In the end, though, they did become romantically involved. Our data do not speak definitively to the issue of whether such a platonic friendship is possible. They do indicate, however, that love and romance do intrude in many apparently platonic friendships, and friendly actions often merely disguise a growing interest in romance.

These two scenarios, of falling upward and platonic intimacy, are of course compatible. Unrequited love may especially arise when two people of unequal attractiveness form a strong platonic bond of friendship, and so the less attractive one begins to dream that the intimacy can be converted to passionate love.

Nor, of course, are these scenarios intended as exhaustive. There may be many other stimuli that give rise to one-sided romantic love, as we suggested earlier in this section. It is even plausible that people may occasionally reject partners *more* attractive than themselves, for fear that they could not sustain the other's interest or make a successful relationship. Moreover, once the beginnings of attraction are there, it may develop for a variety of reasons. Abbey (1982), for example, provided evidence that men tend to misinterpret women's friendly behavior as sexually or romantically inviting. While a woman thinks that she is just being cordial by smiling at the man, speaking in friendly way, or responding to his comments, he may think she is being sexually inviting or seductive. He may consequently develop romantic feelings for her while she has never thought of him in that way. Such processes may fan the flames of unrequited love.

It is even possible that people who have had troubled relationships may become ambivalent about intimacy and may retreat from others even as they are pursuing them. The desire for close relationships appears to be universal, but people who have been badly used by significant others may have reason to fear such relationships too. As adults they may tend to move toward others only if they know that the other is not interested, such as the woman in our study who observed that "It seems like when I can have a guy, I don't want him. And when he is not available to me, I want him." Such patterns are probably limited to a minority of neurotic and insecure individuals and to a handful who may have coped badly with past relationship experiences, but they do suggest another possible route into unrequited love. Individuals like this may respond to their conflicting motivations by pursuing impossible relationships, thus protecting themselves from successful attachment and ensuring that their loves will be unrequited.

Interdependence

A useful method of analyzing human relations, developed by Harold Kelley and John Thibaut (e.g., 1978), is called "interdependence theory." The essence of this approach is to consider how each person's possible actions affect both self and other. Thus, one goes through *options* (i.e., possible lines of action) and *outcomes* (i.e., consequences and results) from both sides of the relationship. It is helpful to apply this method to unrequited love.

Before starting, let us review the essence of the situation of unrequited love. One person has feelings of love (or a related form of strong romantic attraction) toward the other, who does not feel the same way toward the first person. Let us assume that both people recognize this discrepancy, and both regard it as an unacceptable way for things to remain. Either the would-be lover must stop loving, or the other must start. The would-be lover may regard the latter as a possible outcome; if he or she can only do the right things, the other will begin to return the love. For the rejector, however, returning the love is probably not seen as a plausible outcome or as a reasonable choice, because people do not believe that they can fall in love at will. (And in the case of "falling upward," rejectors probably tend to regard the would-be lover as being quite unsuitable as a potential romantic partner.)

Now consider the options available to the would-be lover. He or she can either try actively to win the other's love or can keep silent and passive. The first option, of trying to win the other's heart, offers the would-be lover possibilities ranging from ecstatic happiness to humiliating heartbreak (depending on the other's response). To do nothing, to remain silent and passive, leads most likely to disappointment and slow suffering. The main outcome of that approach is the loss of any chance for a mutual, happy love relationship with this potential partner.

Thus, the would-be lover has an active and a passive option. The active one carries a wide range of possible outcomes, from the sublime to the miserable; the passive outcome offers only a bad outcome. Viewed in this way, the most rational course of action for the would-be lover is to try actively to win the other's love, because only that option contains a significant chance of a happy ending. That course of action only loses its appeal when it becomes apparent that the chances of success are negligible or when the potential magnitude of further humiliation and suffering is too large.

How do these same (would-be lover's) options affect the rejector? The active course, of trying to win the rejector's heart, confronts the rejector with a continuing awkward situation. Annoyance and frustration are likely outcomes. Perhaps more important, the would-be lover's advances may put the rejector in the uncomfortable situation of having to inflict emotional pain.

Rejectors may be especially distressed if the would-be lover persists in making such advances after initial rebuffs. In 1991, as we wrote this book, Americans were fascinated by major public spectacles involving allegations of date rape (the trial of William Kennedy Smith) and sexual harassment (the confirmation hearings of Judge Clarence Thomas and the accusations by Professor Anita Hill). These stories suggest the extreme versions of the problems suffered by victims of unwanted, persistent romantic advances. Although they are more severe than the problems reported by most of our respondents, there is a common theme: Many people do feel persecuted, frustrated, and victimized when they are pursued by would-be lovers who refuse to take no for an answer.

The would-be lover's other option was to do nothing and remain passive. If the would-be lover chooses that option, the rejector's outcome is not anything bad, although it is not anything very good either. At best, the rejector may feel some relief when a persistent pursuer finally gives up and further awkward or embarrassing situations are, it is hoped, ended.

Now turn to consider the options that face the rejector. These choices boil down to rejecting the other's advances or playing along with them—the latter would involve spending time, affection, and possibly other resources on the aspiring lover. To illustrate these choices in a microcosm: When someone asks you to go out on a date, you can either go along, or you can refuse. To go along may be mildly unpleasant, because after all one doesn't really want to spend time with the undesired suitor, and so it may be boring or awkward or costly in other minor ways. It also carries a more significant risk, namely that the would-be lover will take one's positive response as an encouraging sign and may start to become more deeply involved, having stronger feelings and *making further demands*, so that the eventual problem of extricating oneself from the situation will be that much more difficult. Playing along is only a short-term solution that in many cases merely postpones the eventual necessity of firmly rejecting the other. The postponement is purchased at a high price if the other feels encouraged, because the eventual rejection will be that much more traumatic and stressful. In a sense, the option of playing along is an illusory (or at best temporary) option, because ultimately the only way to get rid of unwanted romantic advances is to reject them. But at the time, neither the rejector nor the would-be lover may perceive this. The rejector hopes the problem will go away and puts up with mild unpleasantness; the would-be lover gets mild satisfaction of being in the beloved's presence and seeming to have further opportunities to win the beloved's heart.

That brings us to the rejector's other option, which is to clearly and actively reject the other and discourage further advances. Obviously, this option brings intense pain and suffering to the would-be lover. But it is also hard on the rejector. To inflict painful heartbreak and humiliation on someone else is not easy, and having to do so causes many rejectors to suffer guilt, uncertainty, awkwardness, and other forms of distress.

Such, then, are the outlines of interdependence in the situation of unrequited love. The would-be lover can strive to win the other's love or can give up; the rejector can play along or actively rebuff the other. As we have said, for the would-be lover the seemingly rational course of action is to try actively to win the other's affection. For the rejector, the optimal response is to reject the other, but this is sufficiently difficult and unpleasant that many will be tempted to postpone this, to play along and hope the situation goes away by itself.

There is one further, crucial implication of this analysis. *None of the rejector's possible outcomes are good.* The situation holds no promise, no happy endings, no desirable potential for the rejector; at best, the rejector will merely be relieved when it is over. This is quite different from the situation that would-be lovers find themselves in, which contains a wide spectrum of possible outcomes ranging from ecstasy to misery. It may be true that the worst possible outcome in the whole situation is one that faces the would-be lover, namely the possibility of painful and humiliating heartbreak. But this sad possibility is balanced, in the would-be lover's view, by the possibility of a blissful, wonderful, loving relationship just like in the movies and novels. Unlike this wide spectrum of potential, however, the rejector's range of possible outcomes runs from neutral to awful, without offering anything positive.

To put it simply, the would-be lover sees the situation as a high-stakes gamble, where there is a great deal to win or to lose—but the rejector sees it as a no-win proposition, where there is nothing to be gained and there is a real danger of unpleasantness. In that sense, the rejector's situation is worse than the would-be lover's.

One sign of this discrepancy emerged when we surveyed people about their accumulated experiences with unrequited love. Taken together, they said, their experiences as would-be lovers had a significant element of adventure. Their experiences as rejectors, however, lacked this aspect. Apparently, falling in love may be something of an adventure, and even if it turns out badly one can look back on the experience with some positive attitudes because risk is, after all, part of the nature of adventure. But to be loved in vain is not an adventure.

Anyone who has grown up surrounded by our culture's endless treatments of unrequited love is prepared to recognize that there will be unhappy endings, that aspiring lovers are sometimes disappointed and occasionally suffer to the point of depression and suicide. Yet it may be worth the gamble to them, because the chance of love is worth the risk. For the rejector, there is nothing to make it worth while. As we shall see, rejectors end up in many ways having a more negative and unpleasant experience than would-be lovers. The whole episode may seem merely to be futile and unnecessary suffering.

Attachment: The Need to Belong

The human tendency to form relationships is widespread and pervasive. Some psychologists have begun to think about human relationship as a fundamental, biologically programmed need. Perhaps the best-know among these is John Bowlby (1969, 1973), who laid the foundations of *attachment theory*. In Bowlby's view, infants are born with the need for social attachments to their caregivers (typically the mother), and this need is transferred to other targets later in life. Although in his early thinking Bowlby followed the Freudian approach of seeing adult relationships as repetitions of, or attempts to recapture, the early relationship with one's mother, Bowlby gradually came to see attachment needs as fundamental and pervasive aspects of human motivation from birth to death, and he may have ceased to regard adult attachment needs as deriving from the mother-child relationship. In any case, other theorists have been explicit about this (see Baumeister & Tice, 1990; Shaver, Hazan, & Bradshaw, 1988). The child's need for the mother is thus regarded as merely one manifestation, rather than the cause, of an underlying need for social attachments. The view that people are fundamentally driven by a *need to belong* is supported by a wide assortment of evidence (see also Baumeister, 1991). People without close personal attachments are typically very unhappy, and when one relationship breaks up, people usually try to find a new one to replace it.

Most relevant to unrequited love are recent efforts to understand passionate love as an attachment process. Hazan and Shaver (1987; also Shaver et al., 1988) have elaborated this view of love. As they put it, love is "a biological process designed by evolution to facilitate attachment between adult sexual partners who, at the time love evolved, were likely to become parents of an infant who would need their reliable care." Love is thus related to sexual attraction but goes beyond it. Sexual attraction may be enough to produce intercourse and hence pregnancy and reproduction; but love keeps the adult couple together, which will improve the infant's chances of receiving healthy, nourishing care and hence of surviving to adulthood when it, in turn, can reproduce.

Attachment theory provides a valuable perspective on unrequited love. For one thing, it shifts most theoretical interest away from the would-be lover and on to the rejector. After all, the would-be lover is relatively easy to understand in terms of attachment theory, for he or she is simply trying to form an important, mutually satisfying attachment. That simply follows the dictates of human nature and biology.

The rejector is the paradox: Why would someone refuse to form an attachment? Attachment theory portrays human beings as organisms craving to form social bonds with each other, and so it is surprising to find a person rejecting attachment.

One important implication of attachment theory, therefore, is that rejecting love will be emotionally difficult. To reject another person's offer of attachment is to go against some of the most basic human tendencies and desires, which urge one to form and maintain relationships, not refuse them or break them off. The rejector may have to cope not only with the would-be lover's suffering but with his or her own distress at violating nature's programming. Psychologists have known for decades that people are able to act in ways that thwart their own natural, biological needs and impulses—but to do so often causes an inner struggle. Rejectors may not fully understand why they experience distress, but attachment theory predicts strongly that they will find it difficult and upsetting to reject love.

Moreover, one can well understand why the most common formula for expressing romantic rejection is "Let's just be friends." By sustaining platonic friendship, the rejector can avoid breaking the interpersonal bond to the would-be lover; thus, a relationship is sustained, and the rejection affects simply the *kind* of relationship. "Let's just be friends" is a way of placating the rejector's own inner needs for attachment. Platonic friendship is rarely what the would-be lover wants, and the offer of such friendship was often treated as very meager, inadequate consolation in the accounts of would-be lovers. But rejectors may find that asking for platonic friendship eases their own distress at rejecting love.

The would-be lover's responses to rejection can also be predicted on the basis of attachment theory. Bowlby (1969, 1973) observed that the responses of infants and small children to mother's departure followed a predictable series of stages (see also Hazan & Shaver, 1987). The first involved acute distress and active protest against the other's absence. The second stage involved despair and depression, taking the form of a relatively passive sadness. The third stage involves detachment, in which the child would seem indifferent to the mother and would even avoid her when she came back.

In our work, we will not be able to assess the idea that rejected lovers go through a series of stages in a standard, predetermined sequence—but we will show evidence for each of these three reactions. The initial "protest" reaction will be amply evident among people who refuse to accept the rejection, become extremely upset, and even in some cases seem to go berserk. The "despair" reaction takes the form of people who seem to be in mourning for the lost love. The third, or "detachment," response can be seen among rejected lovers who derogate their formerly desired partners and in some cases refuse any further contacts that the rejector may seek out.

Why People Make Stories

This book is based on the stories people tell about past experiences with unrequited love. It is therefore important to take a moment to consider why people construct such stories, because their motives for making them will help shape how they make them.

People use accounts to make sense of their experiences (Gergen & Gergen, 1988; Harvey, Weber, & Orbuch, 1990). Stories are exercises in self-interpretation. They impose order and structure on the daily events, great and small, of our lives. Indeed, people may often stop short of drawing broad abstract conclusions and making explicit generalizations, and so their stories may be the most important way in which their knowledge about themselves and their lives is stored (see Kihlstrom et al., 1988; McAdams, 1985).

Considerable evidence supports the view that people have several basic *needs for meaning* (Baumeister, 1991), and these needs may provide the impetus and guidelines for the making of stories. The four basic needs for meaning include finding purpose, creating a sense of efficacy, justifying one's actions in the context of accepted values, and maintaining a degree of self-worth. The last two are particularly relevant to unrequited love. Let us consider these two briefly.

Justification, including issues of guilt and appropriate behavior, is an important concern of rejectors. Interpersonal views of guilt (see Hoffman, 1982; Zahn-Waxler & Kochanska, 1990; also Baumeister, Stillwell, & Heatherton, 1991) emphasize that people feel guilty when they hurt someone else, often regardless of whether they intended to do so or not (see McGraw, 1987). Rejectors find themselves in a position in which their only two choices are to form a romantic partnership with someone they do not love or, more likely, to reject that person's advances and in the process inflict heartbreak and its attendant emotional distress on that person. Justifications should not be difficult as long as the rejector did not lead the would-be lover on (i.e., did not provide misleading encouragement). In such cases, however, the person may still feel bad for hurting the would-be lover, resulting in the paradox of feeling guilty despite self-perceived moral innocence.

Issues of self-worth are relevant to both people but especially to the would-be lover, because the romantic rejection can convey a humiliating message that damages self-esteem. Earlier in this chapter, we suggested that unrequited love may often arise when a relatively unattractive person becomes infatuated with a relatively attractive person who does not reciprocate the feelings. The attractive person is in an important sense rejecting the other person because of the other's inferior desirability—which could be a severe blow to the other person's self-esteem. To find out that one is not considered worthy of such a partner may be an unexpected and disheartening judgment about one's personal desirability.

It seems likely that both rejector and would-be lover are aware of the implicitly judgmental aspect of romantic rejection, and probably both are uncomfortable with it. It is difficult to imagine a mutually comfortable conversation in which the rejector says, "Sorry, but you're not intelligent or good-looking enough to deserve me," and the would-be lover replies, "Oh yes, you're right, of course, sorry to bother you." More likely, the rejector would avoid saying anything that would call attention to the esteem implications, lest he or she feel guilty for hurting the other. The rejector might phrase the rejection so as to suggest that the two were equally attractive but simply incompatible on nonevaluative dimensions (see Folkes, 1982). The would-be lover, meanwhile, would want to recall the event in a way that would not cast it as proof of inferior attractiveness. The would-be lover will therefore construct the story in a way that restores or rebuilds self-esteem.

Thus we can postulate one guiding set of motivations behind the stories. For the rejectors, issues of guilt and justification will be central, and so the moral dimension will loom large in their stories. They will judge themselves and the other person on moral terms, and they will use their stories to try to justify what they did. For the would-be lovers, in contrast, the self-worth dimension will be centrally important. Their own coping process, and by implication the stories they tell, will be concerned with repairing the damage to their self-esteem.

One should not expect these themes to be apparent in every story. But they will reflect general themes and broad tendencies. Unrequited love poses a threat to the self-concept of both parties, but the threat will tend to take different forms. For rejectors, it is a moral threat; for would-be lovers, it is an esteem threat.

Having a Script to Follow—or Not

To play a role, one follows a script, in social life as in the theatre. The quality and thoroughness of the script affects the ease with which one plays the role. Scripts come from familiar cultural ideas, practices, and accepted notions of appropriate behavior.

With unrequited love, one important difference between the two roles concerns scriptedness—that is, how well scripted they are. We shall argue that the would-be lover has ample and detailed, if occasionally conflicting, scripts to follow, whereas the rejector may find himself or herself without an adequate script. The would-be lover may therefore know what to do, even to the point of following the script in situations to which it is not well suited. Meanwhile, the rejector suffers from the problems of *scriptlessness*, including uncertainty, confusion, hesitant passivity, and possibly an overriding fear of doing the wrong thing.

The script for the would-be lover comes from a variety of sources throughout our culture. The aspiring lover is a popular theme for songs, movies, operas, novels, plays, and so forth. One can probably hear a song about an aspiring lover in almost any American house within half an hour, just by turning on the radio. And it would be extremely difficult to avoid that theme for very long while watching movies and television.

The details of the aspiring lover's script, though broadly familiar to anyone who has paid any attention to popular or high culture in our society in recent times, deserve some comment in relation to un-requited love. First, it is necessary to recognize that the would-be lover does not know in advance that he or she is going to be rejected—on the contrary, the happy endings so popular among fictional portrayals typically involve success. That is, the aspiring lover may meet with rejection, disapproval, and external obstacles for a while, but by per-sisting he or she (although most often he) will win the beloved's heart, thus enabling them to live together happily ever after. Stories like that of Nicholas and Alexandra are popular precisely because they drive that point home. The script of an aspiring lover may involve rejection and difficulties, but it calls for the individual to persevere in order to reach true happiness.

Moreover, the happy endings of books and movies often em-phasize that *both* people end up living blissfully ever after. The re-luctant person's initial resistance must therefore be overcome *for that person's own good*. This is important to recognize in terms of how people will respond when they love someone who rejects them. Whereas logic, rational pragmatism, and common courtesy might call for leaving that person alone, the cultural script calls for persistence in the face of rejection. Any objections the rejector might have would presumably be outweighed by the eventual joy he or she will receive when finally ready to reciprocate the love. Thus, in an important sense, the script gives the would-be lover license to ignore the wishes of the rejector and persist with romantic advances even after the other makes it clear that those advances are not wanted.

Persisting lovers may try a variety of techniques, which the various fictional portrayals have crowned with success. Some of these may seem devious, but it is unlikely that the would-be lover considers himself or herself to be a villain or evildoer for trying to win some-one's love. There is even a cliche to the effect that any technique is fair in love, just as in warfare, and this view reflects the great power of love as a source of value. Love justifies a wide variety of actions, and a desperate lover expects moral forgiveness for some irrational or otherwise inappropriate acts.

If the rejector does remain firm, then the would-be lover changes from an aspiring lover's script to a victim's script. As victims, brokenhearted lovers are rarely blamed for their woe, because people are not considered to be responsible for their own feelings. Indeed, only if they fail to advance their case aggressively can they be blamed for their heartbreak, which is thus another reason for them to try everything they can in order to win the beloved's heart. The fault may lie in fate or external factors—or with the rejector. If the rejector encourages the love, then the broken-hearted lover is regarded as a victim of a cruel, selfish, exploitative, or negligent villain.

Lastly, it is worth noting that the very multiplicity of portrayals of aspiring lovers is important. The simple fact that the aspiring lover is such a common figure, as is even the broken-hearted lover, entails that to play that role oneself is to participate in a broad drama of cultural significance. True, one may tend to feel at the time that one's own experience is uniquely painful, but soon afterward one may acquire the perspective that one has simply gone through a very common and important experience. Ultimately, many people end up agreeing with the widely quoted lines from Tennyson: "Tis better to have loved and lost/Than never to have loved at all."

Let us now consider the rejector's experience. Unlike the would-be lover, the rejector does not have a detailed and thorough and familiar script to follow. Very few books, songs, or movies describe things from the rejector's experience. The few that do are often unhelpful. For example, the movies *Fatal Attraction* and *Play Misty For Me* focused on the rejector's perspective, but neither depicted a viable, effective way of handling the situation. Instead, both films focused on the the rejector's mystified futility in trying to discourage the unwanted romantic attentions from an increasingly intrusive, maniacal pursuer. The message seemed to be that rejectors are helplessly at the mercy of such would-be lovers, who move from romantic interest to disappointment to hostility and lethal violence in a steady, relentless progression. Ironically, these few portrayals may make it that much harder for ordinary rejectors, who know that their admirers are not deranged killers but ordinary decent people, yet who suffer the same inability to extricate themselves.

The rejector must inflict hurt on someone else, and to that extent the role is a villain's role. Needless to say, that is a strongly unappealing aspect of the role, and when people find themselves having to reject someone they may suddenly see themselves cast in a way they never anticipated or wanted. Thus, the role's central feature is not a pleasant one, and apart from that the role has few guidelines. One may expect people to find it quite difficult to play the rejector's role.

In our sample, a number of people referred to scriptlessness (although not, of course, using that term) as a problem for the rejector. They said they just didn't know how to handle the situation. "I didn't feel attracted to John, I didn't know what to do. I didn't know what to say because I didn't want to hurt John's feelings," as one woman wrote about being suddenly thrust into the rejector's role. A similar comment was made by a man who found himself the target of a woman's affections: "I was very uncomfortable with the situation because I had never actually been chased before and didn't want to hurt her."

Undoubtedly, one result of the difficulty of the rejector's role will be a broad reluctance to face the situation and deal with it actively. One fears to do the wrong thing, and one doesn't know what the right thing is. It is bad enough to have to hurt someone, and one is afraid to make it worse by some inappropriate action. As we shall see, many rejectors did handle the situation by trying to be passive and avoidant. Sometimes this worked and the other person eventually gave up, but other times it failed.

In our sample, some rejectors referred specifically to becoming passive and avoidant because of not knowing how to act. Thus, for example, one woman described how a man who worked in the same office with her asked her out after she had just broken up with a previous boyfriend. She went out with him for two months but just was not interested. Finally she told him, "I don't think this relationship is what either of us want." He said "OK" and nothing else, and they parted. She could tell he had been hurt by the look in his eyes whenever she saw him at work, but they never talked about why their relationship had failed to bloom. Many months later, however, they were both at a party, and after drinking a great deal the man came up and said he wanted to ask her something. She had an inkling of what was coming and did not know how to play her part. For the rest of the party, "I just avoided him, because I didn't know what I was going to say," she wrote later.

This theme—of not knowing what to do or how to act—was an important feature of the rejector's experience, although certainly not all rejectors alluded to it. Uncertainty or scriptlessness was significantly more common among rejectors' accounts than among would-be lovers' accounts. Would-be lovers knew, more or less, what sorts of things they should try to do, but rejectors felt unprepared and uncertain in their roles.

If there is any difficulty with the would-be lover's script, it is knowing when and how to make the transition from aspiring lover to broken-hearted victim—that is, to shift from one role to another. "If only I knew for sure that he definitely was not interested then I could get on with my life," wrote one woman in the midst of that dilemma. Still, she knew both scripts: An aspiring lover tries to win the other's heart, and a broken-hearted victim mourns and then moves on to new undertakings. Her only difficulty was knowing which script to follow. In contrast, rejectors sometimes seem to feel that they have no viable script to follow at all.

One further likely consequence of scriptlessness is that people will consult with their friends and peers to find guidelines for handling the rejector's role. If the culture lacks usable models, people may simply exchange information and anecdotes with their friends on an informal basis. It may therefore be that small, local peer groups exert an important influence on how one should administer romantic rejection.

Care and Need

All loving relationships are not the same, and even within romantic love there is a variety of emotional attitudes one can take. A basic and important distinction is between *caring* for the other and *needing* the other (Steck, Levitan, McLane, & Kelley, 1982). Care involves having concern for the other person, attending to the other person, seeing that person's point of view and wanting what is best for that person. In contrast, need involves a concern with one's own feelings that may be stimulated by the partner. Need is self-oriented, whereas care is oriented toward the partner. A person dominated by need may strive to spend time together with the beloved partner, but it is for the sake of the person's own pleasure and happiness rather than the partner's. Thus, in an important sense, need demotes the romantic partner to a means rather than an end; that is, the partner is a means toward one's own pleasure and happiness. The partner's pleasure, or surprise, or any other reaction to having this effect on the lover is secondary or "incidental to the [lover]'s concerns" (Steck et al., 1982, p. 489).

Loving relationships evolve and change across time (see Sternberg, 1986). One important area of change, apparently, is that need predominates in the early stages of a relationship, whereas later on care becomes more central (Steck et al., 1982). When a relationship is starting, people are especially passionate and emotional, but intimacy is still just building, and commitments may not have been made yet (Sternberg, 1986). In that early stage, lovers are preoccupied with their own feelings, and hence they conform to the need pattern rather than the care pattern.

The predominance of need in the early stages of romantic attraction will presumably apply to most cases of unrequited love. In unrequited love, usually there is no commitment, for a relationship is typically beginning or escalating or does not exist at all. Unrequited love is thus usually a part of the passionate stage, and people in the midst of it will tend to be preoccupied with their own feelings, including love and desire as well as fear and anxiety.

We may expect, therefore, that would-be lovers will be caught up in their own feelings rather than truly attending to the feelings of their partners. Although John's world may seem to revolve around Mary, John does not really attend to what Mary is going through but rather sees her only through the prism of his own wants, hopes, and fears.

This may help explain why the targets of unrequited love are often depicted as aloof, removed, and mysterious, despite being fascinating and desirable, for that may be precisely how the would-be lovers experience them. That popular image may say little about the actual personalities or actions of heartbreakers—rather, it simply reveals the mental state of the person in love.

There are several important consequences of recognizing that the aspiring and unrequited lover is probably in a state of need rather than caring. First, we should not rely on would-be lovers for information about rejectors, because would-be lovers only see the rejector through their own feelings. In this research, therefore, we have been careful to collect accounts from rejectors in order to learn about their experiences in their own words.

Second—and this will be something we find repeatedly in future chapters—would-be lovers may be unaware of some important aspects of the rejector's experience. The rejector's initial feeling of being vaguely flattered, the subsequent struggles with guilt, the problem of scriptlessness, and the escalating irritation and annoyance at the other's persistence—all of these are important aspects of what the rejector goes through, but the would-be lover may be mostly oblivious to them. Because of this, would-be lovers will sometimes act in ways that the rejector will find irrational and inappropriate. A failure to take no for an answer is perhaps the foremost among them. "There were certainly enough cues as to her lack of attraction to me, but I was too preoccupied to notice," as one man wrote candidly about his futile attraction to a woman. He simply didn't pay attention to what she was feeling and so kept after her despite her wishes.

Rejectors, of course, may be less guided by need, because the attraction is not there. They may feel neither care nor need toward the other. Without the blinding effects of one's own needs, rejectors may tend to have a relatively clear notion of what the would-be lover is going through, so that, ironically, the person who is not in love will be the one with the greater level of empathy.

We have suggested that some cases of unrequited love grow out of intimate platonic friendships. In these, care is presumably already present and is mutual, but when one person falls in love need may predominate in his or her feelings for a period of time. Rejectors of platonic friends may be especially guided by feelings of care, which presumably will make it all the more difficult and painful for them to administer the rejection. Consistent with this, several people in our sample described the difficulty of saying no to romantic advances from a close friend. Some used balancing metaphors, such as walking a tightrope, to describe the delicate task of trying to discourage the romance while maintaining the friendship. Above all, they were keenly aware of hurting the other person and sought desperately for a means of rejection that would be painless but effective.

Conspiracy of Silence

The needy attitudes of would-be lovers are not the only barriers to effective communication in unrequited love. Indeed, several factors make it especially hard for one person to discourage another's romantic interest effectively. Although the would-be lover and the rejector are often at cross purposes, they have one (unfortunate) thing in common, namely that they both dread the scene where the one tells the other there is no hope and it is time to break off contact. The result is a kind of conspiracy of silence, in which the two cooperate in avoiding the heartbreaking message. The one doesn't want to speak the message, and the other doesn't want to hear it. No wonder communication is difficult!

The rejector does want the message to be received, but getting oneself to say things that will disappoint and hurt someone often requires an aversive struggle. Telling someone bad news is difficult enough even if you are not responsible for the problem; indeed, there is a general pattern of reluctance to transmit bad news, which has been called the "mum effect" (Tesser & Rosen, 1975). Telling an admirer that her love is hopeless and unwanted, or especially telling someone why one finds him unlovable, must inevitably be very difficult (see also Folkes, 1982).

Several factors increase the rejector's difficulty beyond the basic reluctance to transmit bad news. For one thing, the rejector is at least partly responsible for the other's disappointment and heartbreak, and so he or she may feel guilty, and guilt feelings will not make it any easier to perform the act. For another thing, research suggests that people are especially reluctant to transmit bad news to unattractive others (Rosen, Johnson, Johnson, & Tesser, 1973), perhaps because of sympathy or guilt, and if rejectors are often dealing with less attractive admirers (because of the pattern of "falling upward") then they may be in precisely that situation of extra difficulty.

Even if the rejecting message has to be gotten across in one way or another, it does not have to be thorough and explicit. To avoid making a scene or provoking a hysterical reaction, rejectors may seek to phrase the rejection as gently and vaguely as possible. We have already suggested how difficult it would be for a rejector to say, in effect, "I can't love you because you are ugly, and you bore me, and you are immature, and generally you are just not good enough for me." These may be the real reasons, but because of the mum effect rejectors may avoid saying them out loud and instead express the rejection in more ambiguous, evaluatively neutral terms, perhaps even false ones. The result will often be that would-be lovers will not hear the full or accurate reasons that they are being rejected.

Valerie Folkes (1982) studied the reasons people give for turning down a date, and these reasons shed valuable light on the rejector's dilemma. She found that people are very reluctant to tell an unattractive suitor that they don't want to date him or her because he or she is unattractive. Instead, people will make excuses. Overall, the majority of reasons people gave for turning down dates had a combination of three characteristics. First, these reasons were impersonal (such as work). Second, they were uncontrollable, such as an impending deadline or an illness: nothing could be done about the problem. Third, the reasons cited unstable circumstances that might change. Apparently people find a reason that they can't go out on a date on the particular night the person is asking about, rather than citing a reason that they could never go out with that person. Folkes also demonstrated that people give these impersonal, uncontrollable, unstable reasons for refusing dates even when the true reason is quite different—in fact, even if it is the opposite kind of reason, namely highly personal, controllable, and permanent.

Thus, when people want to refuse a romantic overture, they tend to avoid saying that the refusal reflects their own choice; they avoid saying that the reason has to do with anything about themselves or the would-be partner; and they tend to suggest that their refusal is temporary rather than permanent. All of these responses may purchase temporary respite and avoid guilt feelings, but all of them leave the would-be lover with reason to hope that things might turn out better next time. In other words, if a would-be lover receives any of the standard rejections, he or she would have a sound rational basis for trying again. Rejectors are reluctant to express their true feelings, and consequently they may fail to communicate the true message and may even send out a misleading, encouraging signal.

The would-be lover, meanwhile, does not want to learn that his or her cause is hopeless. We have already noted that would-be lovers may tend to overlook or ignore key aspects of how the rejector is feeling, and this broad tendency toward obliviousness may be multiplied by a specific desire not to see the other's lack of love. The cultural scripts that tell the would-be lover to persist and succeed require that one not give up when confronted with some indifference or rejection. In plain terms, it would simply be too discouraging to realize that the other doesn't love you. Would-be lovers may therefore do their best to avoid hearing a clear and explicit message of rejection.

It is important to realize that there are some valid reasons for the would-be lover's tendency to ignore signals of rejection. Even explicit messages of rejection are sometimes insincere. For example, a survey of university women in the 1980s showed that a majority of sexually active women had said no to sexual advances despite fully intending to have sex with that person on that occasion (Muehlenhard & Hallabaugh, 1988). In those researchers' terms, many women sometimes say no when they mean yes. There was even a significant minority of virgins who had said no despite meaning yes, and their virginity indicated that they had succeeded in preventing themselves from having sex when both they and their partners wanted to have it. None of this furnishes an excuse for date rape or even just insensitive persistence with unwanted sexual overtures. To assume that no means yes, or to ignore refusals, violates all standards ranging from laws to etiquette to simple human decency. No does not mean yes, but Muehlenhard and Hallabaugh's research findings suggest that no does not exactly always mean no, either. It is apparently reasonable and rational to ask again later. One can begin to understand why many would-be lovers remain hopeful and persistent despite discouraging indications or negative responses.

Psychological learning theory furnishes another way to look at the phenomenon of romantic persistence. One basic principle of behavior is that when learning is based on partial reinforcement schedules—that is, when behavior is only occasionally rewarded—it takes a long time to unlearn. If no always meant no, now and forever, aspiring lovers probably would not persist once the rejector came out and said no. But if once in a great while a yes lurks behind a no, and aspiring lovers learn this, then they will be especially slow to get the message when no really does mean no.

Thus, sometimes rejections are not fully sincere or heartfelt. If even explicit rejections are suspect, then equivocal or ambiguous ones may be especially doubtful. It is therefore not surprising that some would-be lovers feel it appropriate to persist in their advances despite negative signals. It may sometimes be appropriate, rational, and adaptive to ignore rejection.

Conclusion

Psychologists have not been able to conduct many systematic studies of unrequited love, so the field presently knows rather little about this phenomenon. The context for unrequited love, however, is that of developing and eventually successful love, and so romantic failures are to be understood—and are experienced by the people involved—in unfavorable comparison to successful experiences of mutual love.

It helps to consider unrequited love from several theoretical perspectives. According to attachment theory, people are innately driven to form and maintain social bonds, and so unrequited love is surprising, not because one person falls in love, but because the other person refuses to reciprocate. To reject an opportunity for love is to go against nature's programming and will therefore be difficult. Another theoretical perspective, interdependence theory, indicates how each person's emotional outcomes depend on what the other person does. For the aspiring lover, the situation resembles a high-stakes gamble, with outcomes ranging from blissful happiness of eventual, successful love, to the misery and humiliation of heartbreak. For the rejector, however, the situation is a no-win proposition, offering only bad and at best neutral outcomes.

Unrequited love may arise from inequities in attractiveness. One common pattern, which we have labeled "falling upward," may be that people fall in love with someone more attractive and desirable than themselves, and such love is unlikely to be reciprocated. There are of course many other possible causes of unrequited love, including intimacy that develops out of platonic friendships.

The culture provides firm and clear scripts for the would-be lover to follow, but the rejector may suffer from scriptlessness and the resulting sense of not knowing what to do or how to act. Would-be lovers may be caught up in their own feelings and needs and may not realize what the rejector is going through, and the would-be lover's script may contribute to not attending too closely to the rejector's feelings. As a result, rejectors may have more empathy and understanding than the would-be lover has.

Rejectors and unrequited lovers have different motives and concerns, and their experiences and accounts should reflect these differences. The rejector role is one that entails hurting someone and is therefore a kind of villain's role; for rejectors, therefore, concerns over guilt and justification become centrally important. Would-be lovers may not regard the experience as having a strong moral dimension, but for them issues of self-worth become very important, particularly insofar as romantic rejection carries the implication that one was not good enough to deserve such an attractive partner.

A variety of problems will plague the communication between rejectors and would-be lovers. Although the romantic rejection is the keystone, the essential and defining feature, of the drama of unrequited love, neither person wants to face it. The rejector feels guilty and does not want to have to inflict the painful news on the admirer, and the would-be lover does not want to find out that his or her love is doomed and hopeless. The would-be lover's preoccupation with his or her own needs and feelings may also tend to hamper an accurate understanding of the rejector's view. These communicative obstacles set the stage for a variety of misunderstandings and problems.

T·H·R·E·E

The Emotional Crossfire

Even when love goes smoothly, it doesn't really go smoothly. There are good days and bad days, pleasure and conflict, elation and despair. Even relatively strong, enduring marriages tend to have some degree of conflict, disagreement, and emotional turbulence, and the early stages of intimate, loving relationships may have times of uncertainty and unhappiness—perhaps inevitably. Part of the reason is simply that to fall in love is to make oneself vulnerable, and it is implausible that such high vulnerability can exist without any suffering.

If ordinary, reciprocated love is associated with a mix of emotions, how much more must unrequited love be! Love means joy, excitement, pleasure at the other's presence, but it can also mean anxiety and despair as the affair approaches its doom. Meanwhile, the rejector is far from the heartless, unfeeling heartbreaker often pictured. To reject another's love is supremely difficult and goes against some of the deepest impulses of nature and culture. And sometimes that is only the beginning, for if the would-be lover fails to get the message or accept it gracefully, the struggle may drag on indefinitely.

This chapter will examine the emotional patterns on both sides of unrequited love. Neither side quite fits the stereotype that casts would-be lovers as relentlessly tortured by miserable obsession and rejectors as cold, casual heartbreakers. The reality is far more complex and multifaceted. In particular, there is much that is positive in the would-be lover's experience, and the rejector's experience is often pervaded with emotional conflict and distress.

Positive Feelings

We begin with positive feelings. To be a young person in love is to participate in one of the culture's ideals. People envy those who are in love, for love is characterized by good feelings—supposedly. To have found someone who appeals to you, someone who makes your heart beat faster, your stomach tighten, and your sex organs tingle—this is a matter of joy. But does this apply even in cases of unrequited love?

The short answer is yes. If the presence of pleasant, desirable emotions is the only criterion, then even unrequited love is a desirable experience. The vast majority of accounts of would-be lovers contained references to positive, desirable feelings. There was pain too, to be sure, but the elation was real. One woman wrote, for example, how this love brought about a powerfully positive transformation in her life: "I [had been] depressed at the time, and being in love gave me an incentive to be happy about something, to wake up in the morning and have something pleasant to look forward to: 'Maybe I will see him today.'"

A common theme was the interlude of intense happiness, which may have been brief but was nonetheless treasured. Looking back on a brief romance, a woman wrote, "We dated for only five weeks. Unfortunately, I will probably never know a time in my life as wonderful as this was. I was in love, without question." Similarly, a young man wrote of meeting the perfect woman for him at a bar, dancing with her, making a date for the next week and exchanging phone numbers. "We talked on the phone every day for a week. Finally we met again the next Friday. By the end of this Friday night I was madly in love with her. I was so happy that I'd met someone I liked so much.

We had a lot of fun together that Friday night, and Saturday night," although after that she abruptly became aloof and evasive. Others wrote of bliss and elation, of the excitement of the first dates and kisses and other intimacies with someone toward whom they felt so strongly.

Even the end of the episode, which often brought heartbreak that some people described vividly as crushing devastation, was not invariably bad. Some people apparently feel out of control during such a period of attraction and hence welcome the end of emotional turmoil and the return to stability and peace. "It was a loss but a great relief when he moved away to Florida," said one young woman about the fellow she had secretly, silently loved through her last two years of high school.

One may readily believe that love always brings good feelings, regardless of what else it brings. But what about the rejectors? It turned out that they too tended to report positive feelings. The reporting of positive affect was far less common among the rejectors than among the would-be lovers, but that is largely because positive affect was so extremely common among the latter. Over half the rejectors reported some positive feelings in their accounts. Most commonly these were friendship feelings toward the other person: The rejector liked the individual but did not have romantic feelings. A few others spoke of enjoying the attention or being flattered by the other's interest.

In short, and contrary to many novels and stereotypes, unrequited love often brings a substantial amount of positive emotion to the would-be lover. If one judges experiences solely by the quantity of positive affect they provide, then one would have to regard love, even unrequited love, as a highly positive and desirable experience.

Bad Feelings

We turn now from the pleasant to the unpleasant and even painful. As one might expect, unrequited love loses much of its appeal once the unpleasant feelings are considered.

Most obviously, heartbreak itself is a source of acute emotional distress. Many people referred to how much they suffered over their broken hearts. An articulate (but otherwise typical) description of this emotional pain was furnished by a woman in our sample. She had thought she was about to make the transition from intimate friendship to romantic involvement, but then abruptly the fellow started dating someone else. "I was devastated . . . I felt that the end of the world had come. I became very, very sad, and my heart literally felt like it was being clamped by pliers. I would cry a lot and lost interest in doing anything. I basically felt hurt and not worthy of anyone."

It is not surprising that romantic rejection hurts. People with broken hearts do suffer. The pain and disappointment are sometimes intense. There is also anger. Some described their intense, painful jealousy upon seeing their beloved with another partner. Indeed, these jealous reactions are often particularly strong, possibly for two reasons. One reason is that seeing one's beloved with someone else is a dramatic and compelling proof that one is not going to be chosen and perhaps has been rejected in favor of someone else. This could also invoke deeply rooted anxiety associated with social rejection or exclusion (see Bowlby, 1969, 1973; Baumeister & Tice, 1990), as well as fears about whether the self is desirable to others.

The other reason is that often would-be lovers are reluctant to allow themselves to feel anger or hatred toward the person they love, but they have no such scruples about the third person whom they regard as "competition," and so they channel all their resentment toward this third person. Thus, they stifle their negative feelings as long as they are only dealing with the person they love, but the accumulated anger and bitterness can all be directed toward the third person. One woman, for example, said the other woman to whom she lost her beloved was "the only person I've ever really hated."

This pattern of directing all one's negative feelings toward the third person was strikingly illustrated in Pamela Des Barres's (1987) account of her life as a groupie. She idolized the rock music stars that she slept with. Even if she just offered them sexual services briefly at odd moments while they were in town, she was overcome with grateful attraction and devotion. Often they moved on quickly to another groupie, and so after having sex with a man she might soon encounter him with another girl on his arm. In her account, she rarely derogated the faithless man, but she spoke in acidic and insulting terms about the girl, such as calling her a "tart" or "whore." This is of course especially ironic insofar as the other young woman was essentially doing the same thing that Des Barres herself was doing, and there was no apparent reason that her condemnations of the other person should not be applied to herself as well.

What is perhaps more surprising, however, is that the heart-breaker suffers too. In fact, the accounts by the rejectors contained more negative feelings directed toward the other person than did the accounts of the would-be lovers. Part of this is because the would-be lovers sometimes suffered their broken hearts alone, without blaming the person they loved. For example, one woman described how the man she dated had treated her shabbily but she had overlooked this because of her strong attraction to him. Even after he jilted her abrupt-ly, leaving her in pain for a long time, "I never completely blamed him or hated him because I liked him so much." Thus, rejectors tend to direct their negative affect outwardly (i.e., at the other person) more commonly than the would-be lovers.

It is important to avoid confusing the mere presence of bad feeling with the intensity of bad feelings. The fact that more rejectors reported bad feelings does not mean that they suffered more intensely than the heartbroken lovers. In a follow-up study, we asked people to rate how intensely they suffered, and on the average the heartbroken would-be lovers endured more intense emotional pain and distress than did the rejectors. Also, in one of the rare sex differences we found, this difference was especially large for females; that is, female would-be lovers reported the highest levels of emotional suffering.

To be sure, a substantial minority of the would-be lovers did sooner or later direct some negative affect toward the person they loved, whether this was frustration, angry feelings of betrayal, or even an attempt to convince themselves that the grapes were sour—that is, to devalue the person who spurned their love. But they were out-numbered by the high proportion of rejectors who expressed negative feelings toward their pursuers. A strong majority of rejectors expressed such negative feelings.

The key to understanding this difference may lie in how the two people make sense of the episode and integrate it with their life stories and self-concepts. The jilted lover cannot usually devalue the person he or she loved without making his or her own initial attraction seem incomprehensible. To recall that "he was a slob, and a pig, and a bastard" leaves one open to the question, "Then why did you love him so much and pursue him so hard?" Hence, to make sense of the episode, it is often necessary to preserve some positive view of the partner.

Meanwhile, the rejector has no incentive to see the admirer in a favorable light. In fact, any unappealing traits in the would-be lover may make it easier for rejectors to make sense of their own actions. That is, one's unwillingness to become involved is readily understandable if the other person was not a desirable partner. In short, in order to make sense of the experience in retrospect, would-be lovers may need to sustain or exaggerate a positive view of the rejector, whereas rejectors may need to sustain or exaggerate a negative view of the would-be lover.

One negative feeling that was common among rejectors was annoyance. Slightly over half of the rejectors expressed some form of annoyance toward the partner. "I became very frustrated with Jeff always being around, and he became more of a nuisance than a friend," said one, who later spoke in disparaging tones about receiving "a sappy letter telling me how much I meant to him." Another spoke of her growing resentment against a man who refused to be turned away. She said after she first told him she was not interested, he came back to say he had found a new girlfriend named Lisa, but she suspected that Lisa was his code word for herself. He would ask her for pointers about how to win Lisa's heart and she would give advice, and then "a couple of days later, the pointers I gave him about 'Lisa' are being used on me." When writing the account, the affair was still in progress and she saw no way to get rid of this man and his unwanted attentions. "Right now, I literally hate [him]," she said, adding that she felt she was almost at her wits' end.

Other rejectors expressed a variety of negative feelings beyond annoyance. Much of the spectrum was covered in one story by a woman whose fraternity "Big Brother" became attracted to her romantically, which caught her off guard because her feelings for him were those of a friend or sister, not a girlfriend. "I felt offended, flustered and hurt. I couldn't trust him. I cringed if he touched me. I sort of felt cheated," she wrote. "There was absolutely no attraction for him, and that was not going to change. I felt angry. I was confused, and didn't know what to do. I started feeling uncomfortable around him and then I would feel guilty because I wasn't treating him as nicely as I used to." When he sent her flowers, she was upset rather than pleased and felt there was no one with whom she could discuss her problem.

Fears and worries were reported on both sides of unrequited love. The would-be lovers often suffered from fears of rejection, fears which in these cases were destined to come true. Such concerns were featured prominently in many of the accounts by the would-be lovers. The rejectors, when asked, seemed to know that the would-be lovers probably felt that way, but their own spontaneous accounts contained hardly any references to this aspect of the spurned one's suffering. Some people are extremely afraid of rejection. "You see," explained one woman, "if I am even remotely interested in a guy and he doesn't reciprocate, I back off immediately." A man said, "I like to be sure of relationships and I dread few things more than a turn-down, so I can say I've rarely allowed myself to go out on a limb to open myself to rejection." A woman described her uncertainties about approaching the man she had a crush on. She put an anonymous classified ad in the student newspaper addressed to him, and then, growing bolder, she wrote a note saying she wanted to get to know him better and had one of her girlfriends slip it under his dormitory room door. "Naturally I didn't sign my name. I am terribly afraid of rejection."

The rejectors, however, suffered their own fears and worries over the necessity of rejecting their pursuers. In most cases, they were quite certain that they did not love this person and did not want a romantic relationship, but they found it very difficult to bring themselves to send this message. Over half of them indicated how hard it was. "Rather than telling him how I really feel I am much more inclined to put him off and make excuses," said one woman, adding "I cannot bring myself to be outright mean or cruel to him, but perhaps that would be the best in the long run." Another wrote, "The only way I knew to make him stop liking me was to shut him out and stop being a friend for a while. This was hard to do because I really did care for him as a friend and it hurt me to see him hurt . . . ." Expressing a common response, one woman wrote "I tried to give him subtle hints to leave me alone. I did not want to bluntly tell him that I didn't like him, because I did not to want to hurt him."

The difficulty of bringing oneself to hurt someone has led more than a few rejectors into moral dilemmas, as they begin resorting to deceptive and dishonest techniques to escape. One woman, for example, related to us that she could not bring herself to give an unwanted admirer a direct, explicit rejection. For a time, whenever he would call, she cajoled her roommates into telling him that she was not home. (In retrospect, she was amazed by her own willingness to put her roommates up to lying for her, *and* by their willingness to do it!) During this time, she recalls having become increasingly annoyed at him for failing to take the hint, even though she was hardly giving him any satisfactory hints. The episode reached the point, however, when each of her roommates had already lied for her twice or more, and they began to get restive about continuing. Rather than face him with the truth, however, she resorted to another deception, taking his call and telling him (falsely) that she had just become engaged to another man and therefore could not see him anymore.

These examples suggest something about what it is like to have to break someone's heart. For many rejectors, this burden becomes the overriding feature of the experience, and their dread of having to inflict this pain drowns out all other aspects of the situation. One young woman told of a first date with a fellow to whom she was only moderately attracted. At dinner, he gave her a gold chain bracelet and asked her to be his girlfriend. She was stunned. "I felt sick for the rest of the night," she said, knowing that she would have to find some way to reject him. The stereotyped images of the aloof, untouched rejector, the heartless heartbreaker, or the casually cruel rejector do not correspond to the reality that is commonly experienced. Instead, it appears that unrequited love is emotionally difficult for both parties. While the one struggles with fear of rejection and futile passion, the other struggles with reluctance to inflict emotional pain and disappointment.

Perhaps the best short summary of the rejector's problem was articulated by one of our professional colleagues, who, recalling her own experiences on the receiving end of unrequited love, said, "It's an imposition on me to make me have to hurt somebody." In effect, the would-be lover forces the rejector to commit a minor crime of the heart, namely the infliction of emotional pain. Hurting someone may be the prototype cause of guilt, and so people are reluctant to do it; but the rejector may feel that he or she has no choice. The rejector's role is thus a matter of being thrust into a moral dilemma. (The rejector's moral dilemma will be examined more thoroughly in Chapter 5.)

The emotional difficulties of unrequited love make it difficult for both parties to express their feelings openly. In our data, there were stories on both sides that contained references to hiding or concealing one's feelings. These were significantly more common among the would-be lovers than among the rejectors, however. These aspiring lovers spoke of the necessity of concealing their passions and yearnings from their beloved, sometimes because they were afraid of the response they would get. In a number of cases, the pair had had a platonic friendship that both parties valued. One person wanted to make the relationship into something more, but was afraid to say anything because to do so would risk damaging the friendship. If the person reacted badly, then the would-be lover would end up losing all contact with that person.

A few people concealed their feelings from their beloved so thoroughly that they were able to believe that the other person never had any idea that the attraction existed. More commonly, however, there was some degree of contact and even dating, which led one person to invest great emotion in the possibility of relationship while the other was simply enjoying a casual good time. The would-be lover showed appropriately casual levels of friendly affection but did not reveal the deeper hopes and feelings. In some ways, it is these unexpressed emotions which mark the most pathetic cases, for these individuals never gave their own feelings a fair chance to be reciprocated. "He never realized how much I liked him or how badly he hurt me," wrote one woman about a relationship that lasted for months and then was ended by the man in a very casual fashion.

Fond and Bitter Memories

In time, love loses some of the urgency, uncertainty, and turmoil that characterize its early stages, and so one should not assume that people's current feelings about a past attraction are the same as they were at the time. After all, it is hardly surprising that falling in love may be accompanied by positive, happy emotions. But after one's passion has come to naught and one's heart has been broken, can one still look back with some positive feelings about the episode? We examined the feelings expressed in retrospect. These suffused the way the person presented the story. In short, was the episode a happy memory, a bittersweet one, or an unhappy one?

A substantial number of these stories expressed some positive feelings in retrospect. Perhaps surprisingly, the would-be lovers expressed more positive feelings than the rejectors. Over half of the would-be lovers were able to look back fondly on the episode, painful as it may have been for them. Some were able to accept, at least by now, that the love was not destined to succeed, and the recollection of their passionate attraction was good.

Apparently, positive feelings can be remembered in a positive way even if the memory is linked to suffering and disappointment. People remember the warmth of their feelings for another person, and the memory is at least somewhat pleasant. Some of our participants expressed gladness at being able to preserve the friendship that could have been jeopardized if their romantic overtures had become too insistent. Others simply treasured the memory or retained a soft spot in their heart for the one they loved. "He's still gorgeous, though, and in a way I'll always like him," concluded one fairly inarticulate account of a powerful yet futile attraction that the woman had finally managed to put behind her. Another woman ended simply by saying that the young man was "a sweet, polite, nice person."

Such pleasant recollections were of course most common when the other person treated them decently or gently. Those who felt misled, used, betrayed, or otherwise mistreated found it harder to experience pleasant emotions in connection with the memory.

But it seems that past love tends to breed forgiveness, at least in some cases. As we already noted, people who retain pleasant memories somehow refuse to condemn the person who jilted them. One woman clearly suggested this. Her story told of a love triangle involving herself, a very appealing young man, and his girlfriend back home. He dated her while at the university but then went back to his old girlfriend during his trips home, especially over the summer. After a summer apart, they were awkward, distant, and she felt he was pushing her away because of his reluctance to make a commitment. They broke up and then he wanted her back, and so they started up repeatedly, each time ending painfully for her. Yet even in retrospect she still refused to condemn him. "I still love him too much to hate him for treating me the way he did."

In contrast, only a third of the rejectors' accounts expressed positive feelings in retrospect. Those that did most commonly spoke about their positive feelings for the person, such as nonsexual friendship. A few mentioned how the experience had boosted their confidence or flattered them. For the majority of rejectors, however, there was not a great deal to remember happily.

The absence of happy memories among rejectors is useful to keep in mind when considering the would-be lover's strivings. Would-be lovers may believe they are offering the other person a marvelous, blissful experience if only he or she will give in to love. They may feel justified in pursuing their cause energetically and even persisting when the desired partner has already turned them down, because they believe that mutual happiness will be the ultimate result. In fact, however, these experiences are far from wonderful for the rejectors, and such energetic persistence by the would-be lover merely makes things considerably worse.

Unpleasant emotions, sometimes sharp and intense, were apparent in a substantial minority of both types of recollections. They were slightly (but not significantly) more common in the rejectors' stories than in the would-be lovers' stories. Indeed, the rejectors were, if anything, more likely to recall the episode unhappily rather than happily. In contrast, the would-be lovers had decidedly more positive than negative affect in retrospect.

The wealth of negative affect expressed by rejectors in retrospect was surprising to us. One can easily understand why the would-be lovers might look back on their thwarted longings with frustration, anger, bitterness, or simple sadness. But why should the ones who inflicted the heartbreak have such negatively toned recollections?

The explanation for this negativity may have several parts, some of which will be clearer after our other findings have been presented in later chapters, but we can anticipate some of those points now. One important difference is that it is often much harder for the rejector than for the would-be lover to see anything positive about the episode. As our interdependence analysis pointed out, the situation offers both good and bad potential outcomes to the would-be lover, but the rejector has nothing to gain from it. The would-be lover may end up disappointed, but the whole affair may have something of the character of a great and challenging adventure, a grand passion, and a powerful and important experience, with a mixture of good and bad feelings. Even though it ended badly, there was perhaps much to appreciate. In contrast, the rejector typically got very little out of the episode. Unlike the would-be lover, it was hard for the rejector to feel that his or her life had been enriched by this experience. For many, apparently, it was a useless and pointless set of aggravations. They were forced to respond to a situation they never wanted, and these responses were difficult for them, bringing uncertainty, guilt, aggravation, all of which went for naught. For some, a valued friendship was destroyed in the bargain. Thus they had plenty to resent and regret.

Would-be lovers had some negative feelings too, but these were often tempered or muted. One of the most common retrospective feelings was embarrassment. As we shall see, the heights of passion sometimes lead people to do things they would not normally do, and they may look back in embarrassment on these. Even more fundamentally, however, people seem embarrassed simply to have loved someone who did not love them. One woman described her inner turmoil and her long struggle to get up the nerve to approach a particular young man for what turned out to be a few awkward, pointless conversations. She concluded her story by saying that after she got over the infatuation she had to avoid him whenever their paths crossed on campus, because she was too embarrassed even to say "Hi" to him.

The negative feelings might seem to contradict the previous section's emphasis on positive feelings among would-be lovers, but the presence of contradictory feelings in the sample, and even in single cases, is undeniable. Unrequited love simply brings a mixture of good and bad feelings for these individuals. For example, a story by a young man told of his protracted encounters with a woman who would lead him on but then push him away whenever she found someone else. He spoke of their times together, of his attractions, and then alternately spoke of her cruel treatment of him when she found someone she liked better. He said other people, even the woman's roommate, told him he was being used, and finally he came to see that this was true. She eventually dumped him abruptly ("Ouch!" he commented) for the man she later married, and he attended the wedding as an invited but very uncomfortable guest. In retrospect, he said he was unable to forgive her fully and still harbored resentment at the way she had treated him. "Yet after all this, I still am attracted to her beauty, intelligence, sunny disposition, and ambitious medical career aspirations. Along with my anger at her, I fondly remember some of the times we had together."

Rejectors were far more willing to express unalloyed hostility and even disgust toward the person who had pursued them, particularly if the person had been extremely persistent. For example, one woman who had recently and with great difficulty extricated herself from such an unwanted entanglement wrote, "The mere thought or sight of him makes me absolutely nauseous," even though she had initially liked the man as a good friend. Thus, episodes of unrequited love are recalled with quite different affective patterns on the two sides of the failed passion. The rejected lover appears to maintain a soft spot in his or her heart for the love object. Love does perhaps conquer all, even to some extent the frustration and disappointment of heartbreak. The rejector, however, is far less likely to look back with positive feelings on this episode. Instead, the rejector's recollections are more likely to be marked by negative emotions.

Lasting Pains and Regrets

Undeniably, the heartbreak of unrequited love sometimes causes lasting suffering. One woman dated a boyfriend for two months and was very enamored of him, to the point where she overlooked the fact that "he never treated me very well." He then unceremoniously dumped her and became involved with someone else. "It hurt me so bad that I couldn't stand to see him or talk to him for at least a year," she said. Another woman said, "It took over a year for me to stop being sad," after the end of a relationship that she had had high hopes for but that apparently meant fairly little to the man. Another said it was many years before she could hear the man's name mentioned without experiencing a painful rush of old feelings, although by now (25 years later) those feelings had mostly subsided except for embarrassment over how she had felt and acted. Beyond such comments, we shall see further evidence of lasting pain in a later chapter where we examine how some people respond to heartbreak by becoming reluctant to allow themselves to trust or love anyone else.

There are several ways to look at the long-range emotional fall-out of unrequited love. A first question is whether the rejected lover is still carrying a torch—that is, still harboring feelings of love toward the other. Such indications were relatively uncommon in our stories, and they were about equally distributed in the would-be lovers' and the rejectors' stories.[1] A related question was whether the would-be lover might still be hopeful of winning the other person's affections, but this too was fairly rare in our sample and was about equally distributed among the two sets of stories.

Of course, it may be unwarranted to assume that rejected lovers had no lingering feelings or quixotic hopes. From these data one may only conclude that such feelings did not find expression in their accounts. It would be unwarranted to conclude that feelings of love are in most cases completely brought to an end. If the beloved object were to come back into the person's life and, at this later time, express great interest and desire in having a romantic relationship, one cannot assume that the would-be lovers would be uninterested or would respond as if to a total stranger. Again, all one may say is that the interpretations and stories people make about these past attractions do not typically express a continuing love or hope or attachment.

Indeed, one must keep in mind that these stories are not simply dispassionate recordings of past experiences, for accounts form an important medium by which people strive to impose order and thus control on their experiences, actions, and feelings (Gergen & Gergen, 1988; Gonzales, Pederson, Manning, & Wetter, 1990; Harvey, Weber, & Orbuch, 1990; Kihlstrom et al., 1988; Schlenker, 1982; Schönbach, 1990). We suspect that many people continue to feel some attachment or vulnerability despite a conscious effort to put it behind them, even if this conflict is only rarely articulated. As an example of this struggle and ambivalence, consider these remarks by a student whose experience was so recent that she could tell it was not over emotionally even if it was apparently over for all practical purposes: "I keep telling myself to forget him and I usually put him out of my mind, but then I'll see him at dinner and my heart takes a leap once again."

At the opposite end of the spectrum, it is worth considering whether the stories express in some clear fashion that the would-be lover did in fact fully "get over" the attraction—that is, make a full recovery and cease to feel attached, attracted, or hurt. Of course, it is not necessary that a story end either with the person carrying a torch or having positively gotten over it; the individual may simply leave the ending ambiguous. But some stories did contain positive statements that the would-be lover had indeed gotten over it. These assertions tended to be more common in the accounts by the rejectors than in those of the would-be lovers. "Eventually he did forget about me and we could become friends again," concluded one fairly typical rejector. In other words, rejectors were more likely to assert that the would-be lover got over it.

This particular result only attained a marginal level of statistical significance, but two points need to be made if the difference is indeed a reliable, genuine one. In the first place, this pattern goes against one broad tendency in autobiographical accounts, namely the tendency for people to feature their own emotions. That is, people tend to make more statements about their own feelings and views than about those of other people who may be involved in the event (e.g., Baumeister, Stillwell, & Wotman, 1990; Baumeister & Stillwell, 1992). Indeed, this broad tendency may have worked to diminish this result, and the fact that it was only marginally significant in our results may be due to this handicap rather than to any weakness of the effect.

The second point is that it seems, in a way, self-serving for rejectors to say that someone recovered from the heartbreak they inflicted on him or her. This is perhaps a first clue to the fact that people feel troubled or even guilty about rejecting someone's romantic advances. When they are fairly certain that the person recovered, it is important to them to point that out. They say, in effect, "I did not do permanent damage to that person." This pattern may in a sense be compared to accounts by offenders or perpetrators who insist that their victims recovered completely or did not suffer any lasting consequences of the offenders' acts (Baumeister, Stillwell, & Wotman, 1990). We shall deal with issues of guilt in detail in a later chapter, but this first hint is noteworthy.

A parallel finding concerns whether the would-be lover still feels hurt by the affair. (This is not the same as what we have discussed so far. One may still feel hurt despite having given up on the chances of love. Persistence of love, hope, attachment, or desire is not the same as persistence of emotional pain.) When we coded stories for clear indications that the would-be lover still felt hurt in the present, we found significantly more of these in the stories by the would-be lovers than in the stories by the rejectors.

This finding does fit the familiar pattern in which people emphasize their own feelings rather than the feelings of others. It is also consistent, however, with the finding about getting over the affair. Rejectors prefer to think that their victims, so to speak, did not suffer for long. They would rather not be aware of continued suffering, and their accounts are silent about any such enduring effects. Indeed, only 6% of their stories indicated that the person they rejected was still hurting. But the broken-hearted individuals themselves have no reason to suppress awareness of their suffering, and they were nearly four times as likely to mention their own lasting emotional distress.

To combine these several findings, then, one may cautiously conclude that rejectors emphasize the brevity of suffering and the recovery of the rejected lover, while the rejected lover tends to emphasize the lasting pain and suffering.[2]

Wishing It Had Never Happened

Before leaving the issue of the long-range consequences of, and retrospective feelings about the incident, it is worth considering one more question, namely whether the individual wishes the incident had never happened. Such a wish is of course a powerful condemnation of the episode and indicates a particularly thorough form of regret. (When we merely coded for any expressions of regret, loosely defined, there were no differences between the two sets of stories.) Only a minority of stories contained such statements. But they were about three times more common in the rejectors' stories than in the would-be lovers' stories. It was the heartbreakers, rather than the heartbroken, who seemed to wish that the whole thing had never happened!

This finding by itself is surprising, and yet it is consistent with the picture that has emerged from our other findings. Despite the disappointment, the pain, the futility, the humiliation, the frustration, and the heartbreak, the would-be lovers seem to have found some value in the experience. They hardly ever wish that the event had not occurred. The positive feelings they enjoyed, and the chance of love that they pursued, may well be linked to some of the most basic and powerful values people in our society hold (e.g., Baumeister, 1991). Of course they may often wish that things had turned out differently, that they had managed to succeed in winning the other person's affections and love. But the failure is not enough to make them wish that they had never tried.

The British novelist Thackeray once wrote, "To love and win is the best thing; to love and lose the next best." We have already quoted

Tennyson's version of this sentiment, which is that never to have loved at all is far worse than to have suffered a broken heart. Apparently, many people come to agree with these sentiments despite their own experiences of heartbreak.

In contrast, a substantial minority of rejectors indicated that they would have been better off if the whole thing had never happened. This too is ironic, for at first glance one might imagine that their experience is enviable. They had someone who admired them, who found them marvelous and attractive, and who offered them an opportunity for a loving attachment. Yet they were the ones who were willing to express the most profound regrets about the experience. "The whole episode makes me sick, and I can't ever even believe he was my friend, or mere acquaintance even!!!" concluded one rejector forcefully.

These sentiments of the rejectors provide a striking confirmation of the apparent aversiveness of their experience. As we have seen, rejectors suffer an abundance of unpleasant feelings, both at the time and in retrospect, and meanwhile they do not seem to get much out of the experience in the way of pleasant emotions or happy memories. For them, the experience is often a bad one with no redeeming value, and so they are willing to wish it had never happened.

To be loved is one of the ideals both of psychological theories and of cultural attitudes. Yet our results cast that ideal in a very harsh light. Contrary to some assumptions, people do not generally or simply or universally want to be loved. To be loved by some people is unpleasant, undesirable, and otherwise bad. Indeed, it is at first surprising that rejectors would prefer that these incidents had never happened. They are saying, in effect, that they wish this person had never loved them.

Unawareness of the Other's Feelings

If true love ideally involves a merging of two selves, in the sense of an emotional sensitivity and communication between two people, then unrequited love can be seen as a failure of merging. The very separateness implicit in the concept of failed love suggests a gap in understanding between two people. That should amplify the general tendency for people to attend more to their own feelings than to those of others. And, indeed, we found that many of the most important emotional reactions in unrequited love were largely omitted from the accounts of the partners. This appeared to be especially true of the feelings of the rejectors. The rejectors had some understanding of what their admirers were going through, but the would-be lovers often seemed oblivious to what it felt like to be the rejector. As we noted in the first chapter of this book, this discrepancy mirrors our cultural awareness, which has dwelt with fascination and imagination on the experience of the hopeless or rejected lover but has largely regarded the experience of the heartbreaker distantly through a haze of vague, misleading stereotypes.

Thus, we have seen that many rejectors found it very difficult to communicate their lack of interest, and their accounts often featured how they struggled to make themselves deliver the message of rejection. Yet these difficulties were largely absent from the accounts of the would-be lovers. This was one of the largest discrepancies in the entire research project. Whereas nearly two-thirds of the rejectors discussed this difficulty, less than a fifth of the would-be lovers mentioned it. If one were to ask the would-be lovers, perhaps they might upon reflection come to speculate that it was indeed hard for the rejector to deliver the rejection. But they failed to bring it up spontaneously or to include it in their story. Apparently, when caught up in one's own struggle and suffering, the struggle and suffering of someone else does not get much attention.

Another huge difference was the annoyance that the lover's behavior may have caused to the rejector. Would-be lovers sometimes realized that their actions, especially when persistent, exceeded the bounds of rationality, but they almost never indicated that their actions might be aggravating or annoying to the person they loved. In contrast, fully half of the rejectors referred to the aggravation or annoyance they suffered because of this unwanted love. The would-be lover who keeps on trying may often fail to realize that he or she is being obnoxious or bothersome. At most, that seems a trivial and minor part of the episode, one that is not worth recording as part of the story. To many rejectors, however, that obnoxiousness is often the centrally salient factor, almost the defining element, of the experience.

For example, one woman's account depicted a platonic friendship with a male who suddenly began trying to escalate it into a romantic involvement. At first she thought he was joking, but he began sending her flowers, letters, and gifts. She was not interested, but he would not be discouraged, and he began to appear everywhere she went. She says she never encouraged him and refused all his invitations, but still he remained persistent. Finally all her feelings of friendship were long gone and she detested him, but even outright expressions of rejection did not seem to work. "Although I kept on telling him that I couldn't stand him and that I probably hated him, all he did was laugh and say that I will get used to him."

Meanwhile, the rejectors downplayed some of the features of the would-be lovers' feelings. The longing and preoccupation of the the would-be lovers were more common in their own stories than in those of the rejectors. (It is possible that the rejectors downplayed those feelings in order to minimize their guilt, for emphasizing those feelings would make the rejection seem a more powerful, painful, or crushing disappointment.) Likewise, the would-be lovers' fears of rejection were more commonly noted in their own stories than in those of the rejectors.

Generally, people in each role found it easier to recognize their own lasting emotional distress than that of the other. We examined all stories for any indication that either the would-be lover or the rejector was still feeling distress in the present while recording the story. Both sides seemed aware that some rejected lovers continued to suffer, although the rejected lovers themselves were more likely to feature this continued suffering. In contrast, the continued distress of rejectors was recognized only by themselves. Only one single account by a rejected lover indicated that the rejector experienced any lasting distress, whereas a number of the rejectors said they still had such feelings.

Another way to look at these findings would be to see which stories contained any acknowledgement that the other party continued to suffer. Whereas 16.4% of the rejectors saw such continued distress in the people whose hearts they broke, only 1.6% of the would-be lovers noted any lasting frustration, guilt, resentment, hurt, anger, dissonance, or other feelings that the rejectors actually felt (see Appendix).

In short, everyone seemed to agree that the rejected lovers suffered more lasting emotional distress than the rejectors did, on the whole. But at least some rejectors were sensitive to the patterns of enduring suffering on the other's part. The rejected lovers were almost oblivious to the distress on the part of the rejector.

We shall return to this suggestion that the would-be lover is indeed oblivious to what the rejector is going through. Would-be lovers do some things that seem insensitive, inconsiderate, and almost shocking to the rejectors and even perhaps to neutral observers. But some of their actions can be understood and even sympathetically appreciated if one recognizes that these individuals may be unaware of the distress they are causing.

The Mystery of Passion

It is worth focusing closely on how the would-be lovers described their own feelings of attraction, even without statistical basis, because their reactions and perceptions provide a valuable context for understanding love. People who are mutually in love may often feel that they have found the person of their dreams, their ideal partner, their soul mate. Likewise, people who are threatened with the loss of a beloved may respond by feeling that they will not find another, because this was the one and only person for them. When friends tell them to forget about that person and find another, they reject that advice, even though in most cases that is what they eventually do. It is tempting to think that love arises when two well-matched people find each other, for cultural theories and personal experience both support such a view.

This myth of the uniquely perfect mate was made vivid to us by a question once asked by a dating partner: "Do you believe that there is only one person in the world for you? Or are there maybe ten or twenty, and it's just a matter of chance which one you meet up with first?" The latter view was presented as the distinctly unromantic alternative, even though it is quite idealistic in the narrow range of possible mates it allows. The possibility that there is an almost un-limited supply of potential mates, or the possibility that people be-come attracted to whoever happens to be available and then marry whomever they are seeing when life circumstances prescribe that it is time to get married, was not even considered. Our culture's love myths continue to conform to the pattern that each person has half a soul and that love occurs only when one finds the person with the complementary half.

But unrequited love reveals passion to be something other than a natural consequence of finding one's optimal mate. Unrequited love shows that people are attracted to others who may be ill suited to them. In retrospect, it is difficult to continue believing that the other person was the "one and only" one for you. (Of course, people who get divorced also cease to give idealized accounts of how well matched they were, and indeed they may portray the initial attraction as acci-dental or arbitrary. But they too have motives, such as justifying their divorce to themselves, and so their views on love are idiosyncratic and suspect; see Vaughan, 1986.) In short, unrequited love can expose the illusion of rationality and optimality that may surround love. Roman-tic attraction can instead be seen as something mysterious and even perhaps almost arbitrary. It is surprising to see the extent to which normal, healthy, well-adjusted people will describe their own feelings as something incomprehensible and out of control. Although this was far from the predominant attitude, its explicitness in some accounts is of interest. The fact that people can love someone without knowing why, or with only vague and speculative reasons, is important in its own right.

"When I look back at the situation, I can't imagine why I was so attracted to her," said one man. "The only reason I can think of is that she was one of the few girls who ever paid me any attention. She was also one of the few girls without her head in the clouds. Also, she was always very depressed with life in general, and I always wanted to help that." The last remark, of course, suggests an attraction based on a dubious desire to change someone for the better, but apart from that afterthought the man seemed mystified by the feelings he had had. By the same token, a woman looked back on her freshman year at college and recalled, "I had a crush on this one guy. To this day, though, I cannot understand why."

Some recalled paradoxical attractions that seemed destructive and senseless. One woman looked back on a turbulent, painful six-year relationship with an ambivalent man who drank too much and alternated between bossing her around and wanting to be left alone. "The more I wanted him, the more he pulled away," she reflected, and in the next paragraph she completed the vicious circle: "The more he pushed me away, the more I wanted him." Looking back, "none of it makes sense now because I really can't say why I loved him, or if I did." She says she was "hooked, bad," and she only broke away when she caught him with another woman.

Several people reported attraction to unattainable or impossible partners. "I think about him all the time," wrote one woman about a recent affair which she was not certain was over. "The only reason, I think, that he became more attractive to me is because he seems unattainable. The more aloof he has been, the more appealing he becomes." She had begun to feel that she was subjecting herself to torture by holding on to this frustrated passion, and she expressed the hope that she would soon stop, although immediately after saying that she went back to discussing whether she should call him soon and how she would react if he called her.

Another woman wrote of being baffled by her own feelings and their destructive consequences. To her surprise, she had abruptly felt powerfully attracted to another woman. The other woman was strictly heterosexual (as she herself had been, for the most part, until this), and so she knew the relationship "would never go anywhere." Apparently she and the woman had become emotionally very close without her ever expressing the romantic side of the attraction. The would-be lover felt that this relationship had had significant costs to her, for her beloved was prone to waste time and money and, in order to be together with her, she had ended up doing the same. She had neglected her own studies and other relationships. When the new school year began, the beloved had moved to the far side of campus, and so the would-be lover never saw her any more, and she claimed to be glad about this. She looked back with relief and embarrassment on the whole episode. In her account, the incomprehensibility of her own feelings and the irrational, hopeless attraction to someone who was no good for her were prominent features.

Of course, many people did have ample reasons for their attractions, and these reasons often featured physical appeal. "I guess I liked the way [he] dressed, spoke, and looked because I really didn't know anything else about him," wrote one woman. Another said, "I liked his ruggedness, physical strength, and insight." A man said when he met Denise he was stunned: "Very pretty girl, nice, distinct personality, and an alternative look... She was everything I was looking for ... She was gorgeous. We had a lot in common." A woman described an airplane pilot she met as "a gorgeous hunk of manhood ... tall, thin, and handsome—blue eyes—blond hair—beautiful teeth and hands. He was an excellent dancer. He interacted socially with great ease—very self-confident." A person whose gender was kept ambiguous wrote, "I felt as though this person was the best looking person I have ever seen in my life." Sometimes the reasons were less attractive in retrospect: "Oh! Sam was very good at being charming and persuasive and because I loved him so much I always fell prey to his deceptions and lies."

It is important to realize that, just as passion may be mysterious, so can its absence. As we have pointed out, people overwhelmingly tend to reciprocate positive feelings that others have toward them, so it is perhaps especially surprising when this fails to arise. The rejector's lack of reciprocal attraction may be the most substantial mystery and enigma.

To be sure, many rejectors were quite explicit about why they did not feel attracted to their admirers or desire a relationship with them. Many recited faults, shortcomings, misdeeds, and other objectionable aspects of their admirers. Still, it is noteworthy that some rejectors simply said they did not know why they were not able to reciprocate the other's attraction. Some even went so far as to suggest that they would have liked to be able to feel attraction and love toward the admirer but could not manage to do so.

We shall return to this issue in the chapter on morality and guilt, because rejectors may invoke their own lack of control over their own feelings to justify inflicting pain on someone else. For now, one example will be sufficient. A woman wrote of a platonic friendship with a man who wanted to be her boyfriend and lover. As friends, they spoke often, and he would frequently comment on what an ideal match they would be, saying things like "You know I would be the perfect boyfriend for you." She agreed with his assessment but nonetheless failed to have the requisite feelings toward him. "As true as that statement [about his being a potentially perfect boyfriend for her] might be, I just did not feel a chemistry between us." She said that he was very popular, tall, well built, with blond hair and blue eyes, but she " just never personally felt attracted to him." Significantly, she added that she regretted her lack of romantic feelings toward him, but there was nothing she could do about it.

Taken together, these comments suggest that unrequited love starts out much the same as any other romantic interest. There is no reason to assume that most cases of unrequited love begin with some doomed passion or rest on some particularly irrational basis. Physical beauty or appeal, social poise and charm, an attractive personality, having things in common, and so forth—these are the familiar bases for successful romantic attractions and for unsuccessful ones too. There is less mystery in the existence of passion than, perhaps, in its absence. For many disappointed lovers, their passion may seem mysterious in retrospect because it was poorly based or directed toward an ill-chosen target. But it is abundantly clear that people do not restrict their feelings of attraction to people who would be the most suitable long-term partners for them.

Why?—Attachment and Interdependence Revisited

Before closing, it is useful to examine the possible reasons for the emotional patterns we have observed. In Chapter 2, we sketched several theoretical perspectives on unrequited love, and these help make sense of the emotional crossfire.

Attachment theory asserts that people are biologically programmed to desire, form, and maintain social relationships with others. The would-be lover's desire to become attached is therefore easy
to understand, as is the joy that would-be lovers feel when they believe
that an attachment is forming. To start a relationship is to satisfy a
basic human urge, and emotional pleasure and satisfaction is the result.

Attachment theory also says that when relationships fail and
people are deprived of the ones they love, responses tend to fall into
three main patterns, and all of these have been observed in our data.
The first response, according to Bowlby (1969, 1973) and others, is
protest, and this is readily seen in the acute distress and occasionally
berserk reactions by newly disappointed lovers. (In future chapters, we
will add considerably to this theme, when we examine some of the
behavioral responses to heartbreak.) The second response, passive
despair, is also exhibited in the profound sadness and depression that
many heartbroken lovers report. The third response, *detachment*, involves derogating the love object and convincing oneself that one
doesn't really want or need the other after all. There was perhaps less
of this than of the other two reactions, possibly because it is a relatively
brief stage, but there certainly were some would-be lovers who fell
into that category and insisted that they would not want a relationship
with that person anymore even if the other person wanted it.

Attachment theory also suggests that to refuse an interpersonal
attachment violates deeply rooted human tendencies and would therefore be emotionally stressful. Consistent with this, rejectors reported
emotional turmoil and distress of various patterns. The rejector's role
is not a happy one.

Turning from attachment to interdependence theory, we suggested that the rejector's situation contains mainly unpleasant possibilities, and so the situation is more stressful and aversive than the
aspiring lover's situation (which, at least, seems to hold the possibility
of something wonderful). The fact that rejectors were more negative
on the whole about the episode may simply reflect this balance of
positive and negative outcomes. Would-be lovers may have seen the
situation as a gamble, and it did indeed offer emotional highs and

lows not unlike gambling. In retrospect, one lost the gamble, but at least one knows that it seemed worth the gamble at the time. In contrast, it was probably never worth it for the rejector. The no-win situation that confronts the rejector was probably stressful and unpleasant most of the time, and there were no desired possibilities to make it worthwhile.

Conclusion

The stereotype of unrequited love portrays pain, suffering, and longing on the one side, with aloof indifference on the other. This stereotype is inadequate on several accounts. It is apparently more accurate to say that both the would-be lover and the rejector are subject to a mixture of good and bad feelings both during the episode and afterward. The rejector is far from indifferent and may sometimes be the one who ends up with the greater load of negative affect. Rather than unmitigated suffering on one side and indifference on the other, the picture of unrequited love that emerges from our investigation is that of an emotional crossfire on both sides.

The unrequited lover does often derive great pleasure from at least parts of the experience. Love is a naturally occurring form of intense pleasure, and it brings moments of joy even if it ends badly. Would-be lovers may pay for a few days of ecstasy with over a year of anguish, but the good and desirable feelings are nonetheless real and important. Rejectors have fewer positive and more (though perhaps less intense) negative feelings than the would-be lovers. Rejectors may enjoy the friendship, the flattering attention, and the excitement of the other's attraction, and some enjoy genuine feelings of attraction themselves even if these seem mysteriously to dissipate fairly soon. On the negative side, rejectors commonly suffer from annoyance, and some report anger, frustration, confusion, resentment, and even repulsion and hatred.

Fears, worries, and uncertainties characterize both sides, although both seem to focus on the response of the rejector. The would-be lover is afraid of being rejected and wonders what to do or how to act in order to elicit the reciprocal attraction. The rejector dreads having to deliver the heartbreaking message of rejection. Both parties become hesitant about expressing their feelings and may even decide to conceal them, and each (partly as a consequence) shows some lack of understanding of what the other is going through.

Thus, would-be lovers sometimes conceal their feelings, but the rejectors are still somewhat sensitive to their suffering and distress. In contrast, rejected lovers seem to have minimal awareness of the emotional distress that the love objects go through in these incidents. These patterns correspond to the broader awareness in the culture, which has models and scripts for lovers (including unrequited lovers) but only a hazy and largely inaccurate notion of the heartbreaker's experience. In our sample, the rejectors often seemed to feel a fundamental uncertainty about how one is supposed to act when one is the target of unwanted romantic interest. This sense of lacking a script is important in understanding the moral dimension of the rejectors' actions, for they do not know how to distinguish right from wrong actions adequately, as we shall see shortly in another chapter.

The mixture of good and bad feelings, and sometimes the attraction itself, can be confusing to the people caught in the emotional crossfire. For the would-be lover, in particular, the bad feelings may be difficult to deal with, because some people find it hard to reconcile passionate longing with anger or resentment. One solution is apparently to direct the negative feelings toward someone else, for instance, if a third person comes along to compete for the attentions of one's beloved.

In many cases, the emotional crossfire is complicated by a preexisting relationship, especially friendship, with the other person. To convert a platonic friendship into a romance is not easy and the attempt to do so is seen by people on both sides as a threat to the friendship. Platonic friends who become would-be lovers have to decide whether to risk destroying the friendship in order to have the chance at love. Meanwhile, platonic friends who do not want to become lovers must reconcile their positive feelings toward their friend with their lack of romantic interest, and they often struggle to find a way to send a firm message of romantic rejection without destroying what may be a treasured friendship.

If feelings are mixed during an episode of unrequited love, they are also mixed afterward. People who suffer rejection and heartbreak may feel resentful for a while, but many of them seem to retain a soft spot in their hearts for the ones they loved. Their recollections of failed love are bittersweet or even, in some cases, mostly positive. In contrast, rejectors are more negative in their recollections, and they may often look back with unmitigated bad feeling on the entire episode.

The discrepancy in retrospective feelings may be partly due to the time course of the feelings. Both parties tend to show an increase in negative affect as the affair approaches its tragic conclusion. For the would-be lovers, however, the negative affect seems to function almost as an opponent process to overcome their very positive feelings of attraction, so their net feelings toward the target gradually move toward zero and, as we have seen, often do not entirely reach affective neutrality even long after they give up any realistic hope for a relationship. Rejectors, on the other hand, are not starting out from a position of strong attraction or love, and the negative affect rises as escalating frustration, resentment, or helpless annoyance at the difficulty of discouraging these unwanted attentions. Thus, at the end of the episode, the would-be lover is approaching affective neutrality from a highly positive state, whereas the rejector is moving away from neutrality toward a heavily negative state.

All told, unrequited love brings more bad feelings than good, and it brings them to both the would-be lover and to the rejector. The rejected lover, perhaps ironically, has more good feelings about the other person than the rejector has, both during the episode and afterward. The rejector has more bad feelings toward the other person, both during and afterward.

Considerable research has established that emotions are strongly affected by events that have a bearing on self-esteem. The next chapter will take a closer look at the dynamics of self-esteem during unrequited love. The self-esteem findings will provide a helpful context for understanding some of the emotional patterns we have described in this chapter—and yet they will also reveal one dramatic, fundamental irony about the emotional crossfire of heartbreak.

Notes

1. This does speak to the issue of whether the two sets of stories refer to different types of incidents. If the would-be lovers, but not the rejectors, were mostly telling stories about affairs that were still in progress in their minds, then some of the other differences might be confounded by the present vs. past time frame. Thus, in a way it is quite fortunate that no difference was found here.

2. There are several possible explanations for how such differences may arise. It is plausible that would-be lovers choose to describe episodes that they are still suffering over, whereas rejectors choose to describe incidents that are firmly in the past. Alternatively, rejectors may not be aware that their victims continue to suffer, possibly because they prefer not to notice. We suspect that the latter is the case, although we cannot rule out the former except by noting that subjects were asked to choose the most important incident that had occurred to them and could only be choosing selectively by violating this instruction systematically. In either case, the motivation is the same: Rejectors want to interpret and present their actions as if they did not inflict lasting harm, while would-be lovers are willing to describe their suffering more or less in full, and possibly in dramatized or exaggerated fashion.

F·O·U·R

The Ups and Downs of Self-Esteem

Self-esteem is one of the overriding concerns in life. People are abundantly concerned with maintaining a favorable evaluation of themselves, as well as with how others evaluate them. The need to preserve and possibly enhance one's esteem is regarded as one of the most basic and powerful human motivations (e.g., Baumeister, 1982; Darley & Goethals, 1980; Greenberg, Pyszczynski, & Solomon, 1986; Hogan, 1983; Tesser, 1988; Zuckerman, 1979). Although contemporary psychologists favor the term *self-esteem*, the concern is hardly unique to modern times. Throughout the ages, the concern with esteem has been central, even though it has been discussed in other terms such as *pride, honor, reputation, acclaim,* and *respect*.

There are strong ties between esteem and emotion. Events that boost or confirm one's self-esteem produce positive emotions, while events that threaten or undermine one's self-esteem produce negative ones. Success and approval produce joy, satisfaction, elation, and other pleasures. Failure or criticism brings worry, sadness, disappointment, anger, and other forms of emotional distress (see Higgins, 1987).

When strong emotions and motivations are at work, as they clearly are in unrequited love, one can expect that issues of esteem are involved.

One important motivational theory that treated both love and esteem was offered by Abraham Maslow (1968). He proposed a hierarchy of needs, which asserted that people seek first to satisfy the most basic motivations (such as needs for food, water, sleep, and oxygen), and when these are satisfied they move on to satisfying higher needs (ultimately reaching self-actualization). He proposed that needs for love and belongingness are an important step in the hierarchy, one that comes before needs for esteem. Thus, in general, love should take precedence over esteem. Maslow's hypothesis provides a valuable context for considering the dilemmas faced by the would-be lover. Such an individual may face a difficult choice between making a dignified withdrawal (to protect esteem) and humiliating persistence (to pursue love).

The would-be lover is not the only one whose self-esteem is affected by unrequited love, however. The rejector's self-image is also involved. It is with the rejector's self-esteem that we shall begin.

A Supreme Compliment?

To have someone fall in love with you should presumably provide a powerful boost to your self-esteem. Indeed, many theories of personality development (such as those of Harry Stack Sullivan, 1953 and Carl Rogers, 1959) have stressed parental love as the the foundation of self-esteem. The unwanted affection of a would-be lover may not contain the emotional power of mother's love, but it still expresses a compliment. It means that someone else found you wonderful, appealing, desirable.

Indeed, one could argue that the esteem boost that occurs during unrequited love should be greater than the esteem boost from mother's love. Your mother, after all, is ineluctably invested in you, and her assessment of you is biased. To win the love of an adult is in some ways a greater tribute to one's positive qualities. "It's an ego boost to have someone attracted to you," as one person in our study pointed out simply.

And unsolicited love is arguably the greatest compliment of all. It signifies that someone became attracted to you without your trying to win it. It is the attributional equivalent to succeeding at a difficult task without trying hard or without preparing. Such successes testify to extremely high ability. To attract love without putting forth any effort suggests that you are extremely desirable.

The accounts by rejectors often referred to the boost in esteem they received, at least initially, from being the object of someone else's attention. On the whole, rejectors got far more positive boosts to self-esteem than would-be lovers got. One young man expressed this articulately: "I consider myself rather modest and have never thought of myself as arrogant, but I could tell that when I walked into the room she had a noticeable quality of excitement. She pampered me with food and drink completely unselfishly and it seemed she believed she could not do enough for me." To have such an effect on another person is indeed an ego boost. A number of others also discussed the flattering impact of things the other person did for them, such as sending flowers, paying compliments, or offering presents and gifts.

The ego boost was of course tempered by the fact that the rejector did not plan to become romantically involved. The majority of references to the self-esteem benefits of being the object of someone else's love took the form of "I was really flattered, but . . . ," or, more ominously, "I was really flattered at first . . . " The boost to self-esteem was typically connected with the initial discovery that the person was attracted to the rejector. Later, amid the struggle to extricate oneself from unwanted attentions and clinging pursuit, the esteem boost may recede to a minor consideration, but the first discovery of someone else's love for you can be a very ego-enhancing message that is all the more striking because it is unexpected. "I was shocked yet flattered at the same time," was one fairly typical description of the first reaction.

Thus we can begin to understand the difficult position in which the rejector finds himself or herself. On the one hand, the romantic interest and attentions of someone else provide a welcome confirmation of one's desirability and attractiveness. This feedback may be especially welcome to young people, who are just having their first romantic experiences and are uncertain about how they may fare and whether they will be able to succeed at attracting lovers and intimate partners. They are therefore reluctant to respond negatively to a source of such positive, wished-for feedback. On the other hand, one does not want to encourage the other too much if one has no intention of entering into a relationship with that person.

The rejector's initial reaction may therefore go beyond surprise to mixed feelings that pull in contrary directions—wanting the positive message but also not wanting it. As one woman summarized her dilemma at being the focus of unrequited love: "It's difficult not to be flattered by someone who likes you that much even if you don't like them back. I'm sure the fact that I was flattered but not attracted gave him mixed messages."

Roughly one out of four accounts by rejectors made some reference to the flattery or ego boost implicit in the other person's attentions. There are two important comments to be made about this rate. First, the recognition that love carries a flattering message to the rejector was much higher in the rejectors' accounts than in the accounts of the would-be lovers. Indeed, the would-be lovers almost never mentioned this aspect. Their accounts largely ignored the fact that the other person might receive a boost in self-esteem from being the object of love. This finding supports the view that would-be lovers are preoccupied with their own feelings and needs and hence do not attend in great detail to the experiences and feelings of the person they love (except insofar as those feelings relate to the would-be lovers' own needs and wants). It is in a sense surprising that would-be lovers would overlook what is often the single most positive aspect of the experience for the rejector.

The second point is that the majority of rejectors did *not* mention any boost to self-esteem. Even if some felt it but did not include it in their accounts, one must conclude that the esteem boost is not a universal feature of the experience of the rejector. In a follow-up survey, we found that there was a general pattern amounting to a weak ego boost overall, although that average was naturally based on a genuine boost for some and a negligible boost for others. Hence it is worth considering why being the target of someone's love should be an ego boost for some and not for others. When does love fail to carry a substantial, flattering message?

One factor is that the lover's own desirability apparently determines the esteem-enhancing value of his or her love. To be loved by creeps, jerks, wimps, sluts, dolts, or other losers apparently has little value for boosting one's self-esteem. To be loved by highly desirable partners, on the other hand, is extremely flattering, perhaps even if one does not want that love. The subculture of groupies who pursue rock and movie stars for sexual favors appears to reflect this truth. A groupie's status with other groupies is determined by the fame and star quality of the people she has slept with. In her memoirs, ex-groupie Pamela Des Barres (1987) spoke with awe about one woman who had reputedly slept with both Mick Jagger and John Lennon.

One reason that some loves remain unrequited is that the love object does not consider the would-be lover to be desirable. If that is the case, then that person's attentions may do little to boost self-esteem. For example, one woman described her admirer in these terms: "This is rude, but Albert is a total turnoff-loser, not extremely well liked outside his circle, not exactly great looking either, personality not wonderful . . . " One can readily see why her self-esteem may have gained little from Albert's declaration of love. In contrast, another woman wrote, "I've noticed over the years, starting with Doug, that all the men that have loved me or been attracted to me have been extremely intelligent, creative, and usually talented." Her esteem apparently did benefit from the attentions of these accomplished, desirable individuals.

The importance of the other person's desirability as a basis for the esteem-enhancing impact of his or her love was perhaps most clearly expressed in another woman's account: " . . . A friend of mine approached me and told me that he knew a guy who was interested in me. Of course, I was flattered and then asked who. My friend gave me some clues and I soon figured out who the guy was. I wasn't all that flattered anymore." Thus, the esteem boost wore off as soon as she learned that the would-be lover was not highly desirable.

In fact, it is plausible that rejectors might even find the other's romantic interest a blow to their self-esteem. Romantic relationships, as we have seen, tend to have some firm basis in equity, such that the two people's "market value" is roughly comparable (Walster et al., 1976). Anna may find George's interest in her flattering if George is a highly desirable partner, for it suggests that she is attractive enough to deserve someone so wonderful. But by the same token, Anna could be offended by George's interest if George is highly undesirable, for his interest suggests that she is unattractive enough to be considered (at least by him) an appropriate match. To be sure, there was very little evidence of feeling offended among the rejectors in our sample, but it may be that rejectors were reluctant to articulate this aspect of their feelings because it reflects badly on them. It would make them seem either elitist and conceited (for falsely regarding themselves as too good for a particular partner) or relatively unattractive (if they did indeed not deserve any better than this undesirable partner). Hence we should not take the absence of this sentiment in our sample as conclusive evidence that it never arises.

Our impression from these accounts is that the would-be lover's desirability is evaluated by several different sets of relevant criteria. For one's own emotional reaction, only one's own feelings matter. For the esteem boost, however, other people's consensual appraisal of the individual's qualities is decisive. Some people said that the person who loved them was a perfectly fine, admirable person, and some even suggested that their own failure to reciprocate the love was surprising or mysterious. But as long as others might consider the would-be lover a desirable partner, his or her attentions may provide an esteem boost even if the rejector has no intention of becoming romantically involved.

Thus, many (but not all) rejectors do receive a boost in esteem from the episode. To be loved, especially when one has not consciously tried to win that love, is a gratifying compliment to one's attractiveness and desirability. This element of flattery is mainly muted or missing when the love comes from people whose love is considered of low value because they are not regarded as desirable partners.

Enduring Humiliation

The other side of the self-esteem story is the effect on the would-be lover. If to be loved is to receive a tribute to one's good qualities, then to be rejected is to receive an implicit but very negative evaluation. Unrequited love can carry a powerful message of disparagement to the would-be lover. If the person you love doesn't love you, there must be something wrong with you, something undesirable—at least, that is what people seem to think.

Loss of self-esteem was far more common in the would-be lovers' accounts than in the rejectors' accounts. In fact, only one rejector indicated having suffered a loss of self-esteem from the incident, whereas half the would-be lovers made some such reference. Over and over in their accounts, the loss of face figured as a prominent feature. They referred to feeling silly, foolish, stupid, embarrassed, humiliated. In some cases, the rejector didn't do anything more negative than fail to respond, but it was still a blow to one's esteem. "I felt stupid talking to someone like that and being put down," said one person whose intended partner walked away without saying anything in response to a friendly opening line. Another spoke about struggling for weeks to get up the courage to approach the man she had a crush on. "One night I got drunk and attempted to talk to him, but he totally blew me off. Total embarrassment." A few even mentioned that the rejection affected them globally and seemed to imply that they would not be a desirable partner in general. Thus, one wrote that after rejection, "I basically felt hurt and not too worthy of anyone".

We have suggested that unrequited love may often arise because of "falling upward"—in other words, because people tend to fall in love with someone more desirable and attractive than themselves. They may convince themselves that they are worthy of this person's love, possibly because they may succumb to the familiar tendency to hold an inflated view of their own attractiveness. The desired partner, however, may see them accurately while seeing himself or herself in a favorably distorted fashion, which quickly furnishes the conclusion that the two are not at all suitably matched. This situation is tailor-made for an ego deflation. Most commonly, the would-be lover will sooner or later have to face the fact that this seemingly ideal partner doesn't regard him or her as an ideal partner.

Indeed, people often say that to love is to make oneself vulnerable. This vulnerability may take several forms, but one major point of vulnerability is self-esteem. Falling upward risks a hard crash on one's ego. Although it may rarely be expressed overtly between the two, and indeed the language of love and courtship takes many forms, one implicit aspect of the aspiring lover's message is, "I think we are well matched," and one aspect of the rejector's message is, "You must be joking," or, more precisely, "You are not good enough to deserve me."

Concerns over esteem seem to play an important role in people's struggle to get up the courage to approach the person in the first place. In the previous chapter, we noted that many would-be lovers suffered a fear of rejection. One big stimulus to these fears was the possibility of losing face, of losing esteem. "I greatly fear making an ass of myself by hitting on [i.e., making romantic overtures to] her," said one young man to describe why he was reluctant to let his feelings be known. Others would drop hints or begin to reveal their feelings but would quickly deny them at the first sign of rejection, apparently in order to save face. It is well known that people are reluctant to make romantic overtures if the probability of rejection is high (e.g., Shanteau & Nagy, 1979).

Of course, the esteem blow may not come in the initial response. But the later it comes, the more devastating it may be. After all, if the person rejects you casually with minimal information, that implies a less thorough evaluation than if someone gets to know you well and then rejects you. A gradual shift toward increasingly negative regard with increasing familiarity is a powerful humiliation that is hard to dismiss (Aronson & Linder, 1965). It leaves one fearful about future relationships. It seems to say that, although you may be superficially desirable enough to attract romantic interest, once you reveal your true self the partner will be repelled.

A woman's account graphically depicted how her self-esteem was undermined when a man she had been seeing for ten months lost interest in her and withdrew his affection. By her own account, she was devastated; yet she still had difficulty acknowledging the blow to her pride, and in her account she began by suggesting that the esteem loss was simply something her friends had suggested: "Lots of my friends felt that maybe the fact that he left me was a great buster for my ego." She said that at the time she refused to accept that a man would lose interest in her, because of the blow to her self-esteem. "I tried to overcompensate, I made excuses for him. I just couldn't believe this had happened to me. We had destructive communication, huge arguments, etc. I kept trying, though I don't understand why I kept hanging on hoping that someday his feelings for me would be rekindled. It was a traumatic experience for me. My self-esteem plummeted so low." She ended by saying that she was better now, but she was still in psychotherapy trying "to rebuild my self-esteem."

The most painful and cruel losses of esteem were suffered by people who became involved with someone who did not reciprocate and then used them. To feel that one is being exploited by someone one loves is apparently a severe assault on one's ego. Exploitation violates the norms of equity in romantic relationships and in fact suggests that the partner did not even consider you worthy of equitable treatment. To the person you loved, you were merely a means, a tool, a toy.

For example, one woman described what started out as a storybook romance with a foreign man: "tall, dark, handsome, etc." She recounted how much she enjoyed their initial time together as her attraction to him grew stronger and seemed to be reciprocated. She took pleasure in their dates and activities, and the only troubling note was that she found him to be "in such a hurry to get into my bed. At first I thought it was because he was really attracted to me, but in actuality, he wanted to consummate the relationship so he would be able to stop the little extras such as going out to the movies, etc. Once he had gotten what he had desired, he stopped calling me except when he was in the mood or had some extra time on his hands." Later she began to suffer over his apparent indifference toward her and she sought to lash out to hurt him in return. "I had learned that he hadn't liked me and that I was just an American conquest for him whenever he was in the mood [for sex]. The relationship hurt me because I was just being used . . ."

Although both sexes referred to the humiliation of being used, women's accounts were more likely to cast this in a sexual form. These accounts described the woman's attraction to a man who simply used her for sexual pleasure. Typically, in such a case, the woman was clearly willing to have sex with the man, but she wanted it to be meaningful and to symbolize a mutual emotional investment. To discover that it had not carried such significance for him was humiliating. This comes through clearly in the following account: "I had never slept with anyone before but I decided it was okay with him because I really cared and [I thought] he must really care if he wanted to take such a big step. Let me tell you, maybe it was a big step for me but obviously it was just a walk in the park for him." In other words, it was his casualness about sex that offended her. She was willing to have sex with him, but only under certain conditions, or only within a certain context that included mutual caring and feeling.

The male would-be lovers who ended up feeling used seemed rather to feel that the woman used them for emotional support or even for an ego boost, or some other goal. One young man described his humiliation at being used as a diversion from another problematic love affair. For some time, he loved a girl who already had a boyfriend. The couple broke up, and our hero moved in for a few weeks of bliss. "And then she decided to go back with her old flame. I was heartbroken. I thought we might have had something special, and all it turned out to be was a momentary escape for her so that she could 'start again' with Joe Kidd." The bitterness in his sarcastic conclusion is apparent, even in the use of a sarcastic name for the rival.

Several additional aspects of the would-be lovers' esteem loss deserve mention. One factor is a parallel to our earlier comment that the rejector's ego boost is increased by the fact that he or she has made no effort to attract the other. The attributional implications of effort may increase the effect on the would-be lover too, but in the opposite direction. Just as it is doubly impressive to have someone fall in love with you when you have not exerted yourself or altered your behavior to win that person's love, it is doubly humiliating to be rejected by the person you have tried your best to win. The more you try, the more devastating failure may be. Many would-be lovers apparently face this dilemma sooner or later. To continue to pursue the beloved is most likely to bring further losses of esteem, although to withdraw is to relinquish any chance of winning the other's affections. The dilemma, then, is at what point do you cease your efforts to secure love, in order to preserve some pride and dignity?

One man, for example, described how several others were attracted to the same woman he desired at the same time. As she began to show a preference for one of his rivals, he was hurt and withdrew from his pursuit of her to protect himself from further blows to his pride. "I gradually came to realize that I was losing this little competition, so I stopped asking her out."

A last point is that one's public esteem may suffer as much as one's private esteem. In their research on jealousy, Pines and Aronson (1983) concluded that the strongest single situational cause of intense reactions to a partner's involvement with someone else is the number of other people who know about the infidelity. People feel least jealous if the partner is discreet and manages to keep the affair a secret. People feel terribly upset, however, to discover that they are the last to know.

We have no systematic data about how much other people's awareness of events influenced reactions, but some observations did seem consistent with Pines and Aronson's conclusion. To be rejected is bad enough, but to be publicly spurned seemed especially galling. For example, one girl described how her boyfriend canceled a date to go to a dance that they had been planning for a long time. "I found out about a week later that he'd been going out with my best friend. I was really upset. Everyone knew before I did. No one told me, I had still been talking to my friend about Dan as if we were still going out, and I felt foolish."

Getting Over It

Many traumas threaten the individual's sense of self-esteem, and so the processes of coping and recovery are often centrally concerned with restoring one's pride (Janoff-Bulman, 1989; Taylor, 1983). Unrequited love is no different. Rejection constitutes a blow to one's pride, as we have seen, and to get over it one may have to do something to restore one's confidence.

This concern with rebuilding self-esteem is primarily associated with the would-be lover. The rejectors showed little concern with esteem at the end of the episode, even though they had many other concerns and may have been quite distressed about the incident. Our impression was that issues of self-esteem had ceased to play any significant role for the rejectors by the end of the episode, and even in retrospect esteem did not loom large for them. Occasionally a rejector said something to the effect of having had his or her confidence increased by the episode, so as to make him or her better able to approach other members of the opposite sex. For the most part, however, references to esteem figured only in the early aspects of the rejector's stories. And even when one did refer to esteem later in the episode, it tended to be a positive consequence (such as increased confidence) rather than a problem.

For the would-be lovers, however, loss of esteem was a significant part of the episode, and recovery had to include dealing with the esteem threat. Would-be lovers used various strategies to restore their self-esteem and minimize whatever loss it had suffered.

A first face-saving strategy was to affirm one's esteem directly. One might say that the beloved was not, in retrospect, worthy of the love that the would-be lover had lavished on him or her. This was sometimes expressed in terms of deserving better: "We broke up and now I realize though it hurts so much I deserved better than to be used by him as a security blanket when he didn't get on with his home girl or he couldn't see her because he was here at college."

Face-saving might also take the form of devaluing the partner, as in the "I don't know what I ever saw in her" reactions we discussed in the preceding chapter. Indeed, occasionally the derogation of the object became explicit, as in this example: "He never called. After a number of months my friend and I saw Jim at the mall. I got a great amount of satisfaction from remarking on how skinny he is and that he doesn't look cute at all." Or, in the more succinct (if more collo-quial) words of another, "I continued to like him for the rest of the semester, even though I now think he is and was a slime bucket."

That this derogation is specifically a phase of coping was suggested by another woman, who wrote, "I bad-mouthed him for about two months, until my next boyfriend." In other words, once she found someone to reciprocate her love, her self-esteem was again secure, and she could afford to stop derogating the one who had jilted her.

Derogating the love object is, of course, a problematic strategy. After all, one has fallen in love with this person, longed for love and pined away over this individual, and perhaps even made a fool of oneself pursuing this person's affections; to then say that the person was not so desirable after all is often unconvincing. Whether it really salvages esteem is even debatable. To have fallen for someone who is a mediocrity does not reflect well on the would-be lover, and the more strenuously one has pursued this person, the worse one looks if the person is pronounced in retrospect to have been undesirable. These retrospective devaluations may have the character of what Leon Festinger (1957) described as postdecisional dissonance reduction—that is, rationalizing one's decision to have been the best when one can no longer change it. A familiar illustration of such a process was furnished by Aesop's fable of the fox who concluded that the unreachable grapes were probably sour anyway.

Some of the accounts clearly struggled with the inconsistency between having loved this person and yet wanting to derogate him or her. For example, one woman described how she lost respect for a man because of his indecisiveness, which she referred to symbolically as a testicular deficiency: "I have no respect for him because he has no balls yet I still feel like he was a great part of my life and I miss it . . . I have no respect for him. I hate him. But I still am hung up on him. I don't understand why, knowing what a jerk he is, I'd still like to go out with him, at least one more time." By her own admission, her feelings make no sense to her; but they make perfect sense to an external perspective. Derogating him is part of her way of coping with the rejection and breaking her emotional attachment to him, but it has not yet succeeded, and so her mind is telling her to despise him while her heart is wishing for another chance.

If derogating the love object may be a dubious means of bolstering one's own self-esteem, perhaps it has other functions. We noted in the previous chapter that reactions to romantic rejection correspond to some of the patterns observed following attachment failure. The third pattern, according to Bowlby's (1969, 1973) observations of children deprived of their mothers, was to decide that one doesn't even want or like the mother after all. Rejected lovers who derogate the ones they loved in vain may simply be exhibiting the same detachment reaction.

Derogating the love object may be an awkward way of coping, but to devalue the third person who stole your beloved's heart can be an effective face-saving strategy. We noted in the preceding chapter that some accounts seemed to aim particular venom toward such third persons. Esteem considerations are clearly central in such episodes. You and another person loved someone, and that someone chose the other person over you. Such a clear judgment of preference contains an unmistakable suggestion that you are somehow inferior to your rival. A number of our accounts appeared to be responding to that specific blow. They took pains to insist that they were superior to the other person after all, contrary to the apparent indication.

Thus, for example, one woman was dumped in favor of another whom she describes as "very unattractive." She was completely unwilling to concede that the other was superior to her in any respect. "Every time I see her or both of them together I keep on asking myself what he sees in her." Recognizing, perhaps, that her remarks seem too blatantly self-serving, she quickly added that other people corroborated her judgment: "This is not just me being vain, but other people also didn't understand why he ended everything with me and started going out with her." The key, however, was that she was able to retain her pride and feel better about the episode as long as she could sustain her sense of superiority over her rival. In her words, "the strangest thing is that I am not even jealous of her because I know that I am much better than she is."

To derogate the third person is also a two-edged sword, however, because of the de facto victory of the other. It is no disgrace to lose to someone who is marvelous, but losing to a loser reflects especially badly on the self. One man expressed this chagrin. He couldn't help but regard his rival in negative terms, but he sensed that losing out to this individual carried some disturbing implications: "The worst part of it for me was that the guy who did 'win' her was a real loser as far as I was concerned. What does she see in him, I kept wondering?"

Perhaps a more reliable strategy for boosting one's self-esteem is to find someone else, preferably someone who is an attractive catch, who will reciprocate one's affections. A number of rejected lovers were careful to point out that others did find them desirable. "I have a boyfriend whom I have been seeing for one year and he treats me so much better than Peter ever did, and he adores me to death," wrote one woman who had been jilted in embarrassing fashion by Peter. A young man was even a bit cynical or sarcastic about this strategy: "By the next year, I could fool freshman girls into thinking I was a cool guy."

Drawing on the fact of one's appeal to others is not simply a strategy for salving one's own wounded ego in private recollections. Some people use it in a highly visible strategy to send a message to the person who spurns them. They may feel that the rejector fails to appreciate them, and they hope that by showing the rejector that others desire them they can rekindle the rejector's interest. Some claim, at least, that this strategy can be somewhat effective. One woman who had been the loser in a triangle wrote that the fellow later began to want her back, "because he realized he was losing me to other guys now . . . " Another was more explicit about displaying the attentions she received from others in order to send a message to her rejector: "After a while, I would deliberately taunt him by making sure that he always saw me with someone else, especially guys. I would be overly friendly with my friends to make it appear as if I didn't need him and that I didn't care what he thought because I had plenty of opportunity to be with someone else."

If the rejector can be moved to want the would-be lover after all, that is the best balm for the wounded ego. Of course, that may be best all around, for one gets what one wants. But even if the would-be lover does not end up having a romance with the rejector, it is very gratifying to be wanted by that person at some point. To reject one's rejector is apparently an especially sweet form of revenge, because one's appeal and desirability are vindicated and so one's self-esteem is salvaged. There were several examples of this strategy. One woman was unappreciated by the man she wanted, who seemed to care little about her despite her strong love for him. When finally she pulled away, he became aware of the loss. "Now he wanted to get back with me because he realized he missed me a lot and regretted his decision." But she stood firm and rejected him despite the temptation to go back to him. Several others wrote of taking control of their emotions and making themselves stop feeling attracted to someone who seemed not to reciprocate their feelings. As a result, any later interest shown by the other person was now unwanted, and the tables were turned, the rejected lover finally able to play the rejector. "I felt really good when he would call me after a party and I'd blow him off," acknowledged one such woman.

The occasional presence of these examples of turning the tables points, however, to the fundamental problem of the rejected lover. In addition to the frustration and emotional pain, romantic rejection is often a severe blow to one's self-esteem, and the only truly effective strategy for nullifying this blow is for the rejector to change his or her mind. Rejection implies a negative appraisal of one's desirability, and as long as the rejection stands, the negative appraisal seems to stand as well. To get the rejector to reverse this appraisal is the best and perhaps the only thoroughly satisfactory way of erasing the blot on one's self-esteem.

This preoccupation with the rejector's assessment was expressed very touchingly by one woman who was still in the relationship that she described. In her account, the man she lived with liked her but had other plans and ambitions, and he did not care enough about her to try to fit their relationship into his plans. She was in the dwindling days of their time together and knew that shortly he would leave her, despite her strong love and attachment. She loved him, but he did not love her and was preparing to move on. "I've kind of settled for just enjoying what time I have left with him before he leaves to find what he needs out of life somewhere else. My biggest hope is that he does miss me when he's gone, even if only a little. But I'd give anything for it to be a lot."

Looking Back

When people look back on episodes of unrequited love, particularly if they have found ways to satisfy their needs for love and belongingness, they may be influenced by their concerns with self-esteem. In that respect, having loved in vain is a defeat, whereas having been the target of someone's love is at least a small victory. For that reason, people should tend to emphasize how many other people have loved them rather than how many times they have been rejected by others. As we noted in Chapter 1, the evidence does support this: People claimed to recall approximately twice as many episodes in which they were loved in vain as episodes in which they loved someone else in vain.

Logically, of course, the two tallies should be equal, insofar as each episode involves one rejector and one would-be lover. Or one might even have predicted the opposite pattern, because people know their own feelings (even if kept secret) but may fail to notice the unexpressed love of others. Contrary to logic, however, people generally insisted that they had been the target more often than the holder of unrequited love. Or, in terms of falling upward, people more often recall having been the superior member of the pair rather than the inferior one. Probably this pattern should be explained on the basis of the general tendency for people to exaggerate things that boost their esteem and downplay those that reduce their self-esteem (Taylor & Brown, 1988).

Our impression is that concern with self-esteem follows opposite time courses for rejectors as compared with would-be lovers. Esteem may be central to the rejector's initial reaction, for as we have seen it is flattering to be loved or admired by someone. Later, the rejector ceases to derive an ego boost from it and becomes preoccupied with other considerations, such as guilt and aggravation and even wishing the whole thing had never happened. For the would-be lover, esteem may not be an issue at first, but it gradually becomes more important. Falling in love, especially until one is rejected, seems not to have particular effects on self-esteem. The rejection raises issues of self-esteem, and during the interval between the first sign of rejection and the end of the episode (when the would-be lover finally gives up hope and disengages himself or herself from the attraction) there may be conflicts between self-esteem and love. That is, love says to keep trying, whereas self-esteem says to salvage one's pride and dignity by not trying.

Therefore, when the would-be lover looks back on the episode, self-esteem considerations may seem to come to the fore, perhaps especially for the would-be lover who wishes he or she had behaved with more dignity. Of course, it's easy to wish that in retrospect, particularly after one has satisfed one's belongingness needs in other ways. Long afterward, you still need dignity, even though you don't need the relationship. At the time, though, you need love and attachment first, and self-esteem can wait (Maslow, 1968).

The concern with esteem may well be integral to the story itself. People tell stories for certain reasons and to make certain points. For the would-be lover, one key function of the story may be to assist in coping with the episode, and coping would almost certainly include rebuilding self-esteem. When we combined all the various esteem-enhancing comments made in the various stories into one large category, including the various ones reviewed in this section and the previous one, it is clear that esteem boosting was a central concern for many would-be lovers but not for rejectors. Nearly half the would-be lovers' accounts contained some statement about their positive traits, deservingness, attractiveness (especially to others), and so on, whereas only a small minority of rejectors made any such boasts.

Several of the would-be lovers' accounts were quite explicit about how their current thoughts about these past events revolved around issues of self-esteem. One woman wrote that she was proud of herself for not having put up more of a fight at the time she lost her lover. She did not say why that should be a source of pride, but one likely explanation is that putting up more of a fight and losing would have led her into actions that in retrospect would have been more embarrassing. By giving in gracefully, she was able to salvage her pride. In contrast, another woman looked back many years later on an unsuccessful romance and said that in retrospect, her main feeling was embarrassment "that I did not have enough pride back then to handle the situation." In other words, she regretted her actions because her later level of pride and self-esteem was hard to reconcile with the way she had acted at the time.

One of the most vivid discussions of self-esteem loss was provided by a young man who recalled a rejection he had suffered in high school. He was a senior, the girl a sophomore, and his supposedly superior status compounded the humiliation of her rejection of him. He angrily recalled the indignities he had endured, seemingly without protest, years ago. As an example, he described one night when he went through considerable difficulty to visit her. He finally "got to her house to find her acting very uncaring as to whether I was there or not. As usual, I played her pussycat and ate crap." Later, when she started to break it off, he wrote a long letter "spilling my guts and telling her how much I 'loved' her. I regret having put something like that in writing to this day." The existence of an incriminating document seemed to stand for him as tangible proof of his humiliation. He concluded his account by saying, "to look back on it, I feel so stupid for the naive way I came off and how much ass-kissing I did."

The rejectors generally did not say much about their own esteem in retrospect (other than recalling the initial feeling of being flattered). They were sometimes sensitive to the would-be lover's loss of self-esteem, but usually their accounts were not fully sympathetic to this aspect of the other person's suffering. Some were quite indignant that the would-be lover should accept humiliations and indignities while continuing to pursue the rejector. They seemed to lose respect for a would-be lover who sacrificed pride for love.

Occasionally, a rejector was even quite aware of being the agent who inflicted loss of self-esteem on the would-be lover. One woman wrote of her difficulty in discouraging the attentions of someone whom she initially liked but never developed strong love for, in contrast to the powerful attachment that he developed for her. "He was very sensitive and after about three months I started making very cruel remarks and making him do things just to see if he would," she wrote, "and the more he did them the more I disliked him for cowarding down to some of my demeaning requests." Thus, faced with conflicting demands of pride vs. love, he sacrificed pride and did what his beloved requested—for which she despised him! She said that soon she could barely stand to be around him and compared him to a puppy who followed her around, even sleeping outside her door until she came home late one night. She said that she would start arguments with him "and he would just sit and say 'it was all my fault, I'm sorry, I'm sorry.'" When she wanted to date someone else, he begged her pathetically to stay with him, offering to do anything she wanted. Contemptuous of him by now, she told him she would stay with him, but she began to date others anyway.

Thus, rejectors may indeed have some awareness of how the self-esteem of the would-be lover suffers. Many would-be lovers are willing to let their pride suffer while they try to win the love they want. Self-esteem appears to be the motive that gets many would-be lovers to extricate themselves from these doomed entanglements. Eventually, things reach a point where the person is not willing to sacrifice any more self-esteem in the apparently doomed hope of winning the other's love. And in retrospect, many may wish that that point had come much sooner.

These last examples bring up another point. If the would-be lover accepts the humiliation and persists in the effort to win love, these efforts may be self-defeating, because accepting humiliation may cost the would-be lover further respect in the eyes of the desired partner. As the blows to the aspiring lover's pride become increasingly palpable, the very incentive to endure them diminishes, even if the pathetic individual cannot see this. For the sake of love, people are willing to make sacrifices and submit to ordeals, but ironically this very submission makes them seem pitiful or even contemptible. Once all respect is gone, the chances for love are probably slim indeed. But some would-be lovers beg and grovel anyway.

Thus, for example, a woman described a case in which a man became obsessed with her after a single date, although she was not interested in him. He kept calling her and she made excuses or had her roommates take the call. He failed to get the hint, she recalled with annoyance. She pretended to be engaged, but he still persisted. She decided to resort to telling him bluntly that she did not like his company: "Even though it isn't my personality to be mean, at this point I felt it was necessary. I told him that I thought he was too deep and consequently that he was boring to be with. And that I did not have an attraction toward him." The man told her he understood, but, she recalls, he insisted on giving his phone number to her in case she changed her mind! She ended by articulating, with cruel bluntness, the moral: "Some guys never learn that . . . desperation is definitely NOT a turn-on." Thus, she went from mere lack of interest to positive contempt merely because he accepted degradation in persisting in his efforts to win her love.

To the would-be lover, in other words, accepting some measure of humiliation and embarrassment may seem like one of several sacrifices that are part of the aspiring lover's lot. But these very sacrifices may be counterproductive, because they help seal the would-be lover's fate. As Maslow's hierarchy suggested, people may be willing to sacrifice pride for the sake of love, but one's willingness to sacrifice one's pride may reduce the rejector's respect, and without that respect, love is unlikely to arise.

The Irony of Retrospect

Before closing, it is worth pointing out one surprising and ironic pattern in these findings. It suggests something quite unusual about unrequited love.

As we noted at the beginning of this chapter, emotional reactions have often been linked to events that affect self-esteem. Most commonly, people feel good about experiences that boost their self-esteem and remember them pleasantly. By the same token, they feel bad when events threaten their self-esteem, and they remember them more negatively or even try to forget them.

The implications of unrequited love for self-esteem are clear. The rejector gets a boost to his or her self-esteem, insofar as it is flattering to be loved or admired (especially when one has not done much to elicit this admiration). The would-be lover experiences a blow to self-esteem, for rejection seems to contain an evaluative judgment that says one is somehow deficient or inadequate as a potential romantic partner.

But as we pointed out in the preceding chapter, it is generally the rejector who ends up with the more negative feelings about the incident and who is likely to wish the whole thing had never happened. The would-be lover's recollected account often seems far less negative.

This pattern can be called "the irony of retrospect." One person has a flattering experience yet ends up wishing it had never happened. Meanwhile, a humiliating experience leaves people with much fonder memories. In the majority of experiences people have, the opposite pattern would be found, for people will generally regret and deplore their humiliating experiences and retain, even treasure, their flattering ones.

To be sure, the humiliation in romantic rejection did apparently contribute to the emotional distress the would-be lovers suffered at the time. And the rejectors did associate the flattery with some pleasant feelings and positive reactions on their part. But in looking back, these patterns were reversed.

These results confirm that the emotional patterns in unrequited love are associated with motivations beyond self-esteem. As we noted, some would-be lovers retrospectively regretted the loss of self-esteem, but many still did not necessarily regret the whole incident. Meanwhile, as we suggested, the flattery experienced by the rejector may tend to be short-lived, and so their memories do not revolve around self-esteem issues. What moves some of them to wish the incident had never occurred is not of course the ego boost but rather the difficult, troublesome, and guilt-inducing developments that arose later and became the central features of the episode. When we analyzed the interdependence of would-be lover and rejector (in Chapter 2), we concluded that the would-be lover's situation resembled a large gamble but the rejector's lot was a no-win proposition. Despite the blow to self-esteem, would-be lovers may look back with fewer regrets, because it seemed worth the gamble, and one eventually understands and accepts that gambling involves losing sometimes. But a no-win situation is extremely stressful (e.g., Weiss, 1971) and can hardly ever be a pleasant memory.

Conclusion

Self-esteem is often implicated in unrequited love. The pattern of "falling upward" may be one reason for this: People fall in love with those more desirable, but not less desirable than themselves, and so unrequited love is a sign of unequal attractiveness and inferiority. Even though rejectors may phrase the rejection in vague, impersonal, or external terms (see Folkes, 1982), the degrading implication does come through. For that reason, there may be some tendency for people to prefer to remember themselves as being loved in vain by others rather than to remember their own experiences of loving in vain.

Generally, experiences of unrequited love tend to provide self-esteem boosts to the love object (particularly if the would-be lover is seen as an attractive or desirable person), and they commonly threaten the self-esteem of the rejected (would-be) lover. The rejected lover often appears to be unaware of the esteem-enhancing aspect of the incident for the love object. But the rejector does seem to have some understanding of the humiliation that the would-be lover suffers.

The rejector may receive an initial boost to self-esteem, but these boosts did not seem to be important features of the accounts in our sample over the long run. We suspect that many rejectors found the other person's interest flattering at first but later it become tiresome or problematic, and so in retrospect the boost to self-esteem played only a small part.

The would-be lover may often face a Maslowian dilemma in which the needs for esteem and needs for love and belongingness make conflicting demands. Our accounts provide some degree of support for Maslow's hypothesis that the needs for love and belongingness take precedence. Consistent with his hypothesis, many people clearly did sacrifice self-esteem for love. They accepted humiliations, sometimes repeated and deliberate ones, in order to pursue their project of winning love. Ironically, the very acceptance of humiliation for the sake of love may further diminish the chances for realizing that love. As the would-be lover grovels and begs, the rejector loses respect for him or her, and love is precluded.

Still, at some point the concern with self-esteem was able to influence the decision to give up on the pursuit of love (or at least this particular pursuit). This suggests that the needs for love and for esteem are more simultaneous than might be suggested by a simple-minded application of Maslow's hierarchy hypothesis. Self-esteem can take precedence over love, especially when a great deal of self-esteem is being sacrificed and the prospects for winning love are beginning to seem small.

We hasten to add that there appear to be fairly powerful individual differences in how people balance the conflicting pulls of love and esteem. At one extreme are individuals such as the one described by the rejector who deliberately demeaned him and was chagrined to see that he continued to accept humiliation rather than break away from the attachment. At the other extreme, some individuals wrote that they tend to back off at the slightest hint of rejection or would even avoid expressing love or attraction because of the danger of rejection. One cannot be sure whether self-esteem is the only motive behind their intense fear of rejection, but it seems safe to assume that it is at least one important factor. They would apparently prefer to do without love than to expose themselves to the danger of a humiliating rejection.

For would-be lovers, concern over self-esteem may loom larger in retrospect than at the time. This is consistent with Maslow's theory, for perhaps later in life people do manage to satisfy their needs for love and belongingness with new partners and then begin to look back with dismay on the degradation they suffered. At the time one is struggling with unrequited love, the concern with maintaining one's self-esteem may seem like a minor or secondary problem. But when one recalls the episode years later, the blow to self-esteem (and especially one's acquiescence in humiliation) may become the central, defining features of the episode. Stories of would-be lovers contained many positive statements about themselves, unlike the stories of rejectors. Romantic rejection is often a blow to one's self-esteem, and recovery may well involve repairing one's self-esteem.

F·I·V·E

Guilt, Justification, Morality: Struggling with Right and Wrong

Conventional wisdom about what is fair in love and war notwithstanding, all is decidedly not fair in unrequited love. There are norms, expectations, and implicit rules about how people should treat each other. This chapter will examine some of the issues of guilt and justification that crop in up unrequited love. As we shall see, these problems tend to be much more urgent and central to the rejector's experience than to the would-be lover's experience.

There are ironies in both the guiltlessness of the would-be lover and in the guilty feelings of the rejector. To understand their respective moral positions, one must appreciate the background. People seem generally to need to find some way of justifying their actions, particularly if someone else might question or challenge or object to those actions—and both would-be lover and rejector are vulnerable to such challenges. To justify one's actions, one can appeal to some basic value or culturally endorsed set of principles. A firm moral foundation is provided by a *value base*—that is, something that is accepted as right and good without needing further justification. In modern Western culture, love is accepted as such a value base: Love is regarded as a fundamental good for its own sake, without needing to be justified (see Baumeister, 1991).

The power of love to justify actions serves the would-be lover well. Although would-be lovers do indeed perform actions that others (most notably their love objects) may question and regard as morally objectionable, they generally do not seem to feel guilt. Love may serve them as a justification.

The rejector, however, lacks any such firm basis for justifying his or her actions. Indeed, to the extent that love is accepted as a basic good and a source of positive value, the rejector is in the position of opposing and rejecting what is good. The rejector is thus vulnerable to being in the position of the enemy of the good. More important, the rejector causes another person to suffer, and causing another's suffering is probably a universal formula for moral blameworthiness. One last moral problem for the rejector is the more particularly American view that one should not regard oneself as superior to others. The rejector is often expressing the judgment that the would-be lover is not good enough to be the rejector's partner—not sufficiently attractive, intelligent, rich, or whatever.

In Chapter 2 we noted that scriptlessness is a central problem for the rejector. Because of the lack of clear guidelines on how to act, rejectors feel uncertain, and their resulting actions may lead them into further areas of moral difficulty. Thus, despite their seeming fundamental innocence, initial lack of responsibility, initial lack of action, and pervasive good intentions, they may end up causing harm and otherwise doing things they regret.

A fairly long account by a young man we shall call Ralph illustrated some of the moral dilemmas that the rejector faces. A longtime friend asked Ralph to lunch and there disclosed her love for him, to his surprise. He thought well of her but did not want to be her lover, for reasons he did not disclose. In the following weeks, he felt awkward and nervous when speaking with her, but he felt the right thing to do was to be honest, and so he told her frankly that he just wanted to be her (platonic) friend and not have any romantic involvement. The woman did not accept this, however, and she insisted that he was refusing to face his true feelings for her.

They continued in that vein for several months. Ralph was frustrated by her persistence and by the loss of the valued friendship, and she was upset by his seeming refusal to allow himself to love her in return. Like many rejectors, he suffered under a sense of obligation toward her because of this love that he did not want. "After all of the crying and harassment on her part, I started to feel as if I owed her something because her feelings were so strong for me. I felt that I should like her or be just as attracted to her as she was to me." He looked back on these feelings as full of confusion, for he liked her and wanted her friendship but did not want romance, and moreover he did not know whether his feelings of guilt and obligation were justified or not.

One day during this confused period they were talking on the phone, as usual discussing their relationship and what form it should take. "I told her that although we were not going to be a couple, *per se,* that we could be sexually involved." In retrospect he says he realizes what a mistake this was, but at that time "it seemed logical to give her half of what she wanted, yet still obeying my true feelings." And so they did become physically intimate, with predictably disastrous results. "We made love or had sex three times through this grueling, stressful, painful, agonizing [period in our] relationship," was how he described it. He insisted "it was happening strictly because I so strongly felt I owed her something in return for her strong romantic feelings for me."

This of course was no resolution, because sexual involvement is not a good way to discourage romantic love and revert to platonic friendship! Instead of finding his sense of obligation reduced, Ralph found it increased: "I kept feeling I owed her more and more as the relationship went on. It was horrible." Talking with her became even more awkward, because she wanted to talk about their relationship and he did not know what to say. And of course the guilt he felt for hurting her increased rather than subsiding. Eventually, when they both felt emotionally drained and exhausted, he realized the impossibility of continuing the relationship.

Ralph's account concluded with a statement that aptly captures the moral difficulty of the rejector's position: He did nothing wrong and was fundamentally innocent, yet was led into feeling guilty and bad, and from this sense of obligation and wrongfulness he acted in ways that made things worse. "It was truly not my fault she felt the way she did about me. Yet I lied or acted the way she wanted me to for her feelings. It was the biggest mistake I have ever made in my life." In those three sentences, he first asserts his innocence and lack of responsibility, then condemns himself for having lied but immediately converts the immoral lie into a morally laudable act of going along with the woman's wishes, and then he concludes with a powerful statement of regret over a "mistake." Even in retrospect, the moral issues are far from clear to him. Many rejectors experience the same uncertainty.

The Urge to Justify

One simple sign of moral doubt is the presence of statements justifying oneself. After all, people who feel no moral qualms do not need to say why their actions were justifiable. By that criterion, it is immediately apparent that rejectors were far more troubled than would-be lovers. Over a third of the rejectors' accounts contained statements of why their acts were justified, whereas only a small minority of would-be lovers felt it necessary to justify their acts. This difference was statistically significant. The urge to justify oneself, in other words, appears much more strongly among rejectors than among would-be lovers.

A variety of justifications was used. A woman said she was asked to go the the prom by a young man she did not know very well. "We went together, basically, because we both wanted to go and we had no one else to go with. At least this was how I felt." But afterward he pursued her aggressively, bought her flowers, asked her for dates, and so forth. "I mean, who wouldn't want that? Except me. I'm just not like that." Thus, she justified not responding to his advances on the basis of the need to be herself. The demands of selfhood, including the need to be true to one's nature, is of course a powerfully appealing source of justification in modern life and is often what people resort to when they need to justify letting another down, hurting someone, breaking a relationship, and so forth (see Baumeister, 1991; Bellah et al., 1985; Vaughan, 1986).

Other justifications included defensive interpretations of the other's actions. "He felt inadequate with himself which led to him buying me things to make up for what he didn't think he was." Likewise, the failings or inadequacies of the would-be lover were an important basis for justifying the rejection. The relationship simply could not work if the people were not equally matched. Mismatches were often described in terms of simple incompatibility, possibly because rejectors feel guilty about asserting baldly that they consider themselves superior to the other. One woman justified the hurt she had inflicted on a would-be lover by saying that " . . . we are too different. I tend to be a very goal-oriented person and I really work hard to get what I want from life. He, on the other hand, is very easygoing—too easygoing. At first I liked his attitude because he helped me 'laugh off' my problems; but when I think about spending the rest of my life with someone who doesn't care about doing things well, I know I would be miserable." She added that their mutual incompatibility would become burdensome to her and require her to act in ways contrary to her nature: "I would constantly feel like I was his mother, forcing him to do everything. In another sense he is too dependent on me. Not only does he look upon me as the one who is going to succeed, but he expects me to constantly bring him out of his angry or depressed moods. I just couldn't handle it anymore. A person can only take so much pressure."

While some justified their actions on the basis of what was wrong with the would-be lover, other rejectors justified their actions on the basis of what was best for the admirer. Thus, a woman described a case in which she was initially attracted to the man but then lost interest, while he was deeply in love with her. She said that she knew it was best for him in the long run to face the truth now. Several males told similar stories. It must be noted that they are probably correct. The story of Ralph, covered in the opening paragraphs of this chapter, suggests that continuing the contact, and especially having sexual relations, simply increases the suffering of the would-be lover.

We have spoken of the alleged need to be true to the self as a form of justification. The self can offer justification in other ways too. It has its rights and interests and people feel themselves entitled to do what they want, even if it means disappointing someone else. Some rejectors made use of such arguments. Justifying the breaking up of a long-distance relationship when moving to a new college, one rejector wrote, "Here I was at college with a whole new bunch of people. I wanted to experience 'life' first. I'm still not ready for marriage and I seriously don't think I will be for a while."

One must not be overly ready to accept these self-justifications at face value. As we said, the urge to justify is an indication that one recognizes doubts or questions about the morality of one's actions. Some rejectors' accounts explicitly articulated their moral uncertainty. For example, one woman described how she debated whether to leave a relationship that meant little to her but much more to the man. "I really do feel guilty for having broken up with him. At times I feel like I was all he had and that I'm really messing him up. I keep telling myself that in the long run, he will be better off than if I had stayed with him, lying about how I felt, but sometimes I even find myself questioning that." Thus, she knew what to say to justify her actions, but she also acknowledged that her exercise in self-justification was not fully convincing.

It is also noteworthy, even slightly amazing, that the woman in the example just given says she contemplated staying in the relationship and pretending to continue to love the man merely to avoid the guilt over leaving. She was not the only one, by any means. Others felt torn, especially if there was some sort of relationship and they felt they had some obligation to the partner. Typical of such dilemmas was that described by another woman, who said that when her romantic feelings for her partner died, she tried to prolong them, to force herself to continue loving him, "just so I wouldn't feel guilty later." Predictably, it didn't work: " I was going nuts and I had to break it off."

This response is of interest in relation to the "suicide ploy"—that is, the stategy of the would-be lover who tries to bind the desired partner (especially an intimate partner who wants to leave a relationship) by threatening suicide. At first blush, the tactic is ridiculous. Who would want someone to stay with you merely out of the mixture of pity and intimidation that you generate by threatening to kill yourself? Pity and intimidation are feeble substitutes for love. On the other hand, comments such as the ones we have quoted in this section suggest that such blatant guilt manipulations can sometimes push toward a more desirable result. Guilt makes the partner try to sustain love. Perhaps it doesn't really succeed (although if it does, our research, which focused on unrequited love, would not have found such cases), but at least it moves the partner to make the effort. That may be the best that some would-be lovers can get. Some disenchanted lovers do apparently try to feel love in order to avoid feeling guilt.

But what else is there to do? If one does not reciprocate the love, then the only alternatives are to hurt the person by breaking it off, or to allow the person to persist in a futile hope—thereby potentially hurting the person more. A young man articulated both sides of this dilemma in a story about a platonic friend who wanted to be his romantic lover, not unlike the case of Ralph described earlier this chapter. This man was direct and honest in telling the woman that they would not be lovers, yet he also tried to preserve the friendship, and these efforts encouraged her romantic hopes. "In retrospect, I feel ashamed of my behavior at these times because my intentions were to have a completely platonic friendship-based relationship yet my being with her seemed to lead her on. As the fall semester approached, I became better and better friends with her, but I selfishly and coldly hurt her when I began to date someone else. Yet I still feel there was no other alternative." The lack of any other alternative is a paradigmatic justification. I couldn't help it, nothing could be done. Or, in the words of another man who had to break off all contact with a female friend who wanted to become his girlfriend (because his actual girlfriend had become quite jealous of her rival's pursual of him), "I felt really bad, honestly, but what could I do?"

Two last forms of self-justification deserve mention. One is the presence of a previous romantic attachment to someone else. In such cases, rejectors are using essentially the same justification that would-be lovers use, namely that love justifies all, and in particular it justifies doing something that another person may not like. If one already has a boyfriend or girlfriend, so the justification goes, then of course one has to disappoint this latest would-be lover. In reality, of course, the meanings and implications may be far more ambiguous. It is quite common for people to leave one boyfriend or girlfriend for another, and the degree to which the rejector had encouraged the would-be lover by flirtation or other means is impossible to establish. Such developments often concerned distant lovers. One can readily suspect that the person may begin to flirt or seek attention nearby while supposedly sustaining a relationship with someone in another city—but when one wants to justify breaking the nearby other's heart, one can always appeal to one's prior commitment to the other relationship.

The final form of self-justification is to become a victim oneself. This requires a fuller discussion, which will be furnished in the next section.

We are not suggesting that the rejectors were dishonest or were fabricating their justifications. Probably all the justifications contained some degree of truth and many may be fully accurate. The point is simply that the rejectors, unlike would-be lovers, tended to feel that their actions needed to be justified. When rejectors tell their stories, they know they are describing how they hurt someone else, and so they feel morally vulnerable. Their stories therefore often needed to include an explanation that they were not as cruel or wicked as they might seem.

Claiming the Victim Role

Generally, in the aftermath of transgressions, victims hold the moral high ground while perpetrators stand guilty, culpable, and vulnerable. As a result, many perpetrators seem to seek to portray themselves as victims after the fact. Thus, for example, Sichrovsky (1988) found that most children of Nazis and war criminals had been brought up to regard their parents as victims of the war, not transgressors, a view that sometimes led to shouting matches between the interviewer and the subject in his study! Apparently, after the collapse of the Nazi regime, many individuals preferred to see themselves as basically helpless pawns who had been coerced by a dangerous system into going along with it, and who had suffered various negative consequences for doing so, rather than seeing themselves as responsible individuals who had voluntarily helped maintain the system. To be sure, there were considerable pressures on individuals to go along with the system, and these individuals' perceptions of themselves as victims can be regarded as a matter of emphasis and interpretation rather than outright fabrication. (For example, the German Wehrmacht executed their own soldiers at a *thousand times* the rate of such executions in the First World War.) Our point, though, is that in retrospect the victim's role has significant moral appeal, and so people may prefer to emphasize it.

Similar implications emerged from our own previous research on modern, relatively minor interpersonal transgressions involving anger (Baumeister, Stillwell, & Wotman, 1990). Transgressors' accounts did often acknowledge their own wrongdoing, but they were also quick to point out anything their victims did to them, particularly including excessive anger or retaliation. Victims almost always portrayed their anger as appropriate, but transgressors often depicted the victims as overreacting to a relatively minor offense. Thus, while admitting to some wrongdoing, transgressors were also able to portray themselves as victims of persecution.

The moral appeal of the victim's role may be especially important in unrequited love, because the rejector is often reluctant to inflict hurt but cannot see any way to avoid this. Contrary to stereotypes, most romantic rejectors are thus *reluctant transgressors*, and any claim on victim status may appeal to them as a moral haven. In other words, rejectors who feel bad about hurting someone else can salve their consciences by regarding themselves as victims. And, in fact, rejectors are often careful to record their own sufferings at the hands of their pursuers.

A number of accounts clearly followed this pattern. For example, the rejector might (in his or her own view) communicate in gentle, considerate terms that he or she was unable to reciprocate the would-be lover's feelings, but the would-be lover would respond to this in an aggressive fashion. Several men described how the women they rejected slandered them and generated substantial resentment and ill-feeling toward them among former friends or mutual acquaintances.

Women likewise report being insulted after refusing unwanted advances. Often the advances take a sexual form, and the woman's refusal leads to reproach framed in those terms. One woman, for example, said that after she rejected a man he continued to approach her, sometimes making sexually suggestive comments that embarrassed her. When she persisted in her refusal, he called her a "frigid bitch," thus seemingly reproaching her for sexual inadequacy instead of accepting the rejection gracefully or acknowledging that the inadequacy could lie with him.

Some rejectors noted more severe forms of suffering. One woman described being pursued by a co-worker who became extremely hostile to her after she rejected him. In her account, his hostility was so disturbing that she had to quit her job "because it was very upsetting to me that I had to work with him when he obviously was really angry with me." It is of course plausible that several reasons entered into her decision to quit her job, but in her account she dwells on the hostility of the rejected would-be lover, which effectively casts her in the role of the wronged victim rather than in the role of the cruel heartbreaker.

Occasional physical acts of desperation by lovers (usually male) crazed with heartbreak are also useful for rejectors who wish to claim the victim role. One woman described how a man she rejected came to her room drunk and tried to choke her. Several who had boyfriends at the time said that their disappointed admirers became physically aggressive toward the boyfriends. Another said her jilted boyfriend actually kidnaped her, eventually leading to his arrest and conviction. And we have already described the case of Jessica, whose rejected boyfriend persisted in calling and harassing her and her friends and eventually embarrassed her by featuring her in one of his "bizarre" paintings.

Becoming a victim oneself does not, of course, actually remove one's own guilt for something one has done. It does, however, recast the story and convert one's own role. Rejectors may feel guilty about hurting someone, but many seem to feel that if they can portray themselves as innocent, long-suffering victims they can escape the villain's role. Victimhood seems to function as if it were a justification.

Morally Innocent But Feeling Guilty

The discussion of justification brings us to a central irony of the rejector's position: guilt without misdeed. Guilt is widely understood as a result of how the person evaluates his or her own behavior—that is, you feel guilty when you think you have done something wrong, especially if it is intentional wrongdoing (e.g., Lewis, 1971). This view of guilt is not adequate to explain the guilty feelings in unrequited love. The rejectors often were quite explicit about saying that they did not do anything wrong, but they felt guilty anyway.

A colleague recently told us a story that still brings her feelings of guilt many years afterward, despite the fact that she did not do anything wrong. The summer after high school, she dated two young men, both of whom gradually became very fond of her. Her own feelings developed a clear preference for one of them, Frank, and she was in the process of deciding to begin an exclusive dating relationship with him. Right at this point the other, Warren, called her and asked her to go out with him to see *Romeo and Juliet,* a local staging that he was involved with. She had not yet decided how to go about breaking his heart, so she just said that she couldn't go. The following week was her birthday, and Frank's parents surprised the young couple by taking them out to see *Romeo and Juliet.* Unfortunately, it turned out that Warren was working as an usher at that night's performance, and he had the sad task of showing the foursome to their seats. She had not meant to hurt him, but she felt terrible imagining how he must have felt, not to mention his having to continue smiling and being pleasant while ushering other patrons.

This confusing problem of guilt feelings despite formal innocence came through in many accounts in our sample. For example, the following excerpt was taken from an account that was mainly filled with the rejector's self-justifications. "We went out a couple of times.

But I noticed that she was somewhat immature and more uptight than I liked. I tried very hard to slow things down, because I noticed that this girl was not the one for me. Then this past week I told her in the most kindest or nicest way that I was not attracted to her." Thus he established his correct intentions and admirable efforts to be restrained and considerate. Following this, however, he conceded that he felt guilty and then quickly launched into a litany of justifications: "I felt really bad for not liking this girl as much as she liked me, but Sue was not the girl for me, I felt. I am being cautious with girls in general because a four-year relationship with one was broken up in the beginning of this summer. Since then I have noticed more women interested in me but I do not want to get involved because I am being cautious. Also, I don't want to get burned again. I don't feel Sue was a bad girl or was not friendly or attractive, I just don't feel ready for another relationship." Obviously, he felt guilty, yet he also was quite insistent that he had not done anything wrong. The surfeit of justifications rightly raises suspicion that he felt morally vulnerable, and indeed he acknowledged that he felt very bad about the affair. Yet there is nothing to indicate that he really acted in immoral or unethical ways. He dated Sue but failed to form any desire for a deeper relationship, and according to his account he tried to be as gentle, considerate, and honest as possible with her. His account effectively portrays him as morally innocent but still records that he felt guilty.

References to guilt feelings were far more common in the accounts of rejectors than in those of the would-be lovers. Ironically, the would-be lovers usually exerted the initiative in terms of trying to start a romance, yet they rarely blamed themselves or felt guilty. In contrast, the rejectors were often (and especially in their own view) quietly minding their own business when this affair was thrust upon them, and yet despite their passive role they ended up feeling guilty about it. In an important sense, the would-be lover is responsible for the episode, but the rejector is the one who ends up feeling guilty.

Part of the explanation for this ironic separation of guilt and responsibility resides in our culture's popular conceptions and perhaps illusions about love. In terms of the active initiation of events in an episode of unrequited love, it is fairly safe to say that the rejector is usually passive, whereas the would-be lover holds the active role. Yet our culture defines emotions as passions in the sense of passive experiences. As James Averill (1980, 1982) has pointed out, the words *passive* and *passion* derive from the same root. The would-be lover can thus comfortably feel that he or she need not accept responsibility for falling in love and perhaps not even for the actions that result from that passion. And even if the passion does not fully excuse the action, love is seen as justifying a wide range of actions. Hence there is no moral dilemma for the would-be lover.

It is also worth adding that the guilty feelings of the rejectors were largely absent from the would-be lovers' accounts. This seems to indicate that would-be lovers do not fully realize how the rejectors may struggle and suffer. The moral dilemmas that preoccupy the rejector may go largely unnoticed by the would-be lover, who is, after all, preoccupied with his or her own passions, feelings, desires, hopes, and fears. When, in a later study, we *asked* would-be lovers whether their partners felt guilty, some of them did acknowledge that the rejector probably did have such feelings. Thus, it may be excessive to say that would-be lovers are completely oblivious to the rejector's struggle with guilt. But only direct questions seem to elicit such a response. In people's spontaneous recollections, would-be lovers pay almost no attention to the moral struggles of the rejectors.

Central to the rejector's sense of guilt was the feeling of obligation toward the other person. It is as if simply by being wonderful one incurs the duty to prevent one's wonderfulness from hurting others. And so people who understandably fall in love with you are innocent victims who need to be cared for. It is akin to noblesse oblige: One has a duty, as it were, to one's admirers. The guilt that results is thus an interpersonal phenomenon, not a private evaluation of self. If you can't give the other person the emotion and attention that he or she wants, you feel guilty.

The sense of obligation came through in many rejectors' accounts. As one woman wrote, fairly typically, "He asked me out and I felt awful about turning him down." Or, in another's words, "I felt angry, . . . confused . . . I started feeling uncomfortable around him and then I would feel guilty because I wasn't treating him as nicely as

I used to." (She had previously been close to him but began to distance herself as his attraction to her grew stronger while her attraction to him faded.) Generalizing about her experiences with unrequited love, another rejector wrote, "The main feeling I got from him and other people [in similar affairs] was this sense of obligation and I felt like this other person had become dependent on me and it was a burden and very stressful, especially if the person was nice."

One man described an incident in which he attended a party and became intoxicated. In that state, he had a long, flirtatious conversation with a woman and said many flattering things to her. Not surprisingly, she got the impression that he was strongly attracted to her, even though when his alcoholic intoxication wore off he felt no such thing. As a result, she came to think of them as a couple and began to interact with him on that basis. He did not know what to do. When, soon after, she mentioned that her birthday was approaching, he said vaguely that they should do something together. He then put it out of his mind, until she telephoned him the day before her birthday to ask what time they should meet. He concluded, "I knew that she didn't have anyone else taking her out, so I felt compelled. I guess that the hardest thing is to have the strength to tell the other person their [sic] true feelings." This incident was unresolved at the time he wrote the account, but one can see his dilemma. He feels somewhat responsible for flirting with the woman in the first place, yet his intoxication should excuse him morally, at least in his eyes. But he nonetheless feels a sense of obligation toward her, and it is hard to refuse each small request she makes, even though acceding to her requests does get him more deeply involved.

Seeing guilt in interpersonal terms (see Baumeister, Stillwell, & Heatherton, 1991) helps illuminate the dilemma. It is the causing of harm, not the self-perception of malicious intent, that leads to guilt feelings. People apparently feel a great deal of guilt over harm that they have unintentionally caused to other people. In fact, McGraw (1987) found more reports of guilt over unintentional than of intentional acts, and she described her own guilt over an incident recalled from her days as a waitress: She spoiled a couple's romantic honeymoon dinner by accidentally drenching them when she opened the champagne bottle.

McGraw's research has thus made a dramatic, even revolutionary point about guilt: People feel guilty about unintentional misdeeds. Unrequited love is full of these. Based on the idealized theory that casts guilt in terms of intentional wrongdoing, these people are innocent, but based on the (unintended and often unforeseen) result of hurting someone else they do feel guilty.

As a typical example of such a case, consider a female student who regularly studied with a male student who secretly developed a crush on her while she, unaware of his feelings, was becoming romantically interested in someone else. Her admirer was doomed to be disappointed before she even realized that he had feelings for her. "On Valentine's Day, when we were doing physics, he pulled out a rose, a teddy bear, and some chocolate and gave them to me. I didn't know what to say. I felt so-o-o guilty because I sent a singing telegram to a guy in one of my other classes and he found out. I just felt really bad." In her view, she was innocent—she even adds, "He thought I led him on (but I hadn't)"—but when he was hurt to discover that her romantic feelings were directed toward someone else, she felt guilty.

One factor that may have contributed to her guilt was that she did have a friendship with the study partner and was benefiting from it, and so to hurt him was to hurt a friend and benefactor. Generally, we think, the strength of the interpersonal bond is a crucial determinant of the magnitude of guilt. Although we have no systematic data on this point, several observations are consistent with it. First, people seem to feel more guilty about breaking the heart of a longtime friend than about breaking the heart of some casual acquaintance. One woman articulated that pattern in her own love life. "A lot of guys are attracted to me that I have no interest in whatsoever. It doesn't bother me so much if I don't know the guy, but all too often he is a friend of mine . . . ," in which case she finds the episode much more difficult and feels worse about it. Likewise, as shown by many of the other stories, it was in the cases where romantic passion intruded on a pre-existing friendship that people felt most guilty. Rejectors referred to guilt feelings in half the cases where there was some relationship but only a third of the time when there was no relationship.[1]

One would also expect that guilt feelings should be substantial when one is breaking off a romantic relationship, if indeed guilt depends on the interpersonal bond. Although a study of divorce is a separate topic, there were several cases in our data in which the couple had begun dating only to find that one fell in love while the other lost interest, and so the result was a form of breaking up. These rejectors tended to report strong feelings of guilt. Thus, one woman described dating a man for six months, and although she was never strongly attracted to the man, he became powerfully attached to her. "When we broke up it nearly killed him. He wouldn't get out of bed and I didn't know what to do. I didn't mean to hurt him, but I did very much. It took four months for us to be friends after that. It really hurt me inside to see him so upset, yet I didn't know what to do." Thus, again, she insisted on her formal, moral innocence (she never intended to hurt him), yet acknowledged that she felt terribly guilty about the pain she caused. She concluded her account with a pessimistic generalization that reflected the degree of her inner struggle with guilt and un-certainty: "Relationships always leave one person hurting."

Of course, one must not overgeneralize the moral innocence of the rejectors. Some probably were responsible to some degree for the would-be lover's attraction. In the next chapter, we will note that one area of pervasive disagreement between rejectors and would-be lovers is whether the rejector had initially encouraged the would-be lover's affections.

And even if the rejector did not solicit the would-be lover's affection and meant well throughout, he or she may have done some-thing to make things worse. The story of Ralph earlier in this chapter exemplifies this. In his account, he did not lead his admirer on initially, but later he did initiate sexual relations with her, and the sex increased the entanglements as well as the woman's suffering. It was also appar-ent that in looking back he felt guilty about his responsibility for at least that part of the episode.

Although the problem of feeling both innocent and guilty is mainly associated with the rejector's position, it is important to note that it can happen to the would-be lover too. Would-be lovers often have the sense that their feelings are out of their control, and if they are overcome by an attraction that is forbidden they too may feel guilty about it. Thus, for example, many people have strong objections to homosexuality, and if they feel romantically attracted to a member of the same sex they may feel some guilt about this. We have already quoted one account in that pattern, in which the woman described being surprised, disturbed, and troubled by her sudden and powerful attraction to another woman. Another set of forbidden attractions involve people who are already married or committed to someone else. One woman wrote of being seriously involved and in love with a boyfriend but then being overcome with a powerful attraction to another man. "I felt very, very guilty about feeling the way I did," she wrote, and she was afraid to discuss her feelings with anyone because it seemed so wrong to have this desire for one man while committed to another. Her sense of guilt was compounded by an impression that her attraction to the outsider was causing her primary relationship to deteriorate, and for this reason she ultimately forced herself to avoid the other and forget about him. In such cases, the doctrine that feelings cannot be controlled makes the would-be lover feel morally innocent, but the rules against those attractions can give rise to guilt.

Thus, would-be lovers may feel guilty for reasons having little to do with the specific interactions with the other person—particularly reasons associated with moral rules about appropriate feelings. Mostly, though, guilt is only a problem for rejectors. The irony remains that the person who is mainly responsible for the episode feels little guilt, while the people who are reluctantly drawn into the episode end up with a much higher prevalence of guilt feelings.

The Uncontrollability of Feelings

We noted in the previous section that the would-be lover can evade moral questions by regarding love as a passion in the sense of a passively generated state (e.g., Averill, 1980, 1982). I can't help my emotions, one may say, and so I cannot be blamed for what I felt—or, perhaps, even for what I did. Such arguments are central to the view of crimes of passion, in which the emotion divests the person of responsibility for action, and indeed lesser guilt is seen (and lesser sentences are pronounced) when the crime was committed in such an emotional state (Averill, 1982).

Rejectors were not unaware of the justificatory power of passive emotion. Just as the would-be lover might claim to be unable to help falling in love, the rejector can claim innocence on the basis of being unable to make oneself reciprocate the other's love. In other words, love cannot be summoned or created on demand, any more than it can be erased or prevented on demand.

Many rejectors' accounts emphasized the absence of feeling, presumably because of its justificatory power. "I am not attracted to him and never will be. I find him boring, and deep down inside I still resent him liking me, even though I have to be his friend," as one woman wrote. Another described the guilt-inducing pattern of breaking a man's heart when she had dated him for a while: "Basically he 'fell in love' with me, and I was in no way feeling the same. Everything about us was different. His background was rural, and I'm a city girl. I knew I would never live on a farm, and I wanted to break off the relationship because I didn't want to hurt him. My feelings just weren't the same." Thus, she repeatedly insists that she did not feel the same way he did. Her lack of feeling for him was perhaps, in the final analysis, the only justification she had for hurting him, and so her account stresses this fact.

Some rejectors dramatized their inability to control their own feelings by suggesting that they would have liked to have been able to reciprocate the other's love. Thus, one man described how a female friend wanted to become a lover and, after declaring her love for him, waited and hoped for similar feelings to develop in him. "She said every night she goes to bed praying that one day I'll fall in love with her. But I don't think it'll ever happen," he wrote. As we have already suggested, hurting a close friend should produce some of the highest levels of guilt, and so the need to justify oneself—such as by alluding to the uncontrollability of one's feelings—is highest. Significantly, he continued, "What's strange though is that I really want to be attracted to her, but I just am not. I want to be attracted to her, because I know she would make me the happiest person on earth." Yet he could not bring himself to reciprocate her feelings. Nothing beyond platonic friendship was possible for him, despite the pain that he knew that this caused her. He concluded, "I really feel bad about the situation, but I can't help my feelings."

A woman's account made the same point. She felt free to praise a young man and suggest that she found him to be desirable in many ways, but try as she might she could not will herself to love him. "He seemed perfect. We had similar interests, backgrounds, my parents loved him and worshiped the ground that he walked on, but I was not physically attracted to him. I really tried to make myself be attracted to him, but I just couldn't think of him as more than a friend ... " Similarly, another woman wrote "I liked him enormously as a friend, and he was quite attractive; but I simply had no feelings for him." Yet another wrote of a man's good points and concluded simply, "I'm sure if I had been physically attracted to him he would have been a good mate."

There is undoubtedly some truth in these accounts. One cannot simply force oneself to fall in love with any given person, especially someone who may in fact have some trait that one finds undesirable. On the other hand, it is also necessary to appreciate how rejectors may focus on their inability to control their feelings in order to justify their rejection and the infliction of harm on the other. By saying that they tried to make themselves love the other, rejectors can free themselves from any moral burden of guilt or blame. As one woman put it explicitly, "I felt bad about not having feelings for him but there was nothing I could do." If there was nothing she could do, then of course she must be innocent. In that way, their accounts can deftly accomplish the function of exonerating them.

Whether people do in fact try (unsuccessfully) to reciprocate love is difficult to say. These few who suggested that they wanted to reciprocate the other's love may be atypical. Their comments do however point to a broader theme, and that is the degree to which the moral, volitional being is simply at the mercy of his or her heart. Psychologists do not have a clear understanding of why people fall in love with particular others and why love sometimes fails to appear under seemingly similar conditions. Neither do individual people fully understand the appearance or nonappearance of love in their own lives.

The mystery is perhaps most apparent to people who initially feel an attraction to someone but find that it vanishes, in contrast to the other's growing attraction to them. Several rejectors expressed their own mystification at the seemingly premature death of their feeling for another. Thus, one woman described how she began dating a man and enjoyed the initial contacts, including holding hands and kissing. Then, rather swiftly, all her physical desire for the man vanished, along with any other interest in being with him. She avoided physical contact, saying that the thought of kissing him now made her "nervous and uncomfortable." She realized simply that she was no longer attracted to him at all, and withdrew, but she could not explain her loss of interest to herself or to him. "For some unknown reason, I became so uninterested in Jack that I didn't even give him the decency of an explanation for my actions and behavior." Her insistence that the reason was "unknown" reveals the mystery of her own lack of feeling.

The same theme is expressed in a longer account furnished by a male rejector. He met the woman in April at college and they became intimate. In May they separated for the summer. Already at that point, "something was starting to leave the relationship for me. To this day I can't figure out what it was." Not knowing why he was losing interest, he began to hold back, and he became reluctant to write to her or to return her phone calls.

At the end of the summer, they were reunited on campus, but he knew that he could not live up to the level of intimacy that she expected. He was reluctant to break up with her definitively, which is perhaps understandable if one is mystified at the disappearance of one's feelings. Yet he was unwilling to restrict himself to an exclusive relationship with her. He told her he wanted to date other women. "I could tell this really hurt her. She wanted to know why, but I couldn't tell her (I didn't know myself)." A couple of weeks later, he called her to break up formally. "She cried again, wanted to know why. I still couldn't [tell her]." Thus, his account repeatedly refers to his inability to understand why he didn't love her.

These accounts probably reflect a common experience among rejectors. The attraction is not there, and nothing can be done to change that. They see the would-be lover along with his or her good and bad points, and somehow the picture is not enough to elicit reciprocal love. In their view, the situation is unfortunate but simple and innocent.

Although the rejector may be mystified by his or her lack of attraction to the other, one must remember that the would-be lover is also far from comprehending this. The would-be lover wonders what he or she could do to win the heart of the other. The would-be lover often thinks and acts as if the rejector were free to decide whether to reciprocate the love or not. Thus, many accounts refer to the would-be lover's wondering and even asking what they should do, what they could do, in order to make the rejector return their love.

Once again, the true controllability of feelings is probably somewhere between the two extremes. People can indeed control their feelings to some degree, but not to an unlimited or even extensive degree. The would-be lover wants to believe that the rejector can exert such complete control, because that maximizes the would-be lover's hope: One would need merely to convince the rejector that one's cause is worthy, and the rejector would presumably change into an acceptor, just by consciously opening the faucet and letting love flow forth. Meanwhile, the rejector wants to regard his or her feelings as wholly beyond conscious control, for that minimizes any feelings of guilt that might arise from hurting the other.

Devious Tactics

Thus far we have addressed the core moral issues involved in unrequited love: feeling guilty about hurting others, the inability to control one's feelings, and so forth. These issues do not exhaust the moral aspects of unrequited love. Once involved in the situation, people may pursue their goals or roles with tactics that are morally questionable. As we shall see in the next two chapters, there is some tendency for unrequited love to cause people to act in ways they would not normally act, and these uncharacteristic actions may include things that one would normally regard as improper.

Shifting our focus to devious, morally suspect tactics will also shift our attention from the rejector to the would-be lover. The would-be lover, after all, is the one who is trying to make something happen, and he or she might be tempted to resort to unscrupulous means to bring this about. Of course, the would-be lover may not necessarily regard his or her own actions as unscrupulous.

When we coded the accounts for references to unscrupulous tactics used by the would-be lover, a substantial difference emerged. A sizable minority of the rejectors' accounts indicated that yes, the would-be lover had done something questionable or objectionable. But none of the would-be lovers' accounts portrayed their own actions that way. At most, one or two of them hinted vaguely that some of their actions at the height of desperation may have exceeded the normal bounds of proper behavior. To the would-be lovers, their own actions were proper and acceptable, at least in their retrospective accounts. Only the rejectors regarded the would-be lovers' acts as improper.

Undoubtedly one factor behind this discrepancy is the general tendency for people to see their own actions in a positive, desirable light. People are undoubtedly quicker to see faults in others than in themselves (e.g., Taylor, 1989; Taylor & Brown, 1988; also Baumeister, Stillwell, & Wotman, 1990). Another cause, however, may be the tendency for would-be lovers to regard love as a justification for unusual or extreme actions. The familiar assertion that everything is fair in love and war seemingly expresses this capacity of love to justify any sort of action, and would-be lovers may subscribe to this to some extent.

Let us examine the rejectors' accounts for some of the objectionable actions that they witnessed. One pattern that a number of rejectors complained about was the tendency of some would-be lovers to act hypocritically as if the rejector reciprocated the affection, in some cases even boasting to others about commitments and intimacies that did not exist. (Hypocrisy, to be sure, is mainly in the eye of the beholder, in this case the rejector; it is difficult to know whether the would-be lovers were deliberately falsifying and exaggerating the intimacy or sincerely believed that the mutual interest existed.) One woman, for example, found that the fellow who had pursued her relentlessly for several months was actually dating other women and telling them that she was his "main squeeze." She also later heard that he had boasted about needing multiple condoms in one night, which may have meant that he was telling others (falsely) that he had had sex with her.

Hypocrisy was also seen in a number of would-be lovers who would, according to their rejectors, illicitly try to betray the explicit terms of the relationship. The rejector would insist that the relationship be merely platonic friendship, or the rejector would agree to go out with the other but on a basis strictly limited to friendship—but then the rejector would find himself or (more commonly) herself the target of affectionate gestures that clearly went beyond platonic friendship. Flowers, candy, compliments, and similar gestures would be forthcoming, even though the rejector would scrupulously insist that there was no romance involved.

Again, it is easy to imagine the would-be lover doing such things without seeing them in an objectionable light. The foot-in-the-door technique is a standard method of eliciting compliance (Freedman & Fraser, 1966): One begins with small requests and favors, and when these are granted one proceeds toward larger requests. If the girl you love finally agrees to go to the prom with you, it may be hard to avoid being carried away with hope, even if she does mention something about going as friends. It may seem like a great step in the right direction, or like an opportunity for further developments, and sending flowers could be a perfectly logical way of trying to keep things moving. The idea that there would be anything inappropriate or immoral may never occur to the would-be lover, even though the rejector may be quite sensitive to apparent betrayals of implicit agreements.

An extreme version of such hypocrisy was covered in our previous chapter on self-esteem, in the story about Steve and the bogus "Lisa." Our subject wrote that she had not wanted to become romantically involved with Steve and had told him so repeatedly, particularly because she already had a serious boyfriend. He would agree that they were just platonic friends, but he would then make advances to her again. After repeated insistences, he told her that he had found a new girlfriend named Lisa. As our informant wrote: "She is involved in activities similar to mine. Further, she has many of the same qualities I have. She even has the same physical appearance as me. In fact we are very similar in all aspects except that our names are different. I have come to believe that 'Lisa' doesn't really exist except in Steve's imagination." She particularly objected to one pattern in Steve's behavior. He would ask her for advice on how to win Lisa's heart, and then a few days later he would be doing just what the woman advised—only with her, not with Lisa.

If this woman is interpreting things correctly, then, the immoral actions of Steve consist of lying about Lisa as an illicit means of ingratiating himself with the woman herself (that is, extorting information about what romantic overtures the woman might find most appealing, in order to use these on her).

The woman who wrote the story about Steve and Lisa objected to Steve's actions in part because she had another boyfriend and she felt it was wrong for Steve to use these underhanded tactics to try to win her away from her real beloved. Similar themes appeared in a number of rejectors' accounts. It is quite understandable that a would-be lover would regard other lovers as rivals and might seek to compete against them, but rejectors often objected to the use of certain tactics. In particular, several mentioned that the would-be lover would say derogatory or unflattering things about the boyfriend or girlfriend, presumably to make the rejector see that person in a less appealing light. Instead, apparently, such remarks generated a negative reaction from the rejectors, who responded by defending their beloved and criticizing the would-be lover.

In general, the rejectors objected to excessively pushy actions by the would-be lovers. We shall cover the differential perceptions of persistence in more detail in the next chapter. For the present, the important point is that rejectors felt that would-be lovers exceeded the bounds of decency, norms of consideration, and even outright promises. Thus, one woman wrote that her pursuer had the annoying habit of dropping by her house without warning. When she insisted that he call first, he agreed, but according to her he never kept that promise and continued to stop over unpredictably. Other rejectors wrote of endless phone calls, of perseverating conversations that wasted their time and detracted from their work or studies or other relationships, of would-be lovers who bothered the rejector's friends looking for some advantage or encouragement when the rejector himself or herself refused to interact with them.

Some rejectors even mentioned that would-be lovers threatened to commit suicide, which the rejectors regarded as a crassly manipulative, underhanded, objectionable ploy. In our sample, suicidal talk was scarcely mentioned, but it is indeed an optional part of the rejected lover's script, and occasionally people do threaten and even commit suicide in response to unrequited love. Several such cases were reported by Douglas (1967). In one case, two brothers who had been inseparable companions both fell in love with the same woman. When she finally expressed a preference for the older one, the younger one threatened suicide, and, shaken, she agreed to marry him instead. But of course threatening suicide is not really a way to make someone love you, and after marrying the younger of the two the woman came to realize that she did actually love the older brother. When she declared her intention to go back to him, the younger brother did in fact kill himself. He left a note saying that his wife and brother had knowingly, deliberately, driven him to suicide and were glad about it. Obviously, such a gesture is ultimately fruitless in terms of winning love for oneself, but it probably did succeed in making it very difficult for the other two to remain together as a couple afterward.

A more general study of suicidal women found that many of them threatened or attempted suicide in order to elicit more affectionate attention from their husbands (Bonnar & McGee, 1977). But like the rejectors in our sample, the husbands regarded their wives' actions as improper, manipulative ploys, and the outcome was counterproductive from the women's point of view—the husbands tended to withdraw emotionally even further.

Although we have featured the devious tactics used by the would-be lovers (as seen by the rejectors), it should not be overlooked that rejectors did occasionally do objectionable things too. Across the entire sample, there were almost as many references to unscrupulous actions by rejectors as by would-be lovers. The improper actions by rejectors, however, were divided almost equally between the would-be lovers' accounts and the rejectors' own accounts, so no significant difference emerged.

Typically, the improper acts by the rejector consisted of efforts to avoid the would-be lover. As we have seen, expressing the rejection in formal, explicit terms was very difficult for many of the rejectors, and so they often sought to deal with the situation by simply avoiding contact with the would-be lover. Some managed this in a reasonably blameless fashion, but others resorted to at least moderate lies or deceptions, such as fabricating excuses for not going out with the would-be lover, or having someone else answer the phone every time the would-be lover called and say, untruthfully, that the rejector was absent.

Such usage of minor lies to avoid the unwanted pursuer is illustrated in an amusing story told by a woman who was strongly attracted to a drummer in a rock band. She dated him several times and even had the band stay at her house when they played a gig nearby. Later, the band was playing in another city not far from where she lived, and she traveled there to see him. She spoke with him before the show and during breaks. When she made plans to "hang out" with him after the show, however, he declined, saying "he was too tired and wanted to go to the hotel and sleep." She accepted this excuse and told him she would be leaving. Unfortunately, she lost her keys in the club and so had to stay until the end of the show. Her own words best express her discovery that his putative exhaustion had been merely an excuse to get rid of her: "He ended up showing up at the club, bright and cheery, 20 minutes later. His mouth dropped when he saw that I was still there. What an asshole. I think it's pretty funny. I didn't at the time, though."

In a few cases the immorality of the rejector's avoidant action went further than such white lies. One woman was initially attracted to a man and dated him briefly, but her interest faded while his grew. She did not know how to tell him that she had lost interest in seeing him, so she tried simply avoiding him. Unfortunately, she had already agreed to attend one social function with him, and so she went. At the party, he was overtly affectionate toward her, standing near her, putting his arm around her while they spoke with others, and so forth, and these gestures were acutely distressing to her. She tried to avoid him by being in other rooms, but he kept returning to her. Finally she met some of her other friends and left the party with them, without telling him.

He called her the next day. She reported that he was very upset. She sympathized with him: "He had every right to be [upset]." Recognizing the inappropriateness of her actions, she felt very guilty about having left the party without him and without even telling him. Even in retrospect, she was quite willing to condemn her own actions. "I felt so bad, I didn't know what to say. That was the worst thing I've ever done to another human being. I was amazed by my own actions."

Leaving a party without informing one's date, while hardly a major crime against humanity, is certainly inappropriate and contrary to prevailing norms. The tactics of rejectors sometimes went beyond the bounds prescribed by conventional morality and norms of obligation. In such cases, they usually emphasized that they felt at their wits' end and simply did not know how to handle the situation. At least their willingness to condemn their own actions did surpass the would-be lovers' willingness to condemn themselves, and that may again reflect the would-be lovers' sense that love justified their acts.

Slander Born of Guilt

We examined all the accounts we received for tendencies to say derogatory, devaluing things about the other person. The rejectors were clearly more negative about the would-be lovers than the reverse. Indeed, over half of the rejectors' stories contained some unflattering remarks about the would-be lovers, whereas only about one-quarter of the would-be lovers had anything bad to say about their rejectors.

We have no way of proving that these derogatory remarks of the rejectors were motivated by guilt. But it is plausible. Other studies have shown that feelings of guilt depend on the esteem or regard that the person feels toward the one he or she has wronged (e.g., Baumeister, Stillwell, & Heatherton, 1991). If that is correct, then one way of reducing guilt feelings is to minimize one's esteem for one's victims. And, indeed, it does appear that when people hurt others, they sometimes try to regard the others as lowly individuals who are unworthy of decent treatment. The great crimes of oppression in the 20th century, from the Nazi and Stalinist murder campaigns to the Cambodian atrocities to the Chinese Cultural Revolution to My Lai, were always accompanied by systematic efforts to portray the sufferers as lowly, execrable, even subhuman beings.

It is indeed a long step from mass murder to simple heartbreak, but there are some common features of the experience of guilt, and it is at least plausible that similar patterns may operate. The less regard the rejector has for his or her victim, the less he or she would need to feel guilty. Thus, for example, in the preceding chapter we recounted a woman's description of her admirer as "a total turn-off loser," unpopular, ugly, and with an unappealing personality. Not surprisingly, she reported no guilt over her rejection of him. Indeed, she described her own actions in terms that seem callous and cruel, such as laughing at him, but if one shares her assessment of Albert as a lower form of life then one can perhaps understand her lack of guilt. In a similar vein, another woman described her admirer as an unethical, malicious, repulsive individual who had deliberately hurt others, and so she too would not suffer guilt over rejecting him.

And so it went. A man described the woman who desired him as "fat and annoying," and he only went out with her because he was "too wimpy to say no." Another justified his loss of interest in the woman on the basis of discovering undesirable personality traits: "She seemed nice at first, so I talked to her. After a while, all I could think of was getting away from her. She was egocentric, self-centered and had the personality (overall) of an ice cube." A woman objected to the immaturity of the male student who liked her. He expressed his affection in ways that reminded her of schoolchildren, such as pelting her with snowballs.

One factor that complicates the link between guilt and derogation is the implicit message of superiority that the rejector's role entails. People are taught from early in life to regard each individual as a worthy, respectable person, to remain modest at all times, and indeed American society is founded on the ideal (or myth, in a more cynical view) that all individuals are created equal. At the same time, however, many parents and peers may convey elitist messages by subtly or even explicitly telling the person that a possible partner is "not good enough for you." In cases of unrequited love, the rejection may often in fact be based on the judgment that the admirer really is not good enough to be one's partner. The harsh but unassailable judgment of personal superiority does violate norms of modesty and equality, however, and this may make some people uncomfortable.

Some rejectors were articulate about the issue of personal superiority and resulting inequity, saying that the other was not financially well off enough for them or not attractive enough. One woman recalled a male admirer in high school who was fairly unpopular at the time. In her blunt words, she had been an outcast in junior high school and was now gaining access to the "in crowd," and she could not afford to jeopardize her newfound popularity by associating with someone less popular than herself. Interestingly, our stories also contained a parallel account by a male who was sufficiently similar as to raise suspicions that he was the same one this woman described. His account, like hers, omits any moral dimension in her rejection of him. He objected to "elitism" in the school on moral grounds, but not to her specific pattern of rejecting him. Here are his words: "I suspect that the main reason she was uninterested in me was due to my unpopularity. I spent a lot of time rebelling against the elitist attitude I perceived (and still perceive) in that school. This left me largely unpopular, and I didn't think she wanted the stigma of being attached to me." He concluded that there was nothing he could have done differently and that things were perhaps fated to turn out this way, and he referred to this romantic failure as "just a large battle I lost." Thus, both his account and hers invoke stigma and elitism in her rejection of him, but both treat these issues as merely pragmatic facts of life and downplay any moral issue.

But we suspect that many rejectors found it difficult to acknowledge frankly that they believed themselves superior beings to their ill-fated admirers. Some of the bland expressions that they simply did not feel physically attracted by the person, or that he or she will someday make someone else very happy, and so forth, may have been diplomatic and evasive ways of articulating this sentiment. As we have pointed out, the rejector's self-esteem was not usually threatened by the episode, and so his or her account has no need to defend or assert this esteem. Moreover, the actual events probably reflected this same difficulty: That is, rejectors probably were reluctant to tell their admirers bluntly that the admirer was simply not good enough for them.

One woman, for example, was briefly involved with a man whom she finally judged was not ambitious enough or likely to be successful enough for her. She clearly felt he was going to be professionally inferior, but she had difficulties expressing this, and chose instead to describe the conflict in terms of differences in values. She valued work, whereas his values were supposedly more on a casual, easygoing lifestyle. She concluded, "I guess in short, I can't love a person who isn't my equal. I need someone who is willing to work for what is important to them and who will work to help others. A relationship in my opinion has to be 50–50 for it to work."

The novelist Joseph Heller parodied a similar conflict in his novel *Something Happened.* In one chapter, he describes how one executive would evaluate his subordinates against harsh, high standards and then, inevitably, would decide to fire them. At this point, however, he would feel guilty, and to assuage his guilt he would seek to arrange another job for the subordinate in the same company working for a different manager. His ambivalence would come through in his recommendation to the other manager, however, when he would say something like, "He'd be perfect for you; he's just not good enough for me." Most people, of course, would be reluctant to make such a bald assertion of personal superiority, and romantic rejectors may often seek to downplay their own flattering self-assessment by portraying the would-be lover as an exceptionally hopeless case or, alternatively, by phrasing the rejection in evasive terms that made no reference to personal quality or worth.

Conclusion: Does Love Justify All?

The majority of moral rules concern how one treats other people. It is right to treat them well, and it is wrong to abuse, exploit, or hurt them. In this view, the would-be lover ought perhaps to feel some degree of guilt, for many would-be lovers do in fact inflict a fair amount of vexation, irritation, and other emotional distress on the people they pursue. But there was very little indication of guilt feelings on the part of would-be lovers in our sample of accounts. There are probably two reasons for their apparent sense of innocence. First, they seem largely unaware of the distress that they cause to their love objects. Second, they may well feel that love justifies their actions. Love is a powerful and fundamental value base in our society, and so most things done for the sake of love are considered to be adequately justified.

In contrast, rejectors often seem to struggle with issues of right and wrong. They do not have the appeal to love to justify their actions. Moreover, the hurt they inflict on someone else is often quite obvious and substantial. They need to have some justification, some proof that they are not cruel heartbreakers or wanton inflicters of pain. It is probably the most basic and widespread lesson of moral socialization that one should not hurt others. Rejectors, however, do hurt someone, and so inevitably many of them will grapple with feelings of guilt.

Rejectors often insist that they were not responsible for the episode. In their view, they did not cause this other person to fall in love with them, and so the other's suffering is not their fault. A fair number also pointed to the impossibility of dictating their own feelings: They could not help it that they did not reciprocate the other's love. In other words, their accounts are careful to portray themselves as entirely blameless, for they are not responsible for the other's feelings, nor for their own lack of feelings.

To the extent that we accept this view that the rejector was not responsible for either person's feelings, we can appreciate the fundamental irony of the rejector's position: morally innocent but feeling guilty. They have caused someone pain, even though they did not intend to do so, nor wanted to do so, nor even did anything to bring about the situation. It is no wonder that some of them end up wishing the episode had never happened, as we saw in the chapter on emotion!

The moral dilemma of the rejector may help to explain the "irony of retrospect" that we noted in the preceding chapter on self-esteem. As we observed, many rejectors end up regretting the incident despite the fact that it did boost their self-esteem, whereas normally people are glad to have experiences that boost their self-esteem. But the flattering aspect was typically early in the episode. In its later stages, the implicit compliment may have been forgotten or overshadowed by the increasing sense of guilt. What they regretted in retrospect was not a boost to esteem but an episode of undeserved guilt.

As we have seen, not all rejectors feel equally innocent. Some may have initially encouraged the other. Guilt over inflicting heartbreak is probably especially difficult for people who begin dating under conditions of mutual attraction but then lose interest while the other's interest rises. Likewise, people who have to break the hearts of close friends—friends who want to become lovers—may be especially prone to suffer guilt.

The issue of encouraging the other's attentions is of central importance. If you have encouraged someone to fall in love with you, your obligation is that much greater, and there are definite norms that people should not solicit romantic attentions that they have no interest in reciprocating. To do so would be to exploit another, to toy with another's feelings carelessly, or to manipulate and take advantage of another for sexual or egotistical benefit. As we shall see in the next chapter, rejectors and would-be lovers differ substantially in their perceptions of the degree of encouragement that was given. For the present, the important point is that rejectors are quite sensitive to the moral implications of misleading the other, and many of their accounts are quite insistent on the fact that they were scrupulously honest, fair, explicit, and consistent. Even accounts like that of Ralph, whose story was summarized early in this chapter, were often full of such assertions. Despite that the fact that he initiated sexual activity with the woman whom he did not love, he attempted to defend his moral innocence by repeating throughout his account that he always told her that no romantic relationship was possible.

There are other means of justification that rejectors use, beyond simply appealing to their technical innocence and inability to control their feelings. They may insist on the impossibility of romance, perhaps especially by derogating the other person. The more they can portray the other in an undesirable light, the less they need to feel guilty for jilting or hurting that person. Other rejectors may justify their actions on the basis of the need to be true to themselves, of doing what is best for the other person in the long run, or of having other commitments or relationships that take precedence.

In extreme cases, rejectors point to their own victimization, suggesting that they (rather than the heartbroken admirer) are the ones who deserve sympathy. These rejectors describe a variety of morally questionable tactics employed by the would-be lovers, such as breaking promises or commitments and misrepresenting the relationship to others. Such accounts effectively shift the focus of blame and guilt away from the rejector. The rejector is no longer the villain inflicting suffering and heartbreak on an innocent admirer, but is instead the victim of intrusive pursuit and unfair, unsavory ploys.

It is not surprising that the would-be lovers' own accounts scarcely ever mention their own use of unfair tactics. People generally tend to downplay their morally questionable actions, and as we have already noted, the would-be lover can appeal to the value of love to justify his or her acts. Indeed, it seems that most would-be lovers do not really do anything that is very bad, for on close inspection even the misdeeds that the rejectors reproach them with are quite minor. The reason, again, is that the rejector can find justification by portraying himself or herself as victim, and so the rejector may tend to make the most of anything the other does that seems morally questionable.

According to the prevailing views in our culture, love is beyond the control of the conscious, moral being. People should therefore not be held responsible for their feelings of love, or for their lack of such feelings. According to this view, unrequited love would hardly be a moral issue at all. In that context, it seems ultimately unfair for so many rejectors to be troubled with feelings of guilt. But as we have said, they lack a firm script or clear guidelines for their role, and so they do not know what their obligations are and whether they are doing anything wrong. It is only clear that they have hurt someone, and for that they feel guilty—and try as best they can to find some way of justifying themselves.

Note

1. Because relatively few rejectors acknowledged a prior relationship, however, this effect was too small to reach statistical significance. It deserves further research.

What Actually Happened?

Woody Allen's critically acclaimed film *Crimes and Misdemeanors* portrays a case of unrequited love that ends when the rejector feels himself compelled to have the would-be lover murdered as the only way to get free of her. The protagonist, a wealthy physician and philanthropist, has been having an affair for several years and now has lost interest. His mistress, frantic over her impending abandonment, writes letters to the man's wife that he intercepts at the last minute. He tries to reason with her. "Promises were made," she insists. "I never said I would leave my wife," he responds. There is no way for the viewer to know what promises were, or were not, made.

When accounts disagree, the objective truth can only be guessed at. Just as in that film, there is no way to know for certain what was, or was not, said between the people who appeared in the accounts we collected. Our rejectors and would-be lovers were not describing the two sides of the same incidents. But overall the two sets of accounts should be compatible—unless there are systematic differences in the way would-be lovers and rejectors perceive, interpret, and recall events. Our work has focused on precisely such systematic differences. This chapter will examine the discrepancies between rejectors' and would-be lovers' accounts as to what actually happened. As we shall see, they contain disagreements like those in the film regarding what promises were made and what encouraging or discouraging words were spoken.

Several of the discrepancies might be dismissed as mere failure to communicate, but such an analysis is too shallow. There are important reasons for communication failure. As we pointed out earlier in our discussion of the "conspiracy of silence," the rejector and the would-be lover, whatever their differences, share one common desire, and that is not to have to endure a situation in which one speaks the cruel, disappointing words of rejection to the other. The rejector does not want to have to articulate the bad news, and the would-be lover does not want to hear it.

Yet the message must somehow be communicated. The rejector's reluctance is merely about speaking the words aloud and suffering the guilt of inflicting pain. The rejector wishes that the would-be lover would come to understand the impossibility of romance without needing it spelled out in explicit, articulate, cruel detail. At most, the would-be lover should take a few hints or understand the deeper meaning of the rejector's avoidance. In contrast, the would-be lover's reluctance is concerned with drawing the conclusion that the love is hopeless and must be abandoned. The would-be lover wants to see positive signs, wants to persist and triumph in the end. In simpler terms, the rejector hopes that a few unreturned phone calls would be sufficient to convey to the would-be lover that the love is doomed. The would-be lover wants to see each unreturned phone call as accident, oversight, inconvenience, indeed as anything except a sign of lack of interest.

And so the communication between mismatched lovers is likely to be poor. Hints and doubts, mixed messages, ambiguous signals, and other sources of confusion and error are likely to intrude.

Was the Love Interest Communicated?

One of the areas of least disagreement concerned the would-be lovers' expression of love. Nearly all the rejectors' accounts included such a communication, and the vast majority of the would-be lovers' accounts likewise included it. There was a significantly higher rate of such communications in the rejectors' accounts (which, as we said, were nearly unanimous with respect to this feature), and the discrepancy can be attributed to the few cases in which people kept their love more or less to themselves.

Of course, lovers do not always express their feelings. Our respondents were asked to describe an especially important and powerful experience of unrequited love, and probably these powerful experiences were particularly likely to include overt communication. Obviously, an episode would not usually qualify as an especially powerful experience for the rejector if the other person never expressed his or her love.

In those few cases in which love interest was not communicated, one may see the beginnings of how communication may fail, however. Consider one man's account of his attraction to a woman that seemed not to lead anywhere even though he says he still thinks about her, long after the episode. He said that as he got to know her, she dated several other men he knew, but he was unable to get close to her. "After a few clumsy attempts at asking her out (more ignored than rejected) I decided to give up and wait." It is difficult to grasp how an invitation for a date could be "more ignored than rejected" if it were expressed in clear, definite, articulate terms. But perhaps if he mumbled something vague about doing something together eventually, she responded to his comment in a similarly abstract or speculative fashion, and so the message would not be communicated. If the woman in his account had participated in our study and been asked to describe an especially important experience she had as a rejector, it is doubtful that she would have chosen this same episode, because she may well have had only an imprecise suspicion of his attraction to her.

Did Someone Lead Somebody On?

Of much greater interest than the would-be lover's communication of love is the issue of whether the rejector expressed affection, encouragement, or love. To show attraction to another and then withdraw it is regarded as inconsistent, teasing, unfair. The common term is "leading the person on," and it violates the norms for appropriate treatment of other people. If the rejector led the would-be lover on, then the rejector's guilt is increased and the would-be lover's confusion, heartbreak, and persistence are especially understandable.

We carefully examined stories for any indications that the rejector expressed encouragement, attraction, love, or affection. A simple and striking discrepancy between the two sets of accounts emerged. Over half the would-be lovers felt they were led on or encouraged, at least initially. In contrast, most rejectors (three out of four) portrayed themselves as never leading the other on, and in fact many of them insisted quite explicitly that they never misled the other and were thoroughly, consistently, scrupulously honest right from the start.

A similar difference emerges even if the criteria are much stricter—that is, when we coded for indications that the love or attraction was reciprocated at some time, such indications were still found significantly more often in the would-be lovers' accounts than in the rejectors' accounts. The would-be lovers thus had had plenty of reason for hope, at least in the way they remembered things. Rejectors, in contrast, tended to imply that there was never much hope and that that message should have been clear all along. This pattern is consistent with Tennov's (1979) observation that people who are in love tend to believe strongly in reciprocity even despite accumulating evidence to the contrary.

These issues were sufficiently important that we examined them in a follow-up study, in which people were asked to make their own ratings of their experiences (Baumeister, Wotman, & Stillwell, in press). The pattern was confirmed. Rejectors denied that they encouraged the would-be lover or led the would-be lover on. Would-be lovers said they were led on. Rejectors said that the would-be lover's attraction was excessive in view of the amount of encouragement they were given, and they said that the other mistakenly believed the love to be reciprocal. Would-be lovers said that the rejectors had encouraged their interest and even initially encouraged their love, which therefore was not excessive or unrealistic.

Thus, it is hard to dispute that would-be lovers and rejectors differ fundamentally in their recollection about whether the would-be lover was led on and encouraged to fall in love. One explanation for these discrepancies is that they could be caused by the diverging motives of the authors. Rejectors want to evade guilt and blame, and so they may choose to describe episodes in which they were honest and forthright, or they may distort their recollections of events so as to give the impression that they were honest. Would-be lovers may be adopting the role of victim and may therefore want to blame the rejector by suggesting that he or she led them on. Or would-be lovers may simply be allowing their own remembered desires to color their recollections—yes, he did love me, at first, I think, it must have been so.

On the other hand, it is very plausible that there were simply mixed and ambiguous signals regarding the rejector's feelings. Often there was friendship between the two, or even some degree of mutual attraction. And even when the rejector is certain that he or she does not want this romance, the rejector does not want to be cruel and so may say kind things as a way of being nice and minimizing the hurt of rejection. But kind words or nice, friendly acts may be interpreted by the would-be lover as suggesting that there is hope after all.

This possibility—of ambiguous comments leading to widely discrepant interpretations—was suggested in the movie we cited at the beginning of this chapter. In one flashback, the man and woman were walking on the beach, and she asks him to teach her things. He says that someday they will have a lot of time together. But what is "a lot of time"—does it imply that he will divorce his wife and marry her, as she eventually believes he has promised? Or does it merely mean that they will someday take a trip together and have several days to talk (which they later did)?

Numerous stories and remarks made by the rejectors in our research suggest how their words and actions may have conveyed unintended messages of encouragement to their admirers. Some recognized the problem explicitly, such as the fellow who wrote, "I never did anything to lead her on, but I was always nice to her, and this seemed to be more than enough." Being nice was all it took to mask the message of rejection.

In the case of platonic friendship, mixed messages may be especially common. Forming and maintaining such friendships requires attending to the other, being considerate, saying kind and supportive things, and all these acts could well be regarded by a would-be lover as signs of another kind of affection. Thus, in the words of another man, "My intentions were to have a completely platonic friendship-based relationship, yet my being with her seemed to lead her on."

Several rejectors described how their own uncertainty, reluctance to be cruel, or pity led them to act in ways that they regarded as merely polite and considerate but that their would-be lovers took as hopeful signs of encouragement. One woman described how she lived with many people one summer in a fraternity house. Among the large group of inhabitants, "there was one guy in the house whom nobody liked—he had a very boring personality, low self-esteem, poor grooming habits, and it was difficult to carry on a meaningful conversation with him." One day, she was preparing to play Scrabble with one of the housemates, and this poor soul came and asked if he could play too. She felt sorry for him: "To avoid hurting his feelings we said 'Yes.'" But he was encouraged by this initial contact, and whenever he encountered her in the following weeks he would express interest in playing again. "Eventually, because I felt sorry for him and because he was beginning to annoy me, I said OK, because I figured it would get him off my back. This was a mistake. He felt that I was being nice to him because I liked him. A couple of days later he asked me out for a date in a very pitiful manner." Thus, she saw her actions as minimally considerate, but she felt he interpreted them as signs of romantic possibility.

The theme of relenting under pressure, only to find that one's seeming change of heart provides further encouragement, echoed through a number of rejectors' accounts. One high school boy approached the girl with notes and calls, but she wanted no part of him. She rejected him bluntly, telling him to go away and leave her alone. He persisted, and she recalls relenting a little toward him: "I think after a while, a month or so, I gave in a little and talked to him more. I suppose this was really bad because it only encouraged him more," but she didn't know better at the time. The result was that it became all the more difficult to extricate herself from him. In another account, a young man approached a young woman who secretly disliked him.

He tried to get her to call him on the telephone. "I do not believe in calling up guys," she wrote, "so I'd never call. . . . One day he approached me and asked why I hadn't called him yet. I do not know what my reply was but I felt very hopeless. I knew that I would never call him so I gave him my phone number." Encouraged by the fact that she gave him her number, he began to call her up frequently.

To appreciate the would-be lover's perspective on these events, it is important to recall the would-be lover's script, as portrayed in books and movies. It involves gradually winning the other's affections through persistence, loyal affection, and devoted effort. The rejector gives in and offers a minimal interaction, which from the rejector's perspective is merely to relieve the burden of constantly being so negative and rejecting. But to the would-be lover it is a sign of progress. Last month she would not talk to me, but this month she will, and sometimes she is even nice to me. In the movies, such changes are often the momentous first indications that the protagonist's suit will eventually be crowned with success. It would be hard not to regard such changes as very positive, hopeful signs.

Several of the key themes we have covered in previous chapters may contribute to the mixed-message problem. As we noted, many rejectors feel profoundly uncertain in this role because of its scriptlessness. Not knowing what to do, they may agree to go out with the would-be lover on a date, may accept and reciprocate compliments, and so forth. The woman quoted above who cited her feelings of hopelessness at being asked to call the young man is one example, and this uncertainty led her to give him her phone number. Another woman wrote, "There was a guy at work who asked me out and I said yes only because I didn't want to hurt his feelings and I didn't know what else to say." Abruptly thrust into the role of target of unwanted affection, she groped for a script to follow, and the least hurtful thing to do seemed to be to agree to go out with him despite her disinclination.

We also noted that some would-be lovers seemed to follow a "foot in the door" pattern of eliciting some minimal promises or favors or responses and trying to build on them. These could easily interact with the rejector's uncertainty and scriptlessness. Would-be lovers may make it difficult for rejectors to say no, but then they may take the positive reply as a hopeful sign. The rejector is just trying to avoid outright cruelty or induced guilt, but the would-be lover capitalizes on these actions.

Thus, one man wrote of meeting a woman from Finland while he was traveling in Europe. They spoke for hours on the train and then parted, a bit awkwardly. She managed to find him again and delivered a note to him at his hotel. He had no romantic intentions and did not respond, and so she called, acting somewhat hurt that he had not called her after getting her note. "I couldn't bear to have her feeling hurt or 'blown off' so I called her."

She took this as encouragement and pursued the matter. Before she went back to Finland, she asked him if he would be opposed to seeing her if she ever came to the United States. He, of course, said he would not be opposed, for to express such opposition would seem needlessly cruel. He did not expect ever to see her again, but she did begin to write him long, intimate letters. Later, back home in the U.S., he received a call from her (from Finland) asking again if he "would mind" seeing her when she came to the U.S. No, he said, he would not mind, are you coming, and when? She told him she would be in Chicago tomorrow! "I almost choked," he wrote, for he was now involved with an American girlfriend who would not take kindly to having him rush off to Chicago at a moment's notice to see his foreign lover. But after telling the woman from Finland that he would be willing to see her if she ever came, he could hardly refuse to see her when she did show up, and he was obliged to do the best he could to calm his girlfriend down and live up to his promise that had un-expectedly come due.

A last aspect of the rejector's experience that is relevant to the mixed-message problem is the fact that there is genuine ambivalence in some cases. Some were initially attracted to the would-be lover, and the disappearance of the rejectors' attraction was mysterious enough even to the rejectors themselves; we can hardly expect the would-be lover to understand or sympathize with the evaporation of attraction that seemed genuine to both. And even rejectors who are not roman-tically attracted may enjoy the attention, flattery, or interest of the other person. As we noted earlier, many rejectors do enjoy a boost to their self-esteem from the other's attraction, and their very enjoyment may seem encouraging to the would-be lover. After all, if the rejector is flattered by your attentions, then he or she is enjoying your company, which must inevitably seem a sign of hope. One rejector expressed this problem precisely in the conclusion of her account: "I'm sure the fact that I was flattered but not attracted gave him a mixed message."

What does all this seem like to the would-be lover? It is confusing. The other person's actions seem almost incomprehensible, for they mix encouraging and affectionate reactions with negative signs and signals. "She sent me a letter, saying but not saying she wanted me again," wrote one would-be lover, articulating the double message he felt he had received. He resumed his suit, only to be totally mystified when she finally told him that it could never work out. Another put it more simply: "I wasn't too sure how well she liked me because I got different reactions on different days."

The bewildering barrage of contradictory messages perceived by some would-be lovers was well illustrated in one woman's account of her passionate attraction to a fellow student. "When Valentine's Day came along, I sent him a card but he didn't respond. He called to say thanks but sounded very cold." Thus, the long-awaited phone call did arrive, but it was disappointing and anticlimactic - and there was neither a definite yes nor a definite no. "By this time, it had been three months since I'd been attracted to him and I was starting to give up. I started realizing that my assumption that he liked me was based on pure flirtation. But I kept hoping. He would always compliment me on my nice clothes, etc. I would still eat meals with him at the cafeteria and he would drop hints at me such as 'people think you are my girlfriend,' etc." As is typical for these stories, she fails to say what she said in response to these "hints," but they were clearly meaningful and positive signals to her—yet ones that contrasted sharply with his lack of overt initiative. "By this time I was really confused. I still liked him, but he never called or asked me on a date. He would only be nice when he saw me somewhere." In short, his words suggested interest, but his actions seemed to indicate a lack thereof. She did not know what to make of him. Under such uncertainty, some would-be lovers began to wish for a clear, definite message from the other, even a negative one so they'd know how things stood. The next section will examine overt rejections.

Was the Rejection Communicated?

Thus far we have focused on mixed messages that the rejector sends to the would-be lover. One way or another, the rejector wanted to avoid any romantic involvement, but meanwhile a variety of actions may have seemed encouraging to the would-be lover. We have considered how rejectors may act in ways that, contrary to their intentions, send out positive signals to the would-be lover. Let us now examine the opposite, namely explicit messages of rejection.

Rejectors and would-be lovers disagreed substantially on the explicitness of the rejection. Fully half the rejectors' accounts indicated a clear and explicit communication that the rejector was not going to have a romantic relationship with the would-be lover. In contrast, only a quarter of the would-be lovers' accounts described such a definite rejection. This was confirmed in our follow-up study, in which we asked people point blank whether the rejection was clearly and definitely communicated. Rejectors generally said yes, but would-be lovers often said no. It was not a matter of would-be lovers simply refraining from mentioning the fact that they were explicitly rejected. On the contrary, they were quite insistent that the message was far from clear or consistent.

An explicit message of rejection and of the impossibility of romance ought to be very salient to a would-be lover. If you are madly in love with someone and desperately hoping that you can entice that person to love you, you will certainly notice it if the person says no, not now, not ever, no chance. There is evidence from other sources that powerful scenes of rejection are very salient to the unhappy individuals who experience them. Newman's (1988) study of executives who lost their jobs found that most of them maintained clear, vivid memories of the day they were fired, even years later. During the months after the firing, they would replay the scene in their memory over and over, discovering nuances in the boss's behavior, thinking of things they should have said, and so forth, and these recollections undoubtedly helped stamp the episode into their memories. It seems farfetched to suggest that rejected lovers would casually forget or ignore the crucial scene on the day their heart was broken, unlike the executives who vividly recalled the day their career hopes and plans were ruined.

Instead, it seems likely that the explicitness of the rejection was often more apparent to the rejector than to the would-be lover. Perhaps the rejector intended to be clear and explicit, but in the act tried to sweeten the blow with some compliments or kind words or other things that enabled the would-be lover to salvage some hope. The effort to be clear and explicit, in other words, may have ended up as another mixed message.

The explicit rejection message brings up both sides of the rejector's dilemma. As one woman put it, "I did not want to go out with him (romantically) and at the same time, I did not want to hurt his feelings by telling him exactly why I did not want to go out with him." On the one hand, the rejector does not want to inflict pain, and bringing oneself to say the words that break someone's heart is very difficult. On the other hand, the rejector feels a moral obligation to be clear about his or her intentions so as not to lead the other on and, in the long run, increase the other's suffering, and so there is a powerful drive to say what needs to be said. The likely outcome of this conflict is that many rejectors may waffle or hedge a little in the event but may in retrospect bolster their moral stance by emphasizing and perhaps exaggerating how scrupulously honest they were.

Not all rejectors even make the effort to be frank. Some rejectors' accounts indicated that they simply avoided contact with the would-be lover and hoped that the situation would resolve itself. Others felt it was their duty to be honest, and so they forced themselves to express their feelings (and lack of feelings). But even they may have failed. Given their guilt, fear of hurting the other, and reluctance to communicate the bad news, the rejection may have come out in a garbled, hedged, qualified, and unclear fashion. To sweeten the bitter news, one may add enough positive statements that the other does come away thinking that she really does like me, he really thinks I am attractive, there may be hope for me yet.

Meanwhile, the would-be lover is hardly in an objective state of mind, able to process information accurately and in an unbiased fashion. As we said, just as the rejector is reluctant to say the heartbreaking words, the would-be lover is reluctant to hear them. Success requires persistence, even in the face of initial failure or setbacks or obstacles, and discouraging words from one's beloved may be taken in that spirit. If at any later time the rejector is pleasant or seems encouraging, the would-be lover may feel justified in deciding that a previous expression of rejection was not final, not complete, not sincere. And in retrospect he or she may further minimize discouraging words.

Ironically, many would-be lovers would probably prefer an explicit rejection in the present, rather than continuing with vain hope that in the end leads to just as definite a failure. Tennov (1979) has suggested that the only cure for being in love is to get indisputable evidence that the target of one's love is not interested. Eliminating the element of hope may therefore be necessary to enable these individuals to begin to put the affair behind them. Several would-be lovers even expressed this wish, saying that they felt suspended in uncertainty and wanted to know for certain whether the other had any feelings for them. One woman wrote, "If only I knew for sure that he definitely was not interested then I could get on with my life." Another said the man she had dated had grown remote and aloof, but "he hasn't said he wanted to dump me, which would make life easier." She said it would be better to hear it from him explicitly rather than simply feeling the emotional distance between them when they were together. She suggested that "he's a wimp and is too scared to tell me," and concluded, "I wish he'd just tell me he wants to see me no longer, so that I can accept the fact and go on with my life."

The longing for a clear message, even a negative one, is rather amazing. One would think that uncertainty at least leaves room for hope, whereas a definitive rejection would be crushing, and so people should prefer uncertainty. Yet we can begin to understand why some would-be lovers would desire a firm answer even if it is negative. The uncertainty is stressful, and as the likelihood of a happy attachment gradually recedes, the would-be lover may begin to long for the episode to be over.

Script theory furnishes further insight into why would-be lovers may eventually desire a firm answer. We have said repeatedly that one source of stress and suffering for rejector is the lack of a script, which leaves rejectors uncertain what to do. Would-be lovers do not have that problem, because they have scripts. We pointed out, however, that there are two basic scripts for the would-be lover role, one of an aspiring lover, the other of a disappointed victim, and there is uncertainty about when to shift from the first to the second script. These would-be lovers who end up longing for a definite yes or no from their desired partners may be precisely at the point where they about to make the shift from the first script to the second. Hence they may feel in limbo. If the desired partner might actually be interested in them after all, they would want to pursue their chances rather than giving up. If the answer is no, then the would-be lover can begin the work of getting over it and moving on to new possibilities. Those two directions make completely opposite demands for how the person should think and feel about the desired partner—whether to focus on him or her as a highly desirable partner, or to devalue, even forget about, him or her. When one is obsessed with someone but can't decide whether to think about him or her in positive or negative terms, the uncertainty may become unbearable.

Thus, would-be lovers may desire a firm answer, even a negative one, in order to allow them to start recovering from the affair. They may be understandably reluctant to start detaching themselves from someone who may yet turn out to be the answer to their dreams and the love of their life. They have presumably already faced rejection and distress, the initial stages of reaction to attachment failure. The final rejection is only the cue to move on to the second script (of recovering victim), to begin the emotional work of detachment, and to set about building a new life structure that does not center around a love relationship with the rejector.

It is also important to note that there is no universal or even general conclusion about the need for an explicit rejection. Some rejectors reported simply ignoring the other who would eventually "get the hint" and give up. Likewise, some would-be lovers insisted that they would approach their intended partners very tentatively and would back off at any sign of lack of interest on the other's part. In one more or less typical example, a young man said he was too shy to approach the girl he had a crush on. Finally he did steel himself to approach her, but to protect himself he phrased his request "in a joking manner. Apparently she took it as a joke. She really hurt me, but I didn't show it." He never asked her out again.

On the other hand, a common pattern in many rejectors' accounts was the fact that mere avoidance had proven inadequate to discourage unwanted attentions. Hints were often not gotten. These rejectors often had to become explicit, whether they wanted to or not, in order to free themselves from the entanglement. When they did finally give up on mere avoidance and forced themselves to make the rejection explicit, often after a period of inner struggle, they understandably expected the situation to be finally resolved. The would-be lover should now accept the inevitable and gracefully move on. If that is what rejectors expected, they were often sadly disappointed. In the next section, we examine how the would-be lovers responded to the rejection.

Was It Accepted Gracefully?

The rejector may have hoped that once the impossibility of the romance was made clear, the would-be lover would accept this truth and spare both of them the distress and indignity of further troubles. In some cases, this hope is realized. Some would-be lovers hear the message of rejection, quietly say "OK," and depart to lead their own lives with little further contact. But these may be a minority. Often the would-be lover responds with an outburst of emotion or action that may be difficult for the rejector. We have often spoken of the rejector's reluctance to come out and say that he or she does not love the other. This reluctance may be well founded, for would-be lovers do not always take it well.

Some responses seem rather extreme, unless one considers that the culture has a long tradition of expecting wild, chaotic actions by people whose dreams of love are abruptly dashed. One woman wrote that the man she rejected went out and got drunk, returning to her room late at night and even trying to choke her. A man described how the woman he disappointed would call him "at every hour of the night to talk (sometimes drunk) and always crying, Why? Why?" These reactions conform to the pattern of protest reactions observed when one is deprived of a social attachment. Like the baby's objections to the mother's departure, the first reaction of the unrequited lover may be active distress and a refusal to accept the separation.

A similar sentiment was expressed in Jessica's account, which was covered in Chapter 1. Her admirer, Ben, turned desperate at her rejection of him. He came to visit her at all hours, crying, sometimes drunk, even threatening suicide. She could not get rid of him, and she felt that her schoolwork was suffering from all the interruptions. When she went further and insisted that he leave her alone—thus breaking off all contact with him—he began to impose on her friends, asking them what he could do to win her heart, crying to them. Her story ended with his including her in a painting he made for his art institute. She felt this painting, which depicted her "next to naked men and ladies French-kissing with statues," was a most ungraceful and embarrassing way for him to cope with her rejection of him.

These reactions are often very distressing to rejectors. Many already feel guilty about hurting someone, and the heartbroken lover's overt and excessive distress must aggravate their guilt feelings as well as causing practical problems. For some, the simple necessity of avoiding the other person becomes paramount. "I practically hid for my life," said one man of this phase. Female rejectors may be more likely than male ones to need to hide, possibly because rejected men may be more likely than women to respond to frustration with aggression. We have already mentioned the woman who said the man tried to choke her. Another one said that the fellow she rejected "turned nasty," which made the unpleasant episode all the more unpleasant.

Several of these themes are combined in an account by a woman we may call Melanie. She had joked around with Don, a fellow student in one of her classes, without thinking much of it. One night he telephoned and asked her for a date. Melanie responded as if he were joking, but it soon became clear that he wasn't, and so she had to respond in earnest. She already had a boyfriend and so she refused to go out with Don. His responses made her feel extremely awkward. First, he began saying how she was breaking his heart, which made her feel quite bad. Then he began to ask about her boyfriend, saying that he wanted to beat the boyfriend up!

When they met after that, Don became physically and sexually aggressive toward her. "Whenever we saw each other he would put his arm around me or put his hand on my legs. I would move etc. but he never got the hint." Finally she had to become blunt and firm with him, saying that she didn't want any physical contact with him and telling him "don't do it ever again." At this, she says, he became very angry and called her insulting names, "but that was the end of it."

Probably the most extreme cases are those where some relationship existed, so that the disappointed lover feels that he or she has a right to express outrage at some perceived breach of obligation. In these, too, the distress over attachment failure is likely to be maximal, insofar as the romantic rejection is perceived as breaking an attachment instead of merely refusing to form one. One woman, for example, said that when she broke up with a boyfriend whom she had ceased to love, he "freaked out," that is, went berserk. "He was suicidal, threatened to kill me and my parents if I broke up with him and he even kidnapped me." The kidnapping led to his arrest, and she was called to court to testify against him. He told her that if she would say it had all been a mistake, he would never bother her again. "For fear that if he did go to jail he'd kill me, I told the court it was a mistake. He got off on a $500 fine. But he is still obsessed with me!" Not honoring his promise to leave her alone, he continued to pursue her, calling her up, asking her for dates, sending her flowers, even giving her expensive gifts such as a gold ring.

Outright criminal actions (such as kidnapping) are fortunately the exception rather than the rule. It is also fairly clear that the majority of rejected lovers accept the disappointing news with reasonably good grace, at least after an initial protest. The minority who do not, however, can make life extremely difficult for the ones who have disappointed them.

Not surprisingly, the majority of accounts of ungraceful response come from rejectors. One can read between the lines of some would-be lovers' accounts and infer that they, too, acted inappropriately or even went berserk after receiving a rejection, but their accounts are almost never explicit about this. At most, they refer to periods of irrationality and denial, to their own inner turmoil and refusal to accept that the desired relationship had no future. Some looked back with regret on these phases of irrational, inappropriate action, but they tend to dwell on the embarrassment and humiliation of their responses rather than on the difficulties they created for the rejector. Thus, we may speculate, if the young man in the preceding story were someday to tell his side of things, he would recall the kidnapping as more a symptom of his inner suffering and as a humiliating episode for him than as a transgression. He would probably look back with embarrassment and feelings of degradation rather than with feelings of guilt. This is consistent with one of the fundamental differences we have observed between rejectors' and would-be lovers' accounts: Rejectors focus on issues of morality and guilt, while would-be lovers focus on self-esteem and humiliation.

All of these, at least, are cases in which the rejected lover has understood the rejection to some degree. Many rejectors have problems getting the would-be lover to reach that point, however. The would-be lover simply refuses to acknowledge the impossibility of his or her suit. We turn next to these cases.

Self-Deception and Refusal to Face Facts

The accounts of would-be lovers and rejectors agreed that self-deception occurred mainly among the would-be lovers. Neither set of stories depicted much self-deception among the rejectors, who after all had little reason to fool themselves at the time. (If rejectors wanted to deceive themselves, it might be in retrospect, such as by minimizing their guilt, and such retrospective maneuvers would not be explicitly noted in stories.) In contrast, a substantial number of would-be lovers seemed to engage in some form of self-deception, such as by constructing illusions about themselves or the possibility of romance, or by simply refusing to face facts when the rejector told them that no romance was possible.

Rejectors were especially sensitive to self-deception by the would-be lover. Two out of every five rejectors' accounts contained some indication that the would-be lover fooled himself or herself or otherwise refused to face facts, and this rate was approximately double the rate at which would-be lovers acknowledged their own self-deception. Of course, even if we look at self-admitted self-deception, there was far more among the would-be lovers than among the rejectors.

One reason that the would-be lover's self-deception may have been more apparent to the rejector than to himself or herself is that, by definition, one does not immediately recognize one's own self-deceptions. Even in retrospect, if one has successfully fooled oneself, one may not realize the extent of the deception and distortion.

Another reason, however, may lie in the garbled communication of rejection that we have discussed. The rejector thinks he or she sent the message but the other persists, irrationally, maintaining hope when there is no chance, believing in the illusory possibility of love. To the rejector, this naturally appears as self-deception, especially to the extent that rejectors think they were clear about the rejection. From the would-be lover's perspective, however, this persistence may be a rational response to mixed signals rather than an irrational response to a definite rejection. At worst, it is taking an optimistic or slightly wishful interpretation of the data. It is not necessarily a matter of refusing to face facts altogether, which is how the rejector may see it.

All of this is not to say that would-be lovers never deceive themselves, for undoubtedly they do, as they themselves admit. We are only saying that the perspective of the rejector may cause him or her to overestimate the other's self-deception. The moral threat and the need to justify oneself shape the rejector's account. This person is pursuing you relentlessly, prolonging the misery for yourself and for himself or herself. It is much better for you to see that person's persistence as a result of self-deception on his or her part, rather than seeing it as a result of the inconsistent, mixed messages you have given him or her. If you led the person on, it is your fault that you both are suffering, but it is not your fault if the individual is kidding himself or herself in spite of your scrupulous honesty.

As one rejector wrote, "It isn't that I didn't inform him, it is because he won't listen!" This sentence clearly reflects the awareness that she would be guilty if she had failed to be clear and honest. And so she insists that the fault is his, not hers.

The rejector's moral vulnerability is greater when he or she has failed to deliver an explicit message of rejection. As we have seen, many rejectors adopt a strategy of avoiding the situation and avoiding the would-be lover, and they realize that the other person may not understand the impossibility of love. Even these rejectors may see some degree of self-deception in the would-be lover, however, and they may also derive some moral exculpation for seeing it. Thus, one woman described her admirer's response to her own strategy of evasion rather than direct rejection. "I think he realizes, at least on some level, that I really don't have any interest in any sort of relationship. But I also feel that he sees what he wants to see. I cannot bring myself to be outright mean or cruel to him, but perhaps that would be the best in the long run." Her own failure to articulate the rejection is thus justified as her not wanting to be mean or cruel, although she is also preparing a justification for being mean should she have to come to that in the near future (as many rejectors eventually find they must). Despite her failure to be frank, though, she thinks her message has gotten through and been ignored.

Whatever the motives of rejectors for emphasizing and exaggerating these distorted perceptions of their admirers, it seems quite clear that many would-be lovers do deceive themselves. The would-be lover probably alternates between passionate love and desperate anxiety, and neither of those emotions is recognized as an aid to rational, objective thought or accurate judgment. We are dealing here with people who want very much for something to come true and are gradually realizing that it will not. They can probably be forgiven (by us at least, if not by their love objects) for postponing this recognition a little. These are certainly facts that they don't want to face.

Would-be lovers referred to both the positive and the negative feelings as sources of self-deception. On the positive side, the would-be lover is swept away with love and desire, and may therefore be preoccupied with his or her own feelings rather than attending carefully to the sober implications of the other's response. In one man's words, "There were certainly enough cues as to her lack of attraction for me, but I was too preoccupied to notice. At that point, my feelings were of the stereotype, 'I'm so happy that I'm with her, I couldn't care less about anything.'" His exuberant love led him, as he put it, to ignore any discouraging signals from her.

On the negative side, would-be lovers may find the message of rejection a threat to their self-esteem and dignity, and so they may try to avoid this message. One woman described an incident in which she gave her virginity to a fellow she loved but who, in retrospect, never cared a great deal about her and regarded her as simply a pleasant sexual conquest. It was painful for her to look back and realize that he never loved her. "Of course, I was blind to this fact for a long time because I refused to admit that I slept with someone who cared less [for me than I cared for him]." By prefacing this statement with "of course," she suggests the seeming inevitability of one's reluctance to face the threatening, heartbreaking, humiliating truth.

Central to many self-deceptive strategies was finding some way to dismiss, discount, or ignore the message of rejection. These responses were especially galling to rejectors, who as we have seen had to force themselves to speak the words in the first place and did not want to have to repeat themselves. Thus Ralph, the man in the last chapter whose platonic friend declared her love for him one day over lunch, knew that the best course was to face up to his unpleasant duty of telling her that he did not and would not love her. He told her this and concluded that they should remain just platonic friends. "She however denied my response, telling me that I was holding my feelings in and not letting them go as they should." Her response seems consistent with the tendency of would-be lovers to think they have been encouraged, for she clearly seems to have thought he did harbor romantic or passionate feelings of love for her. To him, however, she was simply refusing to accept the plain truth of his honest words.

Other rejectors told similar stories of the exasperating dismissals of their messages of rejection. One woman recalled telling the man over and over that she disliked him, but he would laugh and reply, as if she were joking, by saying that she would soon change. Another said that she would grow frustrated by her inability to discourage her admirer's attentions and would sometimes even become "downright rude and nasty" to him. Instead of recognizing her hostile words as an indication of genuine dislike, with the corollary impossibility of love, he would say something like "You're so sexy when you're angry," and would continue his attentions to her. His responses made it impossible for her to get her message across to him, which was extremely frustrating and upsetting to her.

And, indeed, a few would-be lovers recalled how they seized on any possible alternative explanation for the rejecting behavior of their beloved. Not having seen his beloved for a week, one man was overcome with eagerness and hope, but when he picked her up for their date she was cold and distant. He says he knew right then that she did not love him and indeed did not want to see him anymore. But he told himself that maybe she was simply in a bad mood and would come out of it. This thought gave him hope and enabled him to sustain efforts to elicit a positive response from her.

A longer account by a woman we shall call Ellen describes her self-deceptive persistence in the face of multiple and clear messages of rejection. Ellen had become involved with a man whose initial interest soon faded and who eventually wanted to break off contact. At this point, she recalled, he really wanted nothing to do with her at all. "He wouldn't return my phone calls, or answer the door. He even went to the great effort of being at the same place I was at with another girl." If she was correct that her rejector was going to those lengths to discourage her, he may indeed have been quite desperate and frustrated by her persistence. Yet even this seeming cruelty did not deter her. "Constantly his actions showed me that he no longer wanted to have a relationship with me, but I wouldn't pay attention to these actions."

Ellen's own love remained quite strong, and even though his current signals were completely negative, she muted their impact by thinking back to his earlier, more favorable attitude toward her. "I completely ignored what he said and did, because I knew what he used to be before then," she recalled. She told herself, "If he didn't really care for me he would not have led me on like that for two years." She convinced herself that his current actions did not reflect "what he really felt," and she described her efforts at rationalizing things: "I came up with all these conclusions about why he was doing this."

Ellen thus convinced herself that his rejecting behavior was just a temporary problem and not the sign of a definitive end to the relationship. She recalls herself as "obsessed with getting him back." She spent her time thinking up ways to regain his affections, "brainstorming" about strategies that would put the relationship back into what she thought was its true, positive, happy state.

Ellen's account was perhaps the most explicit and detailed one in our sample in its portrayal of her own self-deception. Its conclusion is extremely revealing, however. In her last sentence, she wrote, "I still sometimes think we will get back together." Thus, despite her insight into her own irrationality and futility, there were still moments when she returned to hope and longing. Coming to terms with a broken heart and accepting a romantic failure may often involve a subjective oscillation. At times, one recognizes the futility and hopelessness of one's love, but at other times one thinks that the romance may yet succeed. To put it another way, one shifts from the role and script of broken-hearted victim back into the role and script of aspiring, hopeful lover. Final acceptance of the facts may not be a matter of a single insight and recognition but rather a matter of the gradually diminishing frequency of hopeful moments.

The Persistent, Undaunted Lover

If the would-be lover often refuses to hear the message of rejection, then he or she may well persist in his or her efforts to win the other's love. Indeed, if the rejector's angry, distant, or cruel behavior is seen as a sign of trouble in the relationship (rather than as a sign that the relationship is over), the would-be lover may try even harder. Studies of long-term relationships suggest that when one person expresses discontent or anger, the other may respond by trying extra hard to repair the relationship (e.g., Vaughan, 1986; Levenson & Gottman,

1985). A cycle may even develop, such that the rejector has to become increasingly emphatic to justify his or her leaving, because the other partner responds to each negative sign by stepping up the display of positive feeling and optimism. One woman described just such a cyclic development: "The more I wanted him, the more he pulled away. The more he pushed me away, the more I wanted him."

The determined, often remarkable, sometimes excessive persistence of the would-be lover is an important part of the picture of unrequited love. The script for an aspiring lover is to do all that one can to win the heart of one's beloved, even overcoming initial obstacles such as indifference or rejection, and only giving up when the cause is truly seen as hopeless. As previous sections of this chapter have shown, would-be lovers and rejectors may often disagree substantially over the point at which the cause becomes definitely hopeless. These disagreements should therefore lead to substantial differences in estimating the appropriate degree of persistence.

Sure enough, the would-be lover's persistence was the subject of one of the statistically largest differences found in our research. A few would-be lovers, like Ellen (in the previous section of this chapter), described their persistence in the face of discouragement, but these were a small minority. Only about one out of seven would-be lovers described the persistence of his or her efforts. In contrast, almost two-thirds of the rejectors discussed the persistence of the would-be lover. Clearly, the would-be lover's persistence was far more obvious, important, and central to the rejector's experience than to the would-be lover's own experience. To put it simply, the typical would-be lover's account says that he or she tried and failed, whereas the typical rejector's account says that the would-be lover tried, and failed, and kept on trying and trying and trying.

Nor were these merely matters of emphasis. When we asked people in a follow-up study to rate the would-be lover's persistence, the same difference was found (Baumeister et al., in press). Rejectors perceived much more extreme persistence than did would-be lovers.

It seems likely that this large difference in perceived persistence reflects the fact that for a period of time, the two people are operating on the basis of different scripts. The would-be lover is still the aspiring lover who is trying to win someone's heart; the rejector has delivered the message and is now getting on with his or her life.

This seems an almost inevitable consequence of the poor communication patterns we have documented in the previous sections of this chapter. The rejector has sent the clear message of rejection, as nicely as possible, after a difficult time of getting himself or herself steeled to do so. The case is closed. But the would-be lover did not hear the rejection in such clear, unequivocal terms, and so the case is far from closed. In fact, the would-be lover sees mixed messages and senses reasons for hope. The would-be lover tends to think there was some mutual attraction, so even if the other is being rejecting now perhaps the good times will return. Even if the would-be lover did hear the rejecting message, he or she may have ignored it or rationalized it away.

Many rejectors were quite explicitly frustrated by the would-be lover's persistence, which required them to articulate their feelings over and over. One woman said she constantly had to tell the man that there was no chance of a romance and that they could only be platonic friends, but her words would have only a brief impact. Each time she told him that there would be no love affair between them, he "cooled down for a short time, but not permanently. Every time I think it's over and he got the message, I'm wrong." Apparently he would get the message, but would soon revert to being the hopeful, aspiring lover.

Some rejectors saw themselves forced to adopt extreme, even cruel measures to discourage unwanted attentions from admirers who refused to give up easily. "He kept trying for a long time. He was patient and never gave up," said one student of the fellow who loved her in vain. "It was a very tough situation." The man sought her out frequently, waited for her after each of her classes, asked her about her plans, "wanted to know what I was doing every weekend. After six months I got very sick of the situation and was very mean. He still never gave up." Thus, even her cruelty, born of desperation, failed to discourage him.

In an extreme case, one woman wrote how she had constantly and consistently ignored the young man who had a crush on her. She had refused all invitations and scarcely concealed her strong dislike for him. Despite what she saw as consistent and clear rejection, he persisted until she moved away. After moving, she did not see him for three years. Then, by chance, she encountered him again on a public bus, and he immediately approached her and declared his continued love for her! He began asking her for a date, for her phone number, and so forth. "I could not believe some of the things he was saying to me. I got really frustrated because he was talking in a voice that surrounding passengers could hear. I kept watching my watch and my bus stop." When her stop came, she got off quickly, without even saying good-bye to him. Her alarm and frustration were quite apparent in her account.

If would-be lovers were less likely to feature their own persistence in their accounts, a few of them nonetheless did make it clear that they kept trying for as long as they could sustain any hope. Recalling an obsessive infatuation that made him "crazy," one man described his fruitless persistence thus: "I would constantly talk about her at work. I would talk a long time on the phone. I asked her out many times. I would ask her to hang out, shop, or eat. She always would have a nice excuse, but she wasn't blunt or rude. . . . Everything failed. I finally gave up. I was still fond of her, but it was useless." Significantly, his description does not say that he persisted in the face of clear or explicit rejection, for his beloved simply made excuses rather than telling him that it was hopeless.

Female would-be lovers likewise described persistence. One recalled pursuing a fellow for two and one-half years, without ever definitely telling him that she was attracted to him. Another described how her hopes for love kept overcoming her better judgment that there was no chance: "And even though I knew this relationship would never go anywhere . . . I couldn't pull myself away or stop hoping for something."

Perhaps the most extreme case of persistence described by a would-be lover was furnished by a woman who many years earlier had been in love with a man who was already engaged to be married, but, she said, she "didn't let that stop my pursuit of him—which I did quite recklessly and when I think of it now, I am embarrassed." She tried many tactics, even dating his friends just to be near him! (The dating of a friend so as to increase chances of contact with the beloved was mentioned in a surprising number of accounts. No one seemed to regard it as a devious or immoral tactic, even though it seems to involve a fairly exploitative approach to the friend.) "I plotted ways to see him, I fantasized about his breaking his engagement," she recalled. "I would wait for phone calls promised that never came, phone him at outrageous hours. I never made any demands on him . . . " The latter two statements seem inconsistent, especially when compared with the remark we quoted previously by a rejector who objected to the way his brokenhearted admirer would telephone him "at every hour of the night." The woman said that the "most outrageous thing I ever did" during her pursuit of him was to accompany him on the drive to pick up the plane tickets for his honeymoon, just to be able to spend that hour or two with him. Of course, the man went ahead and married his fiancee, and the would-be lover finally had to come to terms with the impossibility of her love.

Platonic friendship makes the issue of persistence especially painful. The would-be lover may agree to remain "just friends," but the feelings do not necessarily go away, and the continued contact provides a constant reminder and stimulus to the desire. One woman described such a case in which a platonic friend wanted to become a lover and was, with some difficulty, convinced that it was impossible, partly because she already had a boyfriend in another state. Although he agreed to respect that prior commitment, he still found it painful to see her with the other man on a visit. "The look on his face when I introduced him to my boyfriend made my heart break." Later, around the time she wrote the account, he was still occasionally making remarks that indicated his jealousy, but mostly they managed to avoid the topic.

Platonic friendship also increases the difficulty for the rejector. Many noted that they wanted to be clear about discouraging the romantic attentions yet wanted to avoid any cruel or hurtful words because they wanted to sustain the friendship. The would-be lover's persistence was seen as especially vexing because it made it increasingly difficult for them ever to return to the platonic friendship that the rejector may have cherished. And, to be sure, a number of rejectors indicated that they finally had to give up on the friendship and were upset about the loss. They often ended up with some feelings of bitterness toward their former friend and admirer, because this person's seemingly needless and hopeless persistence in the vain attempt at romance had destroyed a valued friendship. After she's laid her heart at your feet and you've had to step on it, after he's begged for an embrace and you've refused, after long anguished phone calls and thwarted kisses and flowers and tears and guilt, it's very hard to go back to just being pals.

Just as the cases of platonic friendship raise special difficulties, so also are there special problems in the cases in which the rejector's initial attraction dwindles to nothing. Although our sample is not large enough for statistical comparisons, our impression was that these rejectors were less critical than others of the would-be lover's persistence. These rejectors had, after all, provided some encouragement to the extent that the attraction had initially been mutual, and so they might well understand that the would-be lover would persist. Still, the degree of persistence often seemed somewhat surprising or excessive to them.

The difficulties of communication and the would-be lovers' opportunities for self-deception may be especially great when the attraction was initially mutual. We suspect that few rejectors will be so explicit about articulating the change in their feelings: "I liked you well enough at first, but I don't like you any more." There are several reasons for this likely reluctance. To say that one's feelings have changed is perhaps to invite an immediate question as to the reason; indeed, several rejectors described their heartbroken admirers asking "Why? Why?" Often the rejector may not know what caused the change, or the rejector may find it hard to put it into words. Even if the rejector does know, it may be difficult to express the reason in a considerate fashion; after all, its essence is, "As I got to know you better I have found you less and less appealing." Further, to change is possibly to violate implicit agreements or commitments, and so admitting change puts one at a moral disadvantage. Lastly, the rejector's hope is often that the would-be lover will quickly find someone else and hence leave the rejector alone and guiltless, but such an articulate rejection may make that hope seem less likely. To say that "to know you better is to like you less" gives the would-be lover little reason to think that he or she will be able to find someone new. Such a message may make the would-be lover cling more desperately to the rejector or even begin to contemplate suicide, and so the rejector's own problems of harassment or guilt will continue.

If rejectors are thus reluctant to articulate their change of heart, then the persistence is especially understandable, for the two are indeed operating on the basis of very different scripts. The rejector is seeing the situation in the context of unambiguous, convincing, unequivocal rejection. The impossibility of romantic future is abundantly clear. In contrast, the would-be lover doesn't quite realize this change and may still be looking at the full set of data containing all the responses and actions by the rejector, including the initial ones. Looking at all this, the would-be lover sees some positives and some negatives. The future, and especially the impossibility of a future filled with the once-mutual affection, is far from clear to the would-be lover.

A particularly potent stimulus to conflicting projections may be contrasting attributional tendencies. Research suggests that when people form impressions of others, they rely most heavily on the first evidence and impressions they get, and so in predicting the future they may discount recent information. In contrast, when predicting how they themselves will act in the future, people tend to rely on the most recent information available and downplay older information (Jones, Rock, Shaver, Goethals, & Ward, 1968). Applying this discrepancy to the various predictions that the participants would make about the rejector's future tendency to love and cherish the would-be lover, we can see ample room for misunderstandings and differences. Rejectors predict the future based on the present and most recent past, and so they feel certain that there is no chance of returning to a state of love. Their partners, however, may see them on the basis of the past, and the earlier days of mutual attraction may seem to outweigh the recent period of disaffection, and so the would-be lover is more likely to think that there is a real chance that the rejector will be loving again in the future.

Ellen's story, covered in the preceding section of this chapter, illustrates this discrepancy of prediction. Her former boyfriend was apparently quite certain that they had no future and was even dating others. She meanwhile sustained some optimism that she could restore the relationship, and she sustained it in part by thinking back to its initial days, when he did indeed feel attracted to her.

Lest we condemn persistence, we hasten to add that it does sometimes lead to success, as the movies and novels and cultural scripts suggest. It is easy to see persistence as misguided and self-defeating when the outcome is bad (Baumeister & Scher, 1988). But one must keep in mind that, from the perspective of the individual involved in the situation, it is often difficult to judge whether a little more persistence is the necessary final ingredient for bringing success—or is merely a matter of compounding failure by throwing good money (or effort, or love) after bad. Our accounts dealt with unrequited love, and so they nearly all ended badly, but that does not mean that there are not other cases in which persistence does finally lead to success. Even in our sample, there were a few hopeful signs for persistent would-be lovers. One man wrote, for example, that a woman was attracted to him and persisted for over a year in the face of his rejections and lack of interest. Finally, however, he did come around and they developed a relationship that, at the time he wrote the account, had been going on for two years. "I'm glad she was persistent," he concluded.

Conclusion

Although rejectors and would-be lovers were writing about similar events and agreed on many features, there were a number of systematic differences in their accounts as to what happened. The would-be lovers were likely to feel that the rejectors had led them on or had actually reciprocated their feelings at some point, whereas rejectors' accounts usually did not indicate that they had given any cause for hope. Rejectors often insisted they had clearly and honestly told the other that no romance was possible, but the would-be lovers tended to recall only confusing and inconsistent signs.

Many factors probably contributed to causing the would-be lovers to perceive mixed messages with regard to the rejectors' feelings. Some rejectors were ambivalent or had indeed initially reciprocated the attraction, and while they focused on the negative side of their feelings in the effort to justify breaking off the romantic contact, the would-be lovers may have focused hopefully on the positive side. The rejector's core problem of scriptlessness may have led to inconsistent behavior, such as occasionally giving in to requests or saying kind things, which the would-be lover might then interpret as signs of reciprocation or positive change. Would-be lovers may also have seen mixed messages as a result of wishful thinking and self-deceptive processes, such as attributing negative messages to bad moods or temporary factors rather than seeing them as proof that there was no chance for their love to succeed.

The rejector's moral dilemma is epitomized in the expression of rejection. The rejector feels conflicting moral obligations to be honest and to avoid hurting anyone (and practical and emotional interests likewise pull in both directions). Yet being honest requires hurting someone. Probably rejectors emphasize their honesty in retrospect, whereas the reluctance to hurt someone is most salient at the moment of speaking their heart to the would-be lover. As a result, rejectors may hedge or qualify or sweeten their message with kind words, any of which may enable the would-be lover to think what he or she wants to think, namely that there is still a chance.

The most obvious consequence of these discrepant perceptions is that would-be lovers may persist with their efforts far past the point that rejectors consider appropriate. The rejector's feelings of being flattered or pleased often wear off soon, and many rejectors soon reach the point of wanting the whole affair to be over. They may communicate this in what they regard as no uncertain terms. But the would-be lover continues to hope, and plead, and try. Many of the rejectors' worst memories of the episode revolved around what they saw as unreasonable, excessive, and intrusive persistence by the would-be lovers.

To the would-be lover, however, the rejection was not so clear as it was to the rejector, and the impossibility of future love is not so apparent. In many episodes of heartbreak, there may be a phase during which the two actors are following different and poorly matched scripts. The would-be lover may be discouraged but is still playing the role of an aspiring lover who seemingly might yet succeed in the end and is now merely encountering obstacles, difficulties, or setbacks. To the rejector, the romantic script should already have ended. It is time to accept the impossibility of this love and move on to new endeavors. The would-be lover presses on, largely oblivious to the rejector's emotional distress and guilt, preoccupied with his or her own feelings. The rejector sees this as an annoying refusal to face facts, and comes to regard the would-be lover as insensitive and self-deceptive.

S·E·V·E·N

Lessons Learned and Mysteries Glimpsed

Almost any experience of love is an unusual and profound one, and as a major life experience it has the power to teach people and to change them. Unrequited love is powerful and unusual too, and so despite its painfulness it may have the power to show people a side of themselves and of others that they had not suspected. If love contains a measure of illusion, failed love may have the power to dis-illusion and thus to reveal truth. Whether people will benefit from these truths and use them wisely is another matter, of course.

Mutual love and unrequited love differ, however, in the degree of intimacy achieved. As we have seen in the preceding chapters, the two people involved in an unrequited love dyad often seem tragically out of touch with each other. It is clear that they fail to understand and appreciate many aspects of the other's experience, and as a result the opportunity for learning may be diminished.

This chapter will look at what unrequited love can teach people. We hasten to note at the outset that despite the findings we shall report, many stories made no mention of learning or changing. Some people go through one of these heartbreaking or aggravating experiences, feel bad for a while, but then resume their lives pretty much as before. For example, one man concluded his account simply by saying, "In all, it was a very bizarre summer," a comment that seems to convey a distinct lack of edifying experience or useful lessons. Some people claim to learn from unrequited love, but not all do. Or, to put it another way, failed love *can* teach but it does not necessarily or invariably do so

The Mysterious, Incomprehensible Other

Intimacy, what Sternberg (1986) calls the common core in all love relationships, enables two lovers to learn a great deal about each other. Love may be one of the most powerful relationships in terms of allowing one human being to get to know another, even though there is good reason to think that love does introduce a measure of distortion into how one sees one's partner. With unrequited love, however, the intimacy does not really develop, and so one does not necessarily get to know the other.

Indeed, the failure of intimacy to develop may reveal a large gap in mutual understanding. Often each had expectations about the other—one regarding platonic friendship, the other regarding romantic potentialities—and both were disappointed. Unrequited love may therefore bring home how little the two people understand each other, and unrequited love might be hypothesized to have the opposite effect from successful, true, mutual love. Instead of furnishing a (possibly exaggerated) sense of heightened intimacy and authentic understanding of another human being, as in successful love, unrequited love may create a sense of mystery and confusion surrounding the other

Yet another reason to expect unrequited love to boost a sense of mystery and incomprehension regarding the other person is that, as previous chapters have shown, people in unrequited love often come away not understanding their own actions or reactions. The appearance of love, or its failure to appear, is sometimes surprising or mysterious to the self, and if people do not understand themselves we can hardly expect their interaction partners to understand them.

In the stories people told us about their experiences with un-requited love, we looked for indications that the storytellers found their partners mysterious or incomprehensible. Of course, many people may find the other mysterious without coming right out and saying so, but if someone expresses mystification about the other person then it seems fair to assume that the incomprehension was a significant aspect of the experience. In fact, we found a substantial number of each type of story that clearly indicated mystification about the other.

Who was more mystified? In general, and as one would expect, authors recognized their own mystification and featured it in their accounts far more than they discussed the other person's mystification. A few people did recognize that their own actions may have been difficult for their partners to understand, but it was far more common to discuss one's own inability to understand the partner. Partly this may reflect the nature of accounts. People construct their experiences into stories in order to help them make sense of their experiences. When they cannot understand a significant element of the experience—such as why the other acted in a certain way—the ac-count-making process is in a sense thwarted, and one's incomprehension therefore becomes a significant element in the story. Expressing mystification is almost an apology for one's failure to make a fully clear and satisfactory story.

It is also apparent that the spurned lovers were more mystified than the rejectors. They expressed confusion, unclarity, or inability to comprehend the other person approximately twice as often as the rejectors. Nearly half the would-be lovers indicated some inability to understand the other person. Thus, although mystery and incom-prehension can be found on both sides of unrequited love, they are especially central to the experience of the rejected lover.

The major area of incomprehension in the accounts of the would-be lovers was the other person's failure to love them. It seems as if people expect others to love them and are surprised when they don't! In many cases, as we have described, there was an initial stage of mutual attraction, and the majority of cases of incomprehension fell into that category. The other seemed to respond and reciprocate the attraction for a week, a month, even a year, but then the person changed abruptly, leaving the would-be lover mystified. This theme was expressed repeatedly: "I still want to know why he broke things up so quickly with no explanation," wrote one disappointed lover. "I'm still not sure why he decided, what seems like suddenly, he doesn't want to be my boyfriend any longer," wrote another, whose boyfriend was in her dormitory room when he abruptly said he wanted to go home—and although she thought nothing of it at the time, she discovered that after that he had no further desire to see her. Several would-be lovers also expressed an inability to understand why their partner left them for someone else who seemed less desirable.

A partial explanation for these mystifying changes is suggested in research findings on romantic breakups and divorce. According to Vaughan's research (1986; see also Duck, 1982a), romantic breakups often begin when one person privately, secretly feels dissatisfied with the relationship and begins to fall out of love. The person may go on spending time with the other and trying to decide whether to initiate a breakup. Only when he or she is fully convinced (and sometimes not even then) will the person break the news to the partner. This often comes as a surprise and a shock to the partner, for even if there were conflicts and disagreements the partner preferred to see them as isolated or minor or unrelated problems and continued to regard the relationship itself as sound.

It seems plausible that a similar process may occur in incipient relationships. People may have a few dates or spend time together, and they may then feel initially attracted, but as they get to know each other one may gradually discover unattractive traits in the other, or indeed the affection may simply fail to blossom for no apparent reason. Just as one person's emotional investment is escalating, the other person abruptly wants to withdraw and discontinue contact. As in Vaughan's sample, it is even plausible that the rejector initially continues spending some romantic time with the other person because of uncertainty as to whether the positive feelings will appear later, because of reluctance to hurt the other person's feelings, or because it would seem needlessly cruel to cancel plans that have already been made. But each additional positive step may encourage the would-be lover's feelings to grow stronger, confident in their reciprocation, and so the change may seem abrupt and incomprehensible.

The time dimension thus contains one crucial difference between incipient and established relationships. In an incipient, escalating relationship, intimate feelings are constantly changing, as the participants become more involved and fall deeper in love, whereas in an established relationship the level of love and intimacy may have reached a plateau. As a result, if the doubtful one passively delays and says nothing until he or she is certain, the effects may be far worse in an incipient relationship than in an established one, because each delay can allow the other to fall more in love. In other words, there is a certain urgency about such decisions in developing relationships, whereas comparable decisions in stable and established relationships do not have such urgency.

Many rejected lovers were clearly groping for an explanation of the other's apparent change of heart. Several, perhaps especially men, assumed that there must have been someone else, and if they did not see a rival the woman's departure was all the more mystifying. "The weird part of this story," wrote one man whose girlfriend of several months left him abruptly, "is that Katie told me that she didn't want to go out with me anymore and gave me no reason. The only reason I can think of is that she wanted to go out with men at her college . . . ." Another described a developing romance that came to a rapid and unanticipated end when the woman gave him what he called "the ever-feared 'let's be friends' speech," which she timed to coincide with moving to a new apartment. She gave her address and phone number to her other friends but not to him. "The most disturbing thing about this event for me is not knowing why. Another man? No—my friends who saw her afterwards didn't report she was going out with anyone." He went on to say he could not understand why she broke contact so completely. Of course, having read the tales of other rejectors, we can well imagine why a rejector would want to break contact completely!

Other spurned lovers wondered whether the fault lay with some unattractiveness or inadequacy in themselves or lay, instead, in the partner. "I think about him all the time," said one broken-hearted and mystified woman, "I wonder is it me, am I not good enough for him? Am I not in the same financial bracket? Or does he have problems sustaining a relationship?" Indeed, several women found it helpful to explain the man's departure on the basis of his inability or unwillingness to make a commitment. Other women concluded that the man had simply wanted to exploit them sexually and moved on after he got what he wanted, having never intended to form an enduring attachment. Ironically, if the man failed to be sexually aggressive and take advantage of the woman's attraction to him, she might be mystified. Thus, one woman described her confusion over the seemingly mixed, inconsistent messages she got from the fellow that she became deeply attracted to, and she found his advances especially confusing because he did not have sex with her, despite her apparent willingness. "I'm still puzzled at why he changed his mind or why he was being overfriendly, since he didn't get anything out of it (and didn't even try)," she wrote.

Two would-be lovers' accounts were particularly interesting and deserve special comment. The ones we have already quoted show that some would-be lovers are left in the dark because of a lack of explanation; and it seems safe to assume that many would-be lovers indeed receive no explanation (because, as previous chapters have shown, many rejectors are reluctant to express rejection clearly). But even when rejectors do give an explanation, the would-be lover may still feel confused and uncertain, as these two accounts make clear.

The first was by a woman whom we shall call Carol. She dated Rob for over two years and was already discussing marriage with him when he told her he wanted to break up. (Clearly, this was one of the most developed relationships in our sample, for there apparently had been a substantial period of mutual, reciprocal love.) Carol listed the reasons Rob gave her. First, he did not love her as much as she loved him. Second, he was not as happy as he had thought he would be. Third, he did not want to center his life around her, whereas he thought that if he were to marry her then he ought to want to do so. Fourth, he said that they were "two very different people and could not work out our differences." And, fifth, "His final explanation was that he was afraid to get married!" Carol's use of the exclamation point with this last reason clearly conveys how outrageously inadequate and absurd she thought his explanation was.

The remainder of Carol's account listed her rebuttals and refutations of his reasons. In a logically developed, systematic argument, she began by pointing out that he and she had never fought and in fact got along very well. She disagreed about their being "two very different people," and to support her point she listed many things they had in common, ranging from goals to values to leisure preferences. She added that their differences were complementary rather than antagonistic. She pointed out that no two people are exactly the same, "and our differences should bring variety to the relationship." Carol felt Rob should have been willing to make her the center of his life, for that is what marriage meant to her. She concluded by saying, "I don't really think I did anything wrong and I don't think there was much wrong with the relationship. We probably could have used more communication—but that's something you can fix in the relationship instead of ending it."

Thus, although Carol's case is at one end of the continuum of unrequited love insofar as it came at the end of a substantial relationship, it is nonetheless very revealing about the possibilities for mystification. Rob apparently did discuss with her his reasons for wanting to break up, and in fact he seems to have given her a list of reasons instead of just one. Yet she remained mystified, for she found his reasons illogical and unsatisfactory.

Carol's story points to a plausible hypothesis about which we can, unfortunately, offer little in the way of solid data. We have seen that rejectors often are reluctant to express their dissatisfaction or disaffection to their admirers. It may be that when they do communicate the rejection, they choose to express it in terms that they think will make the interaction go most smoothly, rather than expressing reasons that might be more upsetting to the partner. To say that "We are two very different people" may hold the promise of getting through the interaction reasonably easily, as compared with saying something possibly more truthful but more threatening, such as "I cannot stand your personal habits," or "You bore me," or "You are sexually inadequate" or "I have found someone else." And so the rejector may phrase the dreaded message in sappy platitudes and vague generalities. The thoughtful would-be lover, however, may well see the inadequacy of these phrases and remain mystified. One has been given a placebo instead of genuine information (see Langer, Blank, & Chanowitz, 1979), and under critical scrutiny or analysis its inadequacy is revealed.

This hypothesis that rejectors may say bland things rather than expressing their real reasons was supported by an account furnished by a respondent in one of our other research projects (Baumeister, Stillwell, & Heatherton, in press) concerned with experiences that create guilt. This fellow described how he broke up with his girlfriend after two years. He had never really cared very much for her, but he could not tell her this. In his account, she asked him repeatedly what was wrong with her that made him want to leave her. "She asked if she was ugly, fat, unattractive, boring, etc.," he wrote, adding that these questions were accompanied by "bouts of tears and self-pity." His account of his own response reveals his unwillingness to be frank: "I tried to explain to her that I still cared for her but I just didn't want to see her anymore. Truly, however, my real reason . . . [was] that I found her extremely dull and boring and that I had gone out with her for such a long time probably just for sex." Clearly, he found the scene difficult enough as it was, and had he told her his true reasons he might have had an even worse time. As a result, he spoke vaguely about caring for her but just not wanting to continue the relationship, an explanation that conveys little information and makes little sense if considered carefully.

The other account of special interest for this discussion was by a woman whom we shall call Barbara. She had been close platonic friends with Jim for nearly two years, after which they began dating. Because the foundations for intimacy had been laid by their previous close friendship, the relationship escalated rapidly, and after dating for less than six months they were thinking of spending their lives together. "We had spoken often of marriage and children during the spring and I couldn't help but daydream about him and our possible future together," she wrote, especially during their brief separation during the university's summer recess. "Everything I did, I did with him in mind."

At the end of the summer, Barbara and Jim were reunited, but she noticed that somehow things were different. The first troublesome sign was that he seemed indifferent to her appearance, whereas before he had shown great interest in her clothing and looks. Their interactions were also increasingly strained, although she could not understand what was wrong. Then Jim told her that he was a homosexual.

This disclosure came as a great shock to Barbara and threw her into a profound confusion. She participated in our study three months after his disclosure, and she was still struggling to make sense of it all. She still loved him but was having to face the fact that her dreams of marriage and family would never be fulfilled, at least not with Jim. "Not only have I been dealing with an attraction that will never be reciprocated, I am also dealing with accepting what I thought was love as a lie." She reported that she was still spending a great deal of time with him and was trying to reinterpret and understand the episode, but without great success, and indeed sometimes she felt lost or felt that the whole world seemed to be falling down around her. "I do not understand his homosexuality nor do I understand why he was able to date me knowing that he was gay, " she said, articulating the heart of the dilemma. She said it was very painful for her to care about him, but she could not simply walk away and leave him, even though to do so might best enable her heart to mend. Barbara's account concluded, "I do love him very much and I just hope that someday my romantic feelings for him can be put aside."

Barbara's account is of special interest for several reasons. First, like Carol, Barbara received an explanation from her lover for the breakup, but this explanation left her with many unanswered questions. In her case, in particular, the explanation undermined her understanding of what had been going on in the relationship. She discovered that the man she had been intimate with for years, first as friend and then as lover and even potential spouse, was extremely and fundamentally different from the person she had thought him to be. Earlier in this chapter, we suggested that love may foster a partly illusory sense of understanding the partner, whereas unrequited love may bring disillusionment and a sense of not understanding the partner, and may even reveal that one never understood the other at all. The powerful feeling of intimacy and mutual understanding is revealed, in retrospect, to have been illusory. Barbara's account provides a striking illustration of that pattern.

Barbara's account also holds special interest because of Jim's homosexuality. There may indeed be special problems of unrequited love for homosexuals, and Barbara's account points toward one of them. Barbara herself was decidedly heterosexual, but her heart was broken through a pattern that may well be far more common among homosexuals than among heterosexuals like herself: She loved someone whose sexual orientation turned out to be incompatible with hers.

Barbara, in short, loved someone who wavered between two sexual orientations and who finally settled on the one that left her with no chance. If one assumes that a fair number of homosexuals struggle with similar issues of sexual self-definition, then many of their partners will be vulnerable to the form of heartbreak that Barbara experienced. When your lover decides to stop dating not just you but your entire gender, your prospects for salvaging that relationship may be bleak. Further research is needed on this pattern of unrequited love, because several of the findings we have covered might or might not apply. For example, we have seen that many people experience a blow to their self-esteem when rejected romantically. If your partner rejects you while declaring a new sexual orientation, does this amplify the threat to your self-esteem, as if implying that your own sexuality was so dismally inadequate as to steer your lover away from your entire gender? Or is the blow to self-esteem cushioned, because of the implication that the rejection really had nothing to do with you personally and instead reflected something about the partner?

Thus far we have discussed the mystification of would-be lovers, whose feelings often do fit the cultural image of the mysterious, aloof love object whose reasons for not reciprocating one's love remain shrouded in doubt and ambiguity. Let us turn briefly to the rejectors and examine their mystification.

Rejectors most commonly expressed mystification at the other's attraction to them, particularly if it was persistent in the face of overt discouragement. Some, as we have seen, expressed their inability to understand the seemingly irrational persistence of the other, and a few used labels of mental illness ("She was crazy," or "He is really psychotic") to characterize this seemingly incomprehensible persistence. Some were surprised by the duration of the other's ardor, such as the woman who wrote "I do not understand why he still likes me even after all this has happened and four years have passed." And some were simply surprised at the attraction itself. One man described the personality of his admirer, and concluded, "It was hard to believe she was attracted to me because I consider myself the opposite, yet I guess opposites attract." The use of a cliché to make sense of the incomprehensible foreshadows one pattern we shall see later in this chapter when we examine the concluding generalizations that were offered in many of the accounts.

Before we examine the lessons that people claim to have learned from their brushes with heartbreak, however, we need to consider one other category of glimpse into mystery: the mystery of self. The next section will examine people's references to acting in ways that were quite different from their normal, habitual patterns.

Acting Out of Character

The popular stereotype of the desperate lover includes the capacity for extraordinary, irrational actions, and it is plausible that this stereotype confers a certain license, even perhaps an expectation, that one may behave in such a fashion during heartbreak. Meanwhile, rejectors are also occasionally driven to extremes of frustration, distraction, and aggravation by their admirers, and so one could expect that they too would occasionally show such extremities of action.

It is difficult, of course, to form an objective standard of what actions are irrational and extraordinary, as opposed to actions that make sense to the person who performs them. The question of whether unrequited love elicits irrational or extreme behavior is therefore resistant to scientific study. We sought to approach this question by coding stories for any explicit indication that the author regarded his or her actions as out of character. The criterion is thus fairly conservative and will almost certainly underestimate the degree of irrationality to which people are driven during unrequited love, but the conservatism confers the benefit that one is on fairly solid ground in assuming that the actions were out of the ordinary even by the person's own judgment.

Both rejectors and would-be lovers reported having acted out of character, but the would-be lovers were significantly more likely to report such actions. Thus, people's accounts of their own experiences do conform to the cultural stereotype which holds that disappointed love makes one act in unusual or abnormal ways, as if to say that the heartbroken person is not his or her normal self.

Some of the would-be lovers found that the love itself drove them to act in unusual ways. In particular, shy people may find that love motivates them to overcome their shyness and approach the target of their affections, especially if the other fails to make the first move. For women, whose cultural scripts for romance have been slowly changing from a prescribed passive role to the possibility of a more active role, a stalled attraction may be particularly salient in moving them from a passive to a more active strategy. One woman described precisely such a dilemma. "I'm not a type of person that would reveal her feelings and pursue them," she said to characterize her normal pattern of behavior, "But I was so infatuated with him that I finally called him and talked to him." It was not easy for her to overcome her passive habits and get up the courage to telephone the man, and the fact that he seemed noncommittal and uninterested on the phone did not help. Yet she overcame this discouraging response and called him again, this time pressing him to see her. He agreed and chose a time that was not convenient for her, because she had a term paper due the next day. Normally, she was a serious, conscientious student, but her concern for her schoolwork faded to insignificance next to her romantic passion, and she agreed to meet him. Their meeting was not satisfactory, despite her sacrifice.

Some would-be lovers were quite chagrined about the ways they acted during the height of their unrequited love, and they expressed clearly negative evaluations of what they had glimpsed in themselves. One woman deplored her inability to control her feelings and actions, saying, "That bothered me, too, because I always considered myself a very self-controlled, rational person, and this whole experience made me feel totally out of control and irrational." Another was concise and blunt about how she had carried on: "Quite literally I was a bitch!"

When rejectors mentioned acting out of character, it was to say that they had violated their usual standards for treating other people in a considerate, polite, and friendly fashion, usually because they felt frustrated and provoked by the would-be lover's persistence. One woman said that she normally felt strong obligations to any man she dated regularly, but in this case she mistreated and abused a suitor, as well as seeing other men surreptitiously on the side. And we already quoted the case of the woman who simply abandoned her date at a party, which she recalled guiltily as the worst thing she had ever done to another person.

Thus, our results do provide some support for the view that love, especially unrequited love, makes people act in ways that they normally would not act. It is impossible to tell whether the cultural stereotype of lovers' irrationality simply recognizes an empirical fact or, instead, is itself a cause, by telling people that it is normal to feel and act in abnormal ways under those circumstances. In any case, it is apparent that both would-be lovers and rejectors (although especially the former) find themselves driven to acting contrary to their normal patterns, personalities, and standards, and that they are sometimes quite displeased with what they see in themselves.

The fact that unrequited love can elicit unforeseen patterns of action and feeling means that it has the capability to reveal new things about the self. This brings us to the next, important section, which will look directly at what people think they have learned from their experiences with unrequited love.

Learning and Changing

People did claim to have learned or changed from their experiences of unrequited love. The frequency of such claims did not differ between the two roles; that is, would-be lovers were neither more nor less likely than rejectors to claim to have learned or changed. But there were differences in what they learned and how they changed.

When we analyzed the data from our first study, we were surprised that people often reported changing for the worse as a result of these experiences. In our follow-up, we instructed people to select an important experience of unrequited love and then we asked them point-blank whether the experience had changed them in some negative way. One category of subjects stood out in saying that the experience had caused such changes: female would-be lovers. Furthermore, we asked people to rate all their experiences (combined, rather than individually) as would-be lovers, and all their experiences as rejectors, and the same finding emerged. Female would-be lovers rated their total experiences as significantly more harmful than anyone else. Apparently, loving someone who does not return your love is especially bad for women.

We noted earlier that females seem to have fewer total would-be lover experiences than males; this is consistent with the view that women are slower than men to fall in love. The greater pain and harm that women report may be a partial explanation for that fact. That is, when a woman does fall in love in vain, she may suffer severely and may become reluctant to make herself so vulnerable again. Although she may perceive this as a change for the worse (because she is shutting herself off from the possibility of love and intimacy), it is understandable. Let us take a closer look at some of the lessons people learn from unrequited love.

A number of would-be lovers (of both sexes) said that the experience had made them less willing to try again. Sadly, but not surprisingly, serious disappointments in love can make people reluctant to expose themselves to any chance of being hurt in the same way. To love, apparently, is to make oneself vulnerable, and perhaps only a broken heart shows one the full extent of this vulnerability. It is understandable that these people may be reluctant to make themselves that vulnerable again: "I have noticed more women interested in me but I do not want to get involved, because I am being cautious . . . I don't want to get burned again," as one man put it. Perhaps such changes are merely temporary reactions, but there is no way of knowing how long people actually remain unreceptive to romance after a major heartbreak.

The pain of unrequited love can be heard in the lessons that people cite. "I will never [again] let another person have that much control over my feelings," concluded one jilted woman. A man wrote with philosophical bitterness, "This taught me a lesson that getting 'hung up' over someone is a preoccupation that generally increases stress and decreases well-being." A woman described an episode in which she believed a true intimacy was developing, for the man toward whom she felt strongly attracted called her, spent time with her, and so forth. Then, when she was already falling in love and was ready to move to a more overt level of romance, he began dating one of her friends instead of her. She was devastated, because it seemed in retrospect that the growing intimacy and passion had actually been a one-sided illusion on her part. "Through this experience, it seems as if now I force myself not to like someone too much at first. I'm really hesitant to admit to the person I'm attracted to that I like him," she concluded, adding that "I guess I'm just more apprehensive to take chances or to get too 'deep.' " She felt that she had been a fool and was determined to avoid repeating that humiliation, even if it meant reducing her chances for falling in love again. Another woman expressed a similar conclusion: "Since then I've never allowed myself to like a guy that much, even the ones I've dated."

One of the basic points of Carl Rogers's theories was that people need a certain degree of basic trust in order to enter into relationships with others, because loving makes one vulnerable, and one needs to trust others not to be hurtful or take advantage of the love. Unrequited love suggests that one's trust has been misplaced or misguided, because one has been hurt after all; and the trust may seem especially misplaced if one feels used, exploited, or mistreated in some other way. "I don't think I can trust anyone again for quite a while because of him," wrote one woman who thought her relationship was developing happily until the man abruptly and inexplicably broke it off. Another woman described her sense of vulnerability after an experience of unrequited love: "When you are in love with someone who likes you less, that person can manipulate you because you don't want to leave even if that person is rude." (Her usage of *rude* probably reflects current colloquial slang, which uses the term to refer to more than mere impoliteness; to be rude is to be exploitative, unfair, inappropriate, or inconsiderate.) She went on to suggest that her lover had manipulated her feelings to extract sexual favors, and her love for him made her act in ways that were somewhat out of character for her: Because she loved him, she said, "Dan was able to get away with things that I've broken up with other guys for." The exploitative implications of the phrase "get away with" are clear.

Fortunately, other broken-hearted lovers managed to learn from the experience in ways that helped them in pursuing futher relationships. They may have recognized the temptation to withdraw from others, but they overcame it. "It was very tough for me to come out of the shell I had made for myself," said one man about his efforts to win the heart of the woman he had become deeply attracted to, "and since I had never let myself get into a situation where I could get rejected it made things worse." Nonetheless, he had not retreated to social isolation despite the pain of rejection. "I think it helped me in the long run because the shell I made around myself doesn't seem to be as thick anymore." A similar point was made by a woman who had fallen in love with a man who had not really cared very deeply about her. She finally concluded that he had just been using her sexually, and although she resisted this conclusion for a time she eventually accepted it and broke off the relationship. Yet she did not decide to remain aloof from further involvements, even after subsequent experiences of the same kind: "It happened to me a couple of times after him but I was much more perceptive in seeing the signals. I have not gotten to the point of paranoia or total mistrust of guys—in fact I think I'm just better at reading people and what they want. I can use all my experiences to learn. Believe me, it helps." At the time of writing, she said she had finally found a satisfactory, nonexploitative relationship, and she suggested that what she had learned from her experiences of heartbreak had enabled her to find and build a good relationship.

It is necessary to keep in mind that we are dealing here not with controlled experiments but with people's analyses and often self-serving acounts of their own reactions and experiences. People's conclusions are of considerable interest in their own right, but it is not safe to assume that their conclusions are valid or correspond to objective reality. People may respond to heartbreak by saying that they learned and benefited from the experience, or by saying that they won't trust someone as much again, but for all we know they will do exactly the same things again if a similar situation arises. It may be comforting to think that one learned something, and one may assert that one has learned even if one has not (see Conway & Ross, 1984). Bitterness, victimization, or the desire to salvage some benefit from a sad experience may shape the stories people construct. These data tell us that people make sense of their experiences by making certain kinds of stories with certain kinds of endings, such as saying that they learned something or will act differently henceforth. To know whether they will actually be different henceforth is another, more difficult question, and one that in any case requires an objective perspective outside the person's own account.

Would-be lovers were not the only ones to come away from these experiences with reduced enthusiasm for love; some rejectors voiced similar sentiments. "Relationships always leave one person hurting," concluded a woman after describing how miserable the man had been when she decided she could not love him. After a couple of experiences in which men loved her but she was unable to reciprocate the feeling, another woman had become cynical about relationships in general: "Through Doug and Steve I've learned that romantic love is rare. Quite rare enough. So what are the chances of mutual love? It is my belief that most marriages do not consist of *true mutual romantic love.*"

One man mentioned that his feelings of guilt over hurting his partner had made him reluctant to get involved with another woman. He described himself as having long been shy and introverted, and he had not had much experience dating. His first serious relationship was initially very welcome, but his girlfriend was not as pretty as the girlfriends of his friends, and this had impaired his affection for her. Eventually he broke up with her because of this. He felt in retrospect that he had "handled the breakup very poorly." His sense of guilt was apparent, for he said, "It's the only time I ever hurt someone that I didn't make up to that person, and I think I have been punishing myself ever since. I haven't let myself get too close with a woman since that event." Although his story was not typical of rejectors in this regard, it is interesting to note that a rejector's guilt can become a cause of reluctance to enter into further relationships.

Both rejectors and would-be lovers claimed to have learned lessons about the nature of love, and their stories contained conclusions and generalizations about human intimacy. For example, one man drew the fairly obvious conclusion that reciprocity is important to love: "I believe that one cannot truly love someone unless there is a reciprocation of feelings . . . Love will fade if it is not returned." Likewise, a woman wrote that her "conclusion is that without a balance in attraction nothing solid can come out of it. A person's feelings can never be secure and therefore the relationship is never secure."

It is easy to disparage the profundity of such lessons. A painful experience of unrequited love teaches the person to avoid unrequited love. Such wisdom is the stuff of clichés, and indeed several of our respondents used clichés to make sense of their experiences. We have already quoted one to the effect that opposites attract. Another man concluded his account with a hackneyed phrase about members of the opposite sex as well as a trite comparison with pets: "Can't live with them, can't live without them! Just give me a good, obedient, friendly canine in the meantime." A woman summed up her decision to break off a developing romance because of its conflicts by saying, "A person can only take so much pressure." Several of the trite conclusions referred used the expression "50–50" to describe the necessity of equal participation for a relationship to succeed, such as the woman who wrote that "A relationship in my opinion has to be 50–50 for it to work." And some of these tritely phrased conclusions sounded like things parents or guidance counselors might have told them, which they probably would have received with groans and grimaces. "It is hard to be in a consistent lasting relationship for young people because we are changing quickly . . . and not necessarily in the same direction." These alleged insights are insubstantial, for they can be reduced to the formula that unrequited love teaches people to avoid unrequited love. Yet when these formulations arise from intense personal experience rather than formulaic pronouncements of overaged, pontificating windbags, young people used them un-self-consciously as if describing important, original, highly personal insights.

Probably the most usable and constructive lessons were the ones that arose from concluding that one had gone about things in an ineffective fashion. Such conclusions might enable the person to do things differently the next time. For example, recall the case of Ralph, whose story was covered in some detail at the beginning of Chapter 5. A platonic friend had fallen in love with him, and he had tried to continue to interact on a friendly basis while allowing her to love him; he had even had sex with her, while still insisting that they were just friends. He had had to curtail his feelings and behave in awkward, inauthentic ways because of the pressures of the one-sided relationship. He learned that that had been a poor strategy. Looking back, he saw that the sexual contacts had been a serious mistake, because they had stimulated her love and made his lack of love all the more painful to her. More generally, he wrote, "I learned that you cannot restrict yourself and your feelings to the point where you are emotionally distraught for the sake of someone else." In the same way, another rejector learned that she had handled things wrong. Her admirer wanted to come visit from overseas, and to avoid hurting him she had avoided telling him that she did not love him and in fact had become involved with someone else. The man had traveled to see her and both had had a miserable time. "I know now I should have told him when I knew my feelings had definitely changed," she concluded.

Rejectors were not the only ones to learn that they had made mistakes, although perhaps because of the scriptlessness of their role and their tendency to handle the situation by ineffective means (such as mere passive avoidance) they may have learned more about how to act differently next time. Still, one would-be lover claimed to have learned an important lesson about love, namely that living together had been a bad strategy for dealing with problems in the relationship, and indeed he concluded that living together had hastened the demise of the relationship. He concluded, perhaps excessively, that living together was unwise, and he said he would advise others against it.

Lastly, some people learned about themselves from these experiences. Perhaps these were the same lessons that others learned, but others generalized them to everyone whereas these individuals recognized that the lessons depended on their particular natures. One woman recognized that she had been drawn into an unsatisfactory relationship and felt peculiarly vulnerable to repeating the mistake. She said, "I don't want to get in such a self-destructive relationship again. That's not love, it's masochism." Another rejector concluded that her lack of respect for her partner had made the relationship impossible, and she concluded "I guess in short I can't love a person who isn't my equal."

Several would-be lovers learned disturbing things about their own patterns of romantic response. One woman summarized a disturbing truth about herself that had emerged from these experiences of both sides of unrequited love: "It seems like when I can have a guy, I don't want him. And when he is not available to me, I want him." Several others criticized themselves for responding to others on the basis of shallow traits such as looks or money, and they expressed the importance of learning to choose partners using more promising and mature criteria.

One prototypical experience of self-revelation was the case in our sample in which the woman found herself attracted to another woman. Clearly, people have expectations about their own romantic responses, and falling in love with someone outside that expected group can be a very surprising revelation. Unrequited love is seemingly always difficult, but when it coincides with a discovery that one has hitherto unsuspected sexual preferences the uncertainty and emotional confusion may well be multiplied.

Thus, again, homosexuals may have special problems regarding unrequited love, because they may (at least the first time) be very surprised at their own attraction to a member of their own sex. For them, dealing with another's nonreciprocation may be complicated by their own uncertainty as to whether they ought to be feeling that attraction in the first place. Self-discovery may raise uncertainty about how to proceed. Of course, once one has accepted one's homosexuality and managed to fall in love with other homosexuals, unrequited love would probably be experienced quite similarly to the way heterosexuals experience it.

Lost Possibilities

Unrequited love is based on a dream of a future that does not come to pass. It is thus a glimpse, if only in one's imagination, of another world, one that is perhaps better and more satisfactory than one's actual world. The sense of lost possibilities is integral to unrequited love. For the would-be lover, it was the romance that was not to be. For the rejector, in many cases, it meant a friendship that was ruined or damaged by the attempt to make it more than it was.

Not surprisingly, would-be lovers made more explicit references than rejectors to the lost possibilities. We have already quoted several would-be lovers who mentioned that even long after the episode ended in failure, they think about the person they loved and imagine how things might have been different. Typical was the comment by a young man who still occasionally looks at the correspondence of love and then rejection from this long-extinguished flame: "To this day, when I read the letter that she wrote to me, I think of what could have been."

The few rejectors who referred explicitly to lost possibilities spoke of the friendship they had had which had been ruined. Some had felt they were attempting a delicate balancing act during the episode, for they wanted both to discourage the other's romantic affection and yet to keep the other's friendly affection. They saw all too clearly that they could not keep that up indefinitely, and the other's persistence at romantic efforts was regarded as upsetting because of the escalating danger to the friendship. Still, the loss of this friendship, even if that is what it came to, was not nearly as tragic as the broken dreams of happy-ever-after togetherness of the would-be lovers. As one rejector summed it up, "I'm sorry that the friendship ended, but I suppose it was no great loss."

Conclusion

For many people, unrequited love provides a glimpse of the unknown, a surprising view of oneself, a confusing perspective on another, or a personally compelling lesson. Unrequited love, after all, is almost always an extraordinary experience for the individual, and as such it can alter the boundaries of our ordinary perception of the world.

Would-be lovers find their rejectors mysterious. Indeed, the sense of mystery may often be compounded by the contrast with love's illusion of unity and mutual understanding. This may particularly affect people who feel that the attraction was initially mutual. The other's change of heart often comes through as abrupt, arbitrary, and even inexplicable. Lovers question themselves and their partners about what went wrong, and even if the rejectors give an explanation it may fail to clarify the matter (partly because rejectors may use innocuous, vacuous clichés rather than telling the honest reasons). Moreover, the ending may reveal the mutual understanding of the previous, more intimate stage to have been illusory. The confusion over the relation-ship's end is thus multiplied by a sudden uncertainty as to what the other had been feeling all along.

Rejectors suffer from a confusion that is less pervasive and less profound. For the most part, their mystification attaches to the other's failure to face facts. They find the other's persistence extraordinary, and perhaps it is.

Unrequited love also offers people mysterious glimpses of them-selves. They may be surprised at the extent, direction, or nature of their attraction, and they may be disappointed (at least in retrospect) at their own actions. It is clear that people have fairly elaborate as-sumptions about themselves, including their patterns of thought, feel-ing, and behavior, and apparently unrequited love pushes some people to violate these assumptions. Would-be lovers are more prone to say they acted out of character than rejectors, although both are liable to feel this to some degree.

Although many people say they learned something or changed as a result of an experience of unrequited love, the substance of their lessons often seems shallow and trite, and the changes seem for the worse. People say they learned not to trust others or that they learned to hold themselves back so as to not to be vulnerable to another disappointment. They say they learned that love (or good relationships generally) have to be mutual, balanced, or in the popular phrase "50–50." These lessons seem to suggest that unrequited love merely teaches one to avoid unrequited love. That is hardly an inspiring insight. And if heartbreak makes people reluctant to take a chance on further love, as some suggest, then the change is perhaps an unfortunate one.

A few individuals were able to articulate particular and useful lessons. Some said they learned that love makes one vulnerable to exploitation, so that romantic involvement has to be tempered with caution and common sense. Some discovered that they pursued relationships in futile or destructive patterns and that they would have to change their own habits and inclinations if they wanted to be happy. Some said they learned better how to deal with others, and the lessons from failed relationships were useful for building successful ones. Some saw things about themselves that they did not like, such as discovering new actions or feelings that they had not previously suspected, and they became determined to change. (Others may have discovered more positive or neutral things about themselves, but they were less articulate on this.) Rejectors, in particular, learned by concluding that they had handled things wrongly, a lesson that once again must be understood on the basis of the fundamental scriptlessness of the rejector's role; that is, rejectors don't know how to handle the situation, and so sometimes they learn by painful trial and error.

Still, there is no escaping the impression that the majority of lessons were banal and trivial, even phrased in some cases in clichés. We suspect that if we asked people simply whether they had learned anything from their experiences of unrequited love, many would say they had—but if we asked them then to articulate those lessons, we would hear much of the same unprofound and unoriginal commentary. Why is unrequited love so apparently unedifying?

One possible answer is that it is unfair to ask people to express what they have learned in the form of abstract, general principles. In our sample, the richness of people's stories contrasted dramatically with the poverty of their abstract deductions, and perhaps it is the latter that is deceptive. A powerful or unusual experience of unrequited love may make one personally familiar with an important area of human experience, and even if one's experience does not lead to articulated insights that are much different from what other people have already said, at least one's direct personal familiarity with that realm of experience may be a valuable resource for the individual.

Love, after all, is an extremely important issue, even a central preoccupation, in our culture. Love is one of the most popular topics for discourse in our society, among friends, at parties, on television, in movies, in books, and so on, and people may well feel that they can participate in this discourse only if they have some personal experiences on which to draw. Unrequited love is an important part of this, and its very dis-illusioning nature may help one to participate with greater confidence and insight in this discourse. A capacity to understand the dramatic entertainments in the media, the discourses of putative experts, the jokes of comedians, the subtleties of novels and even the complaints or stories of friends, may benefit from one's own experiences. Such lessons would be difficult to articulate and may come out, if they do at all, as clichés, but they may nonetheless be real and useful.

Conclusion:
The Two Sides
of Heartbreak

These chapters have covered what we have learned about unrequited love. They have portrayed the humiliation and anguish along with the bittersweet joys of broken-hearted lovers, and they have covered the anger and guilt felt by rejectors. In this final chapter, we shall not attempt to review all of our findings but shall focus on a few broad themes.

It is important to recall that our conclusions refer to roles, not personality traits. We asked every respondent to tell both a would-be lover story and a rejector story. Less than 5% of the people we asked replied that they had no such story to tell. In our sample, therefore, the rejectors and the would-be lovers are by and large *the same people*. There is no basis for saying what kind of people are rejectors and how they differ from the kind of people that broken-hearted lovers are. Rather, our results shed light on what it is like for anyone and every-one to find oneself cast in the role of would-be lover or rejector. Both sides of unrequited love can (and sooner or later do) seem to happen to almost everyone.

Why It Happens

Early in this work we raised the question of how unrequited love may be possible. That is, if there is such a strong tendency to reciprocate another person's feelings, why might strong feelings of romantic attraction fail to elicit similar feelings in reply? Two particular scenarios were suggested early in this book. Both of them were found in abundance in our sample.

One scenario, which we labeled "falling upward," involved uneven attractiveness. Past work suggests that people become attracted to maximally desirable others but then eventually mate with others equal to themselves in desirability. When someone falls in love with someone of higher attractiveness, this love is likely to go unrequited. There were ample indications of this pattern in our stories. Rejectors were sometimes quite explicit in describing how unsuitable or inadequate as partners their admirers were. The would-be lovers were less likely to dwell on this aspect, perhaps in part because it was degrading to them to learn that they were considered below the other person's acceptable level of desirability. Still, some of them did recognize that a possible explanation for their rejection was some inadequacy on their part.

Another scenario involved the intrusion of romantic feelings into platonic friendship. A man and a woman might be intimate, nonsexual friends, but based on this intimacy one might begin to harbor deeper feelings while the other remained content with the nonromantic friendship. This pattern was also abundantly evident in our sample. It is clear that friendship does sometimes turn into love—but this emotional transformation is often one-sided. Moreover, these episodes pose an especially troublesome dilemma for both people, because they are quite aware that the friendship is jeopardized if the romance fails. "Let's just be friends"—that is, let us have a platonic friendship but not a romance—has become a cliché for expressing romantic rejection, but it is apparently not always easy to maintain a friendship in the wake of a romantic failure.

A third pathway into unrequited love revolves around the transition from casual dating to serious, possibly exclusive romance. Many stories described a series of romantic dates in which, presumably, both people shared the casual romantic assumptions. (Sometimes, to be sure, the rejector simply agreed to go on the date due to the lack of a valid excuse or due to reluctance to insult the other by rejecting a friendly overture.) But then one person would become strongly attracted to the other and might want to escalate the level of intimacy to something more powerful. The other person, however, failed to develop strong feelings and did not want to make that transition.

This third pathway has its own special problems. Because there was some initial romantic contact between the couple, the would-be lover may be especially prone to feel that the rejector had encouraged him or her and perhaps had reciprocated the attraction to some degree. Moreover, the rejector's dilemma is acute, because the aspiring lover's feelings are escalating steadily and so there is pressure to make a decision rapidly as to whether to go along into a more serious romance or to end the affair abruptly. The rejector may, ironically, be content to continue a casual relationship, but the escalation of the other's feelings make that option less and less viable. The rejector may not realize this immediately.

These pathways are not mutually exclusive, of course. Unequal attractiveness may be an important reason behind unequal desires to move into a romantic attachment from either casual dating or platonic friendship. Nor are they exhaustive, for there may well be other causes. But they do appear to be major factors in setting the stage for experiences of unrequited love.

The broader context for understanding unrequited love is the social (i.e., interpersonal) causation of emotion. Human feelings are often dependent on other people, and perhaps no phenomenon shows this as clearly as unrequited love. In unrequited love, two people may inflict almost the entire gamut of emotions, from love to hate, on each other, and mostly without intending to do so. Indeed, ironically, the one emotion that someone *intends* to generate in the other—the would-be lover's desire to make the rejector feel love toward him or her in return—misfires, which is the defining feature of unrequited love.

Attachment and Interdependence

Early in this book, we offered two broad theoretical contexts for thinking about unrequited love. Now, at its end, let us examine how well our findings have fit into those two contexts: attachment theory and interdependence theory.

The basic point of attachment theory is that people are biologically programmed to form and maintain interpersonal relationships. Unrequited love poses one challenge to this view by the very fact that people sometimes do reject someone else's offer of love and intimacy. Critics of attachment theory might point to the fact of romantic rejection to challenge the fundamental argument that people are innately programmed to form and maintain attachments. After all, if people are always longing for attachment, why would someone refuse attachment?

In our view, this criticism is not justified. Attachment may still be a fundamental, innate part of human nature even if some people sometimes refuse opportunities to form relationships. Indeed, people occasionally behave in ways that run contrary to nearly every basic pattern of human nature and motivation. Fear of falling is almost certainly an instinctive reaction in human beings, but skydivers learn to leap out of airplanes, and cliff divers plunge off rocks into the sea. The desire for sexual pleasure is instilled by our biological makeup, yet some people such as monks and nuns choose to live lives of sexual chastity and purity. The desire for food is also undeniably part of our innate programming, yet dieters, hunger strikers, and others thwart that desire and refuse food. Even the desire for self-preservation is sometimes overcome by conscious effort, such as among people who commit suicide, or among infantry soldiers who must march forward toward people who are shooting at them. Abraham Maslow (1968) used the term *instinctoid* to refer to the role of instinct in human nature.

Like animal instincts, people are biologically programmed with innate wants and fears, but people are capable of overcoming these wants and fears—of refusing to act on them. Attachment may likewise be a basic human need that people can sometimes refuse to translate into action.

A fairer test of attachment theory, perhaps, is whether people find it difficult to refuse attachment. If the need to belong is programmed into human nature, then to go against it should produce inner conflict. Sure enough, we found that rejectors experience considerable difficulty in bringing themselves to do this. Guilt, frustration, annoyance, anger, and other forms of emotional distress characterized the rejector's role. There are often particular events that account for these reactions, but it is also plausible that underneath specific events and specific reactions is a more general difficulty of violating nature's programming. According to attachment theory, to refuse love is to thwart your own deeply rooted desires, and some emotional struggles and inner turmoil are to be expected. What we have learned about rejectors in this study is consistent with that view.

Attachment theory would predict that people would mainly refuse love when it is offered by an unsuitable, undesirable partner, or when one already has enough social attachments to satisfy the need to belong. Our findings fit this pattern too, with some exceptions. Rejectors often portrayed their would-be lovers as unsuitable or unattractive or in some other way undesirable. Other rejectors noted simply that they were already committed to a girlfriend or boyfriend and hence were not amenable to someone else's offer of intimacy, which may be translated into saying that their needs were already being satisfied and so they did not desire to form a new relationship. Of course, these prior commitments must always be taken with a grain of salt, because it is abundantly clear that people are quite capable of dumping one romantic partner in favor of a new one.

The only exceptions were the rejectors who said that the would-be lover seemed like a potentially suitable partner but failed to arouse feelings in them anyway. Some of these may reflect efforts to be diplomatic and to be consistent with what one says to the aspiring lover. As we noted, the norms of modesty and consideration make people reluctant to come right out and say that the aspiring lover is not good enough to deserve them.

The remaining cases do perhaps pose a challenge to attachment theory. If one is unattached and an eligible potential partner offers love, how can one fail to accept the offer? Yet people occasionally do, at least if our data are taken at face value. One man noted that the woman who was attracted to him later graduated from college with honors *and* won a state beauty contest, so we may assume that she had both brains and beauty, but he simply did not feel any sexual desire or romantic passion toward her. Here, we can only invoke the mysteries of sexual arousal and romantic attraction, just as the individuals themselves do in their stories. One doesn't know why one does not have feelings for this seemingly eligible person, but one doesn't, and it cannot be helped. Possibly this phenomenon bears some resemblance to the mysteries of taste aversion: For unknown reasons, some people just do not like the taste of certain foods. Interpersonal intimacy and especially sex appeal may have some of the same patterns, which may occasionally doom an otherwise likely matchup. Fortunately, these cases appear to be only a rather small minority.

From the point of view of attachment theory, the would-be lover's desires are simple to explain. One desires attachment, one finds a suitable partner, and so attraction begins. We noted further, however, that studies on attachment have suggested three patterns of response to loss (e.g., Bowlby, 1969, 1973), and it is worth considering how our own observations about unrequited love resemble these three patterns.

The first pattern of response to attachment failure has been called protest, characterized as an active phase of acute distress that may include refusal to accept the loss. There was plenty of evidence of this type of response in our stories. We cannot say that this response is always evident, and in fact it was omitted from many stories, and so the theory that this is always a phase of response to interpersonal loss cannot claim support here. But it certainly does occur in many cases. Rejected lovers shout, scream, and cry. They argue with the rejector and insist on detailed explanations. They make demands on the rejector, they telephone at all hours, they show up unexpectedly, and in general many thwarted lovers simply refuse to let go. To judge by the rejectors' accounts, would-be lovers do not simply accept the rejection gracefully, by and large. They do protest, sometimes with a few words, sometimes by going berserk for weeks, even threatening or kidnaping the person who refuses intimacy.

The second response involved passive despair. This, too, was evident in the stories we have studied. Many would-be lovers reported feeling sad, helpless, depressed, and so forth. To the rejectors, the protest reactions were the most vivid, but would-be lovers themselves tended to focus on their despair and sadness. The silent enduring of emotional pain was one hallmark of the experience for many rejected lovers.

The final response was detachment, which may be marked by an active disregard for the lost attachment and even by saying that one would no longer want a relationship with that person. This pattern, too, was evident among unrequited lovers (although, again, it was far from universal). Many derogated their rejectors, wondering what they ever saw in such an individual. Some took satisfaction in finding fault with the person they had loved. A few even went so far as to insult the rejector to his or her face, a pattern that rejectors themselves found especially unpleasant.

Ultimately, as we have said, many unrequited lovers end up keeping a soft spot in their hearts for the individuals they loved. They find themselves able to look back with a bittersweet mixture of plea-sure and pain on these failed romances. That does not, however, contradict the fact that initial responses may involve protest, despair, and derogation, as attachment theory predicts. When one has rebuilt one's self-esteem and found new relationships to satisfy one's needs for attachment, then it may be a suitable time to reappraise these episodes. But it may take people a long while to reach that point.

Turning now from attachment to interdependence, we offered an analysis that indicated how in unrequited love each person is to some extent at the other's mercy. This was abundantly confirmed. Indeed, one of the supreme ironies of unrequited love is that both parties may end up feeling like helpless victims. In unrequited love, at least to some extent, each person has the power to make the other miserable. Usually the other's misery is not the person's purpose or intention, but it often emerges as a major side effect. The would-be lover tries to persist and persuade the other to initiate a romance, sometimes to the point where the rejector feels hounded or persecuted. The rejector simply wants to keep things as they are and decline the offer of romantic attachment, which breaks the would-be lover's heart.

A further point that emerged from our interdependence-theory analysis was that the rejector's situation was, in total, worse than the would-be lover's. To the would-be lover, the situation offers a wide range of possible outcomes, from bliss to despair, and so the episode resembles a gamble or an adventure. Would-be lovers may suffer acutely when they lose the gamble, but on the whole it was probably worth a try. Rejectors, on the other hand, had little to gain and much to lose, and so for them the episode was probably not worthwhile. Consistent with this, we found that rejectors' accounts were more uniformly negative than would-be lovers, in a variety of measures: bad feelings toward the other person, regrets, and even the implied wish that the whole thing had never happened.

Still, these broad issues and background contexts are somewhat speculative extensions of our work. The core of this book has been to illuminate the respective, divergent experiences of rejectors and would-be lovers. We have covered them together in theme after theme. Let us now take a moment to consider them individually, according to the composite portrait that our findings suggest. Of course, these portraits are not intended as checklists or norms, and it would be foolish to argue that every rejector or every broken-hearted lover has exactly the same experience or even conforms to every generalization. These are merely the broad, typical outlines.

On Causing Someone to Love in Vain

One theme of this work has been a concerted effort to understand the rejector's experience in unrequited love. Many people go through episodes in which they find themselves the target of romantic attentions without feeling the same way in return, and their story has largely remained untold.

Literature has offered various stereotypes of rejectors—such as aloof, casual, teasing, or sadistic heartbreakers—but these do not correspond to what we have found. Instead, rejectors emerge as ordinary, well-meaning people who find themselves caught up in another person's emotional whirlwind and who themselves often suffer acutely as a result. Indeed, it appears that rejectors have on the whole a more thoroughly, uniformly negative and emotionally unpleasant experience than the broken-hearted lovers, even if most of them do not suffer any moments quite as intensely bad as the most acute pain felt by broken-hearted lovers. For would-be lovers, the event at least brings a mixture of good and bad feelings, and overall the good and bad emotions are roughly balanced in their accounts. In contrast, for the rejectors, the bad emotions far outweigh the good ones. Rejectors were the ones most likely to wish the event had never happened and to report pervasive, unpleasant feelings about it.

This is not to dismiss the intensity of the suffering of a person whose heart is breaking. Our collection of first-person accounts does not measure the degree of suffering, simply its frequency. When we asked people to rate how severely they suffered, the would-be lovers reported more intense suffering than rejectors, on the average. It may well be that rejectors very commonly suffer mild doses of negative affect, whereas would-be lovers suffer less common but more extreme forms of emotional distress. Still, it is clear that people recall their own futile loves with mixtures of good and bad feelings, whereas their recollections of playing the rejector's role are more uniformly negative and unpleasant.

Scriptlessness was an important feature of the rejector's role. Over and over, people said they did not know how to reject their admirer, did not want to do the wrong thing, did not want to hurt anyone, did not know what to say or do. The one seemingly central requirement of the rejector's role—telling the other person that one does not love him or her, that no romantic attachment is possible—was something they found it supremely difficult to do. With neither cultural wisdom, familiar role models, nor fictional portrayals to guide them, rejectors struggled with the uncertainty of how to handle the task of breaking someone's heart. Understandably, many retreated into passive avoidance, at least for a time.

The rejectors' difficulties were compounded by their moral dilemma. Guilt feelings are rooted, perhaps, in the knowledge that it is wrong to hurt someone (e.g., Hoffman, 1982; Zahn-Waxler & Kochanska, 1990), and rejectors find themselves thrust into a position where they have to hurt someone. Despite their self-perceived innocence in sophisticated moral terms—for example, they never intended to mistreat anyone or to violate any ethical principles or standards—they come face to face with feelings of guilt. The rejector's role is a villain's role, in that it must thwart someone's needs and inflict pain, and many people find themselves tormented by that aspect of the role. The combination of guilt and scriptlessness makes the rejector's role especially hard to play. Without a script, they cannot know the right way to act, and the lurking presence of guilt means that it is easy to do something wrong. The rejector's role may be experienced as a moral minefield: Disaster threatens any false step, but it is hard to tell in advance what is a false step and what is not.

Indeed, moral concerns were central to the rejector's experience, unlike the would-be lover's experience. A substantial part of the rejectors' accounts revolved around guilt and misdeeds. Many rejectors felt guilty. Many worried about doing the wrong thing. Some dwelled on their justifications for how they acted, acutely aware of the need to defend themselves. Some rejectors also reproached the would-be lovers with morally wrong behavior, such as breaking promises, lying, or using deceptive tactics. In short, rejectors show a strong tendency to see the episode of unrequited love in terms of morality, guilt, and justification, a dimension that was largely absent from the would-be lovers' accounts.

For most rejectors, the experience had little that was good or positive about it, and for others the only positive aspect they mentioned was a boost to their self-esteem. Simply put, many found it flattering to have someone attracted to them. This esteem boost was not, however, an important aspect of the experience for most rejectors. Even if it was noted, it typically occurred early in the episode and was overshadowed by other events later on. Moreover, if we recall that many would-be lovers are rejected because rejectors perceive them as inferior in attractiveness, then it becomes clear that the boost to self-esteem must be rather trivial. Being loved by a relatively un-attractive partner may be rather like receiving a compliment from a servant or subordinate: vaguely nice, perhaps, but without much im-pact. The fact that this other, inferior person thinks that you would be a suitable match for him or her may even be slightly insulting, which would further diminish the value of the compliment.

The later stages of the episode, seen through the rejector's eyes, often involve an increasingly unpleasant struggle. Any initial ambiva-lence or pleasure may be long forgotten. When one does finally bring oneself to confront the other and make the rejection explicit, the admirer may not accept it gracefully and go away; all too often the other person simply fails to get the message and keeps persisting. Many rejectors' accounts accorded a central place to the scene of rejection, in much the same way that men's war stories often feature a focal scene in which the man thought briefly that he was about to be killed. To the rejectors, that scene was the central event which they had hoped to avoid and toward which they had had to marshal all their moral courage and interpersonal skills. It was supposed to be the climax and the end. And then, to their surprise, the drama turned out to be far from over.

Thus, for many rejectors, the final scenes involved excessive, even obnoxious persistence by the rejected lover. Many rejectors por-trayed their admirers in highly unflattering terms, as self-deluded or even mentally ill individuals who needlessly prolonged the mutual ordeal.

One ought not, of course, to accept the rejectors' accounts at face value and uncritically. There may be exaggeration, distortion, shading, and even self-deception in their accounts, just as in the would-be lovers' accounts. Possibly they exaggerated in retrospect the clarity and finality of their message of rejection. Undoubtedly, rejectors wanted to be firm and clear but also gentle and considerate in rejecting the other person, and these motives pull one in contrary directions. For example, we quoted one woman who described her admirer in her account as "a total turn-off loser" and then elaborated by saying that he was unintelligent, shallow, and rather ugly. If rejectors would state such feelings in similarly plain words directly to their would-be lovers, we suspect that there would be far less excessive persistence. But of course the wish to be gentle and considerate militates strongly against any such candor.

When it actually comes down to telling the other person the bad news, therefore, rejectors may often surround the rejecting message with clichés, consolatory words, compliments, and even expressions of their own friendly affection. To the rejector, these may seem to be merely a way to ease the blow, but the would-be lover may end up perceiving the message as a mixture of good and bad things and may conclude that there is still hope after all.

Ultimately, it is necessary to realize that the function of the rejector's account (and hence of the stories that rejectors told us) is often to deal with the implication of guilt. The rejector's self-justifications often depend crucially on not having encouraged the other person and in fact on having made clear the impossibility of romantic attachment. It would not be surprising if rejectors' retrospective accounts embellished the clarity and moral purity of their actions.

All we have is the stories people told us, and so there is no way of knowing for certain what actually happened and what was actually said. Still, it is clear that rejectors struggle with feelings of guilt because of the central moral problem of their role: It is wrong to hurt someone, but it is also wrong to allow someone to go on loving in vain (because that will produce more hurt in the long run). The rejector walks a tightrope between being too harsh and not being harsh enough. Holding still—doing nothing—is often both morally unacceptable and pragmatically impossible. And even if the rejector manages this feat perfectly right, the other's response is likely to be distress and unhappiness. Without a script, the rejector must play a difficult and unpleasant role fraught with moral danger. It is not surprising that many rejectors look back with unmitigated negative feelings on these episodes.

Detour into Heartbreak

The would-be lovers' experiences have also received careful attention in these pages. Of course, no one sets out on a romantic quest knowing in advance that it is futile and hopeless. Would-be lovers see themselves on a journey to love. When it takes a wrong turn, often they still hope that the other's resistance is merely a delay or detour and that eventually they will succeed in winning the other's heart. Only gradually does the typical would-be lover recognize that the intended, desired love will never come to pass.

Their recollections have a bittersweet quality, capturing both ends of the affective spectrum, from elation and thrill to pain and disappointment. Many people clearly look back with some fond and pleasant feelings on their futile loves. To be sure, others are scarred and bitter, but as a group the would-be lovers showed a balance between good and bad feelings that was absent from the rejectors' accounts. Would-be lovers recall their experiences as emotional roller-coasters and often, in the final analysis, as adventures. As we have said, risk is part of the essential nature of adventure, and eventually people seem to accept that these adventures are worth having even if the risks do sometimes materialize in the form of heartbreak.

We have said that morality and guilt were central to the rejectors's stories while self-esteem issues comprised a relatively unimportant dimension. The reverse is true for the would-be lovers. Scarcely any would-be lovers spoke of feeling guilty, felt pressured to justify their actions, or described the incident in moral terms. Possibly one reason for this was that love does seem to justify a wide range of behavior, and to the extent that would-be lovers are motivated by love (the highest and purest of motives, in their view) they do not need to worry about guilt or moral reproach.

But esteem issues were central. From the initial fears of rejection that hamper one's efforts to declare one's love, to the retrospective efforts to restore one's pride, self-esteem issues permeated the would-be lovers' accounts. It was clear that romantic rejection is often a powerful blow to self-esteem. Moreover, broken-hearted lovers appear to endow the episode with meaning in such a way that will begin to restore their damaged sense of self-worth. Their accounts included a fair number of statements designed to reassert their personal worth or provide other evidence of their attractiveness and desirability. The implication is that rebuilding one's self-esteem is an important part of the coping and recovery process that follows heartbreak.

Just as the rejector's role is centrally concerned with the moral dilemma of how to hurt someone without doing anything wrong, the would-be lover's role revolves around an esteem dilemma. We have cast this in terms of Maslow's (1968) hierarchy of needs. According to Maslow's theory, love and belongingness needs take precedence over esteem needs. Unrequited love puts the two sets of needs in sharp opposition, and would-be lovers often have to choose between continuing their humiliating ordeal in the quest for love and attachment—and, alternatively, abandoning the quest for love in the hope of salvaging some dignity. Cultural scripts allow and even call for aspiring lovers to humble themselves and accept some loss of pride in pursuing their romantic suits, but these losses of esteem are often portrayed as temporary trials on the way to eventual romantic success. In unrequited love there is no success at the end. In many cases, longer persistence just brings more humiliation without altering the outcome. Accepting degradation can even make one's situation worse, because it sometimes lowers the desired partner's respect for the aspiring lover, thus making love impossible and producing the opposite of the intended result. (As one woman wrote, "desperation is NOT a turn-on!") It is not surprising that some would-be lovers wish in retrospect that they had salvaged more pride and dignity by making an earlier, more graceful exit.

For would-be lovers, then, the decisive issue in determining persistence is the impact of the episode on pride and self-esteem, and not the propriety of their actions or the discomfort of the rejector. Of course, they would probably not persist long in the face of certain failure or unambiguous rejection, but few aspiring lovers seem to have felt they received such clear rejections. In their views, typically, the person they loved was mercurial, and they saw a confusing mixture of both encouraging and discouraging signs.

The problem of mixed messages made it difficult for would-be lovers to know when to give up, and this uncertainty may be partly responsible for their long persistence that so vexed some of the rejectors. Unlike rejectors, aspiring lovers do not suffer from a problem of scriptlessness, for their roles have been well described and frequently portrayed. Their main script problem is the fact that unrequited love involves two scripts—aspiring, hopeful lover and recovering, heartbroken victim (or failure)—and they must somehow determine when to abandon the first script and take up the second. All the issues of persistence, mixed messages, self-deception, and so forth refer to this problem of script transition. In other words, there are fairly clear and standard guidelines for pursuing love, and there are also guidelines for how to recover from disappointment, but there are no clear guidelines for making the transition.

We noted at the start of this work that the early stages of romantic attraction have been linked to a need-based preoccupation with one's own feelings (Steck et al., 1982). This view has been amply confirmed by the accounts of would-be lovers. They emerged from this study as fairly unaware of what the rejector goes through. Their accounts acknowledged that they did not understand the rejector, that they became preoccupied or even obsessed with the episode, that they acted out of character, and even that they engaged in some degree of denial and self-deception. Meanwhile, they expressed little knowledge of the rejector's problems and reactions. Perhaps they did, dimly, sense that their attentions may have become unwelcome or even intrusive at times, but, being themselves overwhelmed with the catastrophe of doomed passion, they had little sympathy or compassion to spare for anyone else. From the rejector's point of view, it may eventually become a matter of simple courtesy and common decency to leave someone alone when that person doesn't want your love or finds your company upsetting, distasteful, or bothersome. But simple courtesy and common decency may be far from the mind of the person in the grip of unrequited romantic passion. Bourgeois conventions of ordinary politeness may seem much too petty to guide the actions of someone who sees himself or herself more or less as the star in an epic tragedy.

Ultimately, the aspiring lovers realize that the other is not going to change—that the detour is in fact a dead end. Some become angry, hurt, embittered, and some even harden themselves against taking another chance or seeking another love. But in time, most seem to get over the incident and even become able to look back on it with some positive, if wistful, feelings.

Common Ground

Although we have emphasized the differences between rejectors and would-be lovers, it is necessary to recognize that their experiences with unrequited love do have some similarities. Thus, for example, both sides find it difficult to express their feelings. The basis of this difficulty may differ somewhat: Would-be lovers are reluctant to express their attraction because they fear rejection, and rejectors are reluctant to express their lack of interest because of guilt and a fear of hurting the other person (and possibly out of a well-founded fear that the other will make an unpleasant, difficult scene; e.g., Tesser & Rosen, 1975). But both find it difficult to speak their hearts.

Likewise, neither may really want to hear about the other's feelings. Rejectors often cited their chagrin at the other's declaration of love. And aspiring lovers dreaded hearing the message of rejection.

Partly as a result of the bilateral reluctance to express one's true feelings, communication tends to be poor and muddled, and mutual understanding suffers. Our rejectors and would-be lovers expressed some inability to understand each other. Part of this is what we have called the *conspiracy of silence* in unrequited love. The one person doesn't want to speak the words of rejection, and the other doesn't want to hear it. Hence, inevitably, communication is poor and the two often disagree about whether there was mutual attraction and whether there was explicit rejection.

Perhaps ironically, both rejectors and would-be lovers sometimes end up feeling like victims. Would-be lovers are victims of heartbreak, of their own feelings, and perhaps of (someone they see as) a cruel or heartless rejector. Rejectors feel themselves to be victims of an intrusive, relentless, distressing pursuer whose unsought, unwanted affections seemingly cannot be discouraged. Not all rejectors or would-be lovers end up with such feelings, but there is a strong current of victimization on both sides of unrequited love.

The bilateral sense of victimization is related to a broader, and equally bilateral, sense of helplessness to control one's feelings. Rejectors insist that they did not deliberately or knowingly attract the other person's affections and, moreover, that they cannot help their inability to reciprocate the love. Would-be lovers do not see themselves as deliberately or knowingly causing themselves to fall in love, and they feel powerless to turn their feelings off. And, ironically, both sides occasionally appear to assume that the other person ought to be able to control his or her feelings. Would-be lovers sometimes act as if the other is being merely obstinate in refusing to reciprocate the love, and rejectors think the would-be lover ought to just give up and move on. The utter inability to exert conscious control over emotional states is mainly experienced in relation to one's own feelings, not the other person's.

Associated with the victimization and helplessness is a broad sense of passivity that runs through both sides of unrequited love. This is not to say that people fail to take action, and in fact many accounts contained both active and passive attitudes. But there is a strong element of passivity that is shared by the participants in unrequited love. There seems to be a sense that one is thrust, not by choice or inclination, into a powerful and unpleasant experience. A key aspect of this passivity is the interpersonal emotional contingency. Both rejectors and would-be lovers abruptly find that their lives and their emotional states have become heavily dependent on someone else. Thus, the suddenly enhanced awareness of being unable to control one's own feelings is compounded by feeling that someone else has a great deal of power over one's feelings.

And, ultimately, both rejectors and would-be lovers tend to be dissatisfied with the outcome of unrequited love. The tragedy is compounded by the fact that no one gains much of anything from it, except perhaps for the trite wisdom that often comes in the aftermath of sorry experiences. For society, perhaps, unrequited love has some value as part of the mating process, but individuals do not seem to benefit much from particular experiences of unrequited love, regardless of which side they are on.

Limitations and Unanswered Questions

This book was intended as a first step toward achieving an understanding of the phenomenon of unrequited love, and we hope it will not be the last. Before closing, therefore, it is helpful to say a few words about the limitations of our research and the questions that remain for further investigators.

Our sample consisted mainly of young, unmarried, white, American, heterosexual, middle-class adults. They are the logical place to begin a study of unrequited love, because one can assume that it is a recent and pressing concern for many of them, and clearly the majority of them were able to relate recent experiences on the themes we assigned them. But it would be desirable to check some of our conclusions with substantially different samples. In particular, people from non-Western cultures may find that love and its scripts and roles have been defined very differently for them than for us, and their experiences might be radically or fundamentally different. Another group that may be especially important to investigate is homosexuals, for (as we have noted at several points in this work) their love lives have an additional set of obstacles beyond those that heterosexuals have to contend with, and these additional obstacles may further complicate their experiences with unrequited love.

We were not centrally concerned with finding gender differences, and in fact very little in our data suggested a need to compare men with women. We did note a few areas, such as sexual exploitation, where unrequited love may follow different paths depending on gender. We noted that women report suffering more intensely then men when their hearts are broken, and (perhaps for that reason) we found a slight tendency for women to have more rejector experiences while men have more would-be lover experiences. For the most part, however, men and women seemed to tell rather similar stories.

Still, other researchers may find it desirable and valuable to develop and test hypotheses about how men and women may have different experiences in unrequited love. Moreover, the similarities between men and women in our sample probably reflect the liberal, progressive, egalitarian norms that govern gender relationships at modern Western universities. We suspect that the most valuable and fruitful research on gender differences in unrequited love would use non-university populations that have rigid, traditional norms and radically different roles for men and women. Perhaps the most important such extension of our work would be to include women who are culturally or normatively forbidden to take any initiative in pursuing love, because in our sample both men and women were relatively free to disclose their affections and initiate romantic contact.

Such work might also benefit from studying populations with substantially unequal sex ratios. One of the classic recent works on sex roles showed that patterns of interaction between men and women change dramatically depending on whether there is a relative surplus of men or of women (Guttentag & Secord, 1983). To belong to a statistical minority is to have more options for partners, and so perhaps unrequited love would be less traumatic in such a situation. In contrast, to belong to the majority gender might multiply the threat of unrequited love, because it will be that much harder to find another partner if there simply aren't enough members of the opposite sex to go around. The availability of alternative partners has been shown to have a significant effect on the maintenance and dissolution of romantic relationships (Rusbult, 1980, 1983), and we suspect it would have a definite if subtle effect on the beginnings of relationships too.

In our view, the most important and desirable extension of this work would look at personality differences and experiential patterns among people who characteristically or frequently find themselves in either the rejector's role or the would-be lover's position. We have assiduously avoided that aspect of the problem in our methodology, even to the extent of ensuring that our rejectors and would-be lovers were exactly the same people. This followed from our interest in how people in general experience unrequited love. But the study of particular types of chronic heartbreakers or frequently disappointed lovers also holds the promise of generating useful, scientifically interesting findings. A complete account of unrequited love should probably incorporate both aspects, that is, both the general principles that apply roughly to everyone in that situation, and the specific patterns and configurations that apply to the individuals who play those roles on a regular basis. It would also be useful to learn about how accounts or views change through repeated experiences of unrequited love.

Conclusion

For centuries, Western culture has increasingly espoused the view that to love someone is one of the highest, most pleasant and fulfilling states available to human beings. To be in love is regarded as one of the epitomes of human experience, and society indulges and envies people who are in love. But this view is plainly wrong. For the would-be lovers in our sample, being in love was painful, disappointing, and humiliating, even if it did have its pleasant aspects. Ultimately, persisting in love was intolerable.

In recent decades, psychological theory has increasingly advocated another view: that the most desirable and enviable state is *being loved* rather than loving. Whether this involves being the recipient of unconditional positive regard from a few intimately related other people (Rogers, 1959), or being the object of loving admiration by masses of strangers (Braudy, 1986), the point is that fulfillment comes to the recipient of love. This view, too, is inadequate. The rejectors in our sample had someone to love them, but the situation brought most of them neither joy nor satisfaction, let alone fulfillment. For many of them, it was acutely troubling and aversive.

It is the *mutuality* of love that is crucial for fulfillment. Neither loving nor being loved is desirable in itself, and either without the other eventually becomes unpleasant. Unrequited love is not generally fulfilling for either person. Love may yet hold the promise of some of the highest and most pleasant of human experiences, but only if one both loves and is loved in return.

Mathematicians use the term *zero-sum* to describe games in which there is a winner or a loser (as in chess) or in which the positive winnings and negative losings add up to zero (as in poker). Love is very definitely not a zero-sum affair. In some cases of love, especially those in which love is mutual, everyone wins. With unrequited love, everyone loses.

The importance of equity in human relationships has been asserted by social psychologists (e.g., Walster, Berscheid, & Walster, 1976). Equity exists when everyone involved contributes and benefits roughly the same amount as everyone else. Although one might suspect that people would want to find a relationship where they get more benefits and contribute less than the others, research shows that people are generally unhappy on *either* side of an inequitable relationship (Rook, 1987; Walster et al., 1976). Our investigation of unrequited love provides further support for that conclusion. Neither the would-be lover nor the rejector is pleased or satisfied with unrequited love. And both would-be lovers and rejectors sometimes concluded their accounts with specific statements that they had learned how essential equity is for a satisfactory relationship.

Unrequited love is not usually sought out or deliberately fostered by either person. It arises, instead, as a by-product of the mating process, stimulated by some contradictions in human nature. Patterns of desire do not match patterns of mating, and the result will be many futile desires—such as when people fall in love with someone more attractive than themselves, someone who is therefore unlikely to reciprocate that love. And people tend to overestimate their own good qualities and attractiveness while perhaps seeing others in more accurate terms. As a result, they may think themselves good enough to be an equitable, suitable mate for someone who will not agree at all with that appraisal.

Unrequited love, then, may be part of the mechanism that takes people who are driven by desire and illusion and channels them into the sober satisfactions of properly matched, equitable relationships. Finding the right mate is, to some extent, a matter of trial and error. Unrequited love contitutes the "error" part of trial and error, and it provides the painful stimulus to learn, perhaps, how to make a better choice on one's next trial.

Yet some might object that such a characterization is too banal and unromantic, and they may be right. It is perhaps too reductionistic to describe love, even unrequited love, merely as part of a channeling or mating function. Romantic love is, perhaps above all, one of the supreme adventures in human life, and adventures carry risks. Mountain climbers sometimes fall; swimmers and sailors sometimes drown; fliers sometimes crash; and lovers sometimes come to grief and heartbreak. None of this is likely to be much consolation to the person whose love is unreciprocated, and it offers even less solace to the vexed, helpless, and uncertain target of unwanted affections. Then again, it is not entirely fair or appropriate to ask someone's opinion of a sport right after he or she has broken a bone while playing it. Heartbreak reveals some of the main risks and dangers of love, and it punctures some of people's illusions about life, love, and precious self-worth. Yet who, except perhaps for a few unrequited lovers and their equally hapless rejectors, would wish that human beings could find their mates on the basis of sober logic and passionless common sense?

Appendix

This book is based on a research project conducted at Case Western Reserve University. We collected the data during the fall of 1989 and did the bulk of the coding during 1990. We wish to thank Rebecca Lasek for her assistance with the coding. A follow-up study was conducted in the fall of 1991 (Baumeister, Wotman, & Stillwell, in press).

Research participants were 71 subjects enrolled in upper-level psychology courses. All students in the course were asked to participate and most of them complied. They were assured of anonymity and were requested not to use real names on the questionnaire materials. Informed consent and extra-credit forms were kept separate from the questionnaires, so that no responses would be individually identifiable. Although some older, nontraditional students took part, the majority of respondents were in their early 20s and predominantly middle-class. Both males and females were well represented in the sample, with a slightly higher (62%) proportion of females.

Each subject was asked to furnish two stories. Seven subjects failed to write the second story, so only one story was obtained from them. One of the missing stories was a rejector story and the other six were would-be lover stories. Thus, the final sample consisted of 134 stories.

The data were collected in a series of group sessions. Subjects were given an initial oral briefing that emphasized the study of personally important, emotionally powerful experiences. Each subject wrote two stories, one from the rejector's perspective and one from the would-be lover's perspective. The instructions for the rejector condition began by saying, "Please write a true story from your life in which someone was romantically attracted to you and the attraction was not mutual (you were not romantically attracted to that person). Nearly everyone has experienced such things more than once; please choose an especially powerful and memorable experience." Further instructions asked subjects to be thorough and "tell the full story." The instructions for the would-be lover condition were identical except for the first sentence, which was changed to read, " . . . in which you were romantically attracted to someone and the attraction was not mutual (the other person was not romantically attracted to you)."

Subjects then wrote until they were finished. Upon handing in their questionnaires, subjects were given written debriefing forms that explained the purposes, goals, and methods of the research.

The handwritten stories were typed by a secretary in order to prevent any effects of handwriting on the coding and to provide a further shield for the anonymity of participants. One judge, blind to the main hypotheses, coded all the accounts in a random order. Two other judges each coded part of the stories for the purpose of computing reliabilities. Discrepancies were discussed briefly, and the final coding reflected the consensus.

Coding was done on dichotomous dimensions rather than continuous or quasi-continuous scales. Coding thus involved judging each story as to the presence or absence of the specified feature. We have found dichotomous coding to be clearer, more reliable, and more effective than quasi-continuous scales in previous research (see Baumeister, 1988b, 1989; Baumeister, Stillwell, & Wotman, 1990).

Some stories could not be coded because of ambiguity or irrelevance of the dimension. These "maybe" codings were kept to a minimum (less than 1%) by the rule that if a feature was absent from a story, it was coded as "no." Stories coded "maybe" were deleted from analyses on that dimension, and so different analyses have slightly different Ns. In the analyses, the number of "maybe" codings is the difference between 134 and the N.

Interrater agreements (prior to discussion) were computed for 57 items. The proportion of agreements between raters ranged from .750 to .972, with a mean of .9039. Cohen's kappa ranged from .500 to .944, with a mean of .809. The codings thus appear to have been adequately reliable. "Maybe" codings were not used for the computation of reliabilities. A few dimensions were coded later as conceptual analysis yielded further or supplementary questions, and since they were done later they were not available for the interrater reliability analyses; because the same raters and procedures were used for these late ratings, reliability on those dimensions is presumably similar to what was obtained on the other dimensions.

Percentages and statistics are presented for the major findings in the following tables. In all cases, the number under the "Rejectors" column refers to the percentage of rejectors who were codable on that dimension and whose accounts contained the feature being coded. The number under the "Would-be Lovers" column represents the same for would-be lovers. The Chi^2 column represents the computation of that statistic for the difference between the rejectors and would-be lovers. All Chi^2 analyses are based on one degree of freedom and $N = 134$ minus the number of "maybe" codings, which ranged from 0 to 12. The "Significance" column refers to the statistical significance of the Chi^2 result, according to the following (standard) notation: $\star$ p<.05; $\star\star$ p<.01; $\star\star\star$ p<.001.

The first table presents the findings relevant to emotion. They refer to whether the story referred to the existence of positive or negative emotions during the episode and, also, in retrospect; the indication of some wish that the event had never occurred, which included portraying the incident as a wholly negative or undesirable experience; indications of reluctance to reject, fear of being rejected, feelings of longing or preoccupation with the love object; and indications that the rejector was flattered or annoyed by the would-be lover's attentions.

TABLE 1. Emotion

| Dimension | Percent coded as yes | | | |
	Rejectors	Would-be lovers	Significance	Chi²
Positive emotions	57.1	98.4	★★★	32.061
Positive affect in retrospect	33.3	53.1	★	5.311
Negative emotions	70.0	43.8	★★	9.42
Wish it never happened	21.4	6.4	★	6.157
Rejector felt reluctant to deliver rejection	60.9	17.5	★★★	24.174
Would-be lover feared rejection	7.1	22.2	★	6.157
Would-be lover had feelings of longing, preoccupation	27.0	46.0	★	4.930
Rejector felt flattered	23.5	1.6	★★★	13.704
Rejector felt annoyed	51.4	3.1	★★★	38.396

*p<.05
**p<.01
***p<.001

The key dimensions on self-esteem are presented in Table 2. All of these refer to the author of the story. That is, did the author indicate that his or her self-esteem was raised or lowered during or by the incident? And did the account contain some self-enhancing statements by the author?

Next, Table 3 focuses on issues related to guilt and morality. The first item refers to saying that the rejector felt guilty in the incident. (Would-be lovers did not feel guilty.) The self-justification item refers to the author of the story, whether rejector or would-be lover, and represents whether the author offered any statements that would assert the moral correctness or defensibility of the way he or she acted. The last two items refer to indications of unscrupulous, underhanded, or morally objectionable tactics.

TABLE 2. Self-Esteem

	Percent coded as yes			
Dimension	Rejectors	Would-be lovers	Significance	Chi²
Self-esteem raised	15.7	4.7	★	4.34
Self-esteem lowered	1.4	49.2	★★★	41.426
Self-enhancing statements	7.1	42.2	★★★	22.588

*p<.05
**p<.01
***p<.001

Table 4 involves references to various events. Stories were coded as "yes" if they contained the relevant event.

Next, Table 5 involves interpersonal perceptions and judgments. If the item mentions a role, then that role relationship was what was coded for all stories. Otherwise, the item refers to the story's author. Thus, "praising statements about other" refers to whether the author of the story made praising statements about the person in the coun-

TABLE 3. Guilt and Moral Issues

	Percent coded as yes			
Dimension	Rejectors	Would-be lovers	Significance	Chi²
Rejector felt guilty	33.8	3.1	★★★	20.238
Self-justifications	35.7	12.5	★★	9.706
Unscrupulous tactics used by would-be lover	21.7	0.0	★★	7.254
Unscrupulous tactics used by rejector	5.7	14.1	ns	2.66

*p<.05
**p<.01
***p<.001

TABLE 4. Events

| Dimension | Percent coded as yes | | | |
	Rejectors	Would-be lovers	Significance	Chi²
Feelings were initially reciprocated	19.1	35.5	★	4.415
Love was communicated	97.1	82.1	★	8.124
Rejector led the other on	24.2	54.8	★★★	12.572
Overt, explicit rejection	49.3	23.8	★★	9.026
Would-be lover persisted	61.4	15.6	★★★	29.337

*p<.05
**p<.01
***p<.001

TABLE 5. Perceptions

| Dimension | Percent coded as yes | | | |
	Rejectors	Would-be lovers	Significance	Chi²
Praising statements about other	43.5	59.4	<.10	3.358
Would-be lover idealized other	10.3	26.6	★	5.866
Devaluing statements about other	52.2	25.0	★★★	10.297
Self-deception by would-be lover	40.6	18.8	★★	7.524
Self-deception by rejector	4.3	3.1	n.s.	<1.
Rejector mysterious to other	2.9	39.1	★★★	27.238
Would-be lover seemed mysterious to other	20.0	1.6	★★★	11.433
Rejector was considerate	55.9	37.7	★	4.262

*p<.05
**p<.01

TABLE 6. Additional Analyses.

	Percent coded as yes			
Dimension	Rejectors	Would-be lovers	Significance	Chi²
Conceal own feelings	7.1	19.1	★	4.215
Lost possibilities	7.3	18.8	★	3.941
Self acted out of character	4.3	15.9	★	5.048
Author portrayed self as passive	78.6	63.5	<.10	3.694
Author felt guilty	33.8	0.0	★★★	26.2148
Deny that rejector led would-be lover on	38.6	15.6	★★★	22.588
Author indicated scriptlessness	18.6	6.7	★	4.582

★p<.05
★★p<.01
★★★p<.001

terpart role: The first column indicates that 43.5% of rejectors made praising statements about their admirers, and the second indicates that 59.4% of would-be lovers included praise of their beloved rejector.

The previous tables are grouped for the sake of convenience. Additional dimensions are covered above. All of them except one refer to the author of the story; the exception is the dimension "deny that rejector led would-be lover on" which codes whether the story included some explicit or clear statement that the rejector did *not* act so as to encourage the romantic feelings of the would-be lover.

References

Abbey, A. (1982). Sex differences in attributions for friendly behavior: Do males misperceive females' friendliness? *Journal of Personality and Social Psychology, 42*, 830–888.

Aronson, E., & Linder, D. E. (1965). Gain and loss of esteem as determinants of interpersonal attractiveness, *Journal of Experimental Social Psychology, 1*, 156–171

Averill, J. (1979). The functions of grief. In C. Izard (Ed.), *Emotions in personality and psychopathology* (pp. 339–368). New York: Plenum.

Averill, J. (1980). A constructivist view of emotion. In R. Plutchik & H. Kellerman (Eds.), *Theories of emotion* (pp. 305–339). Orlando, FL: Academic Press.

Averill, J. (1982). *Anger and aggression: An essay on emotion*. New York: Springer-Verlag.

Banagi, M. R., & Crowder, R. G. (1989). The bankruptcy of everyday memory. *American Psychologist, 44*, 1185–1193.

Baumeister, R. F. (1982). A self-presentational view of social phenomena. *Psychological Bulletin, 91*, 3–26.

Baumeister, R. F. (1988a). Masochism as escape from self. *Journal of Sex Research, 25*, 28–59.

Baumeister, R. F. (1988b). Gender differences in masochistic scripts. *Journal of Sex Research, 25*, 478–499.

Baumeister, R. F. (1989) *Masochism and the Self*. Hillsdale, NJ: Erlbaum.

Baumeister, R.F. (1991). *Meanings of Life*. New York: Guilford Press.

Baumeister, R. F., & Scher, S. J. (1988). Self-defeating behavior patterns among normal individuals: Review and analysis of common self-destructive tendencies. *Psychological Bulletin, 104*, 3–22.

Baumeister, R. F., & Stillwell, A. (1992). Autobiographical accounts, situational roles, and motivated biases: When stories don't match up. In J. Harvey, T. Orbuch, & A. Wever (Eds.), *Accounts, attributions, and close relationships* (pp. 52–70). New York: Springer-Verlag.

Baumeister, R. F., Stillwell, A. M., & Heatherton, T. F. (in press). Guilt as interpersonal phenomenon: Two studies with autobiographical narratives. In J. P. Tangney & K. W. Fischer (Eds.), *Self-conscious emotions: Shame, guilt, embarrassment, and pride*. New York: Guilford Press.

Baumeister, R.F., Stillwell, A., & Wotman, S.R. (1990). Victim and perpetrator accounts of interpersonal conflict: Autobiographical narratives about anger. *Journal of Personality and Social Psychology, 59*, 994–1005.

Baumeister, R. F., & Tice, D. M. (1990). Anxiety and social exclusion. *Journal of Social and Clinical Psychology, 9*, 165–195.

Baumeister, R. F., Wotman, S. R., & Stillwell, A. M. (in press). Unrequited love: On heartbreak, anger, guilt, scriptlessness, and humiliation. *Journal of Personality and Social Psychology*.

Bellah, R.N., Madsen, R., Sullivan, W.M., Swidler, A., & Tipton, S.M. (1985). *Habits of the heart: Individualism and commitment in American life*. Berkeley, CA: University of California Press.

Berscheid, E., & Walster, E. (1978). *Interpersonal attraction*. Reading, MA: Addison-Wesley.

Bonnar, J.W., & McGee, R.K. (1977). Suicidal behavior as a form of communication in married couples. *Suicide and Life-Threatening Behavior, 7*, 7–16.

Bowlby, J. (1969). *Attachment and loss. Vol 1: Attachment*. New York: Basic Books.

Bowlby, J. (1973). *Attachment and loss. Vol 2: Separation anxiety and anger*. New York: Basic Books.

Braudy, L. (1986). *The frenzy of renown: Fame and its history*. New York: Oxford University Press.

Byrne, D. (1971). *The attraction paradigm*. New York: Academic Press.

Conway, M., & Ross, M. (1984). Getting what you want by revising what you had. *Journal of Personality and Social Psychology, 47*, 738–748.

Darley, J.M., & Goethals, G.R. (1980). People's analyses of the causes of ability-linked performances. In L. Berkowitz (Ed.), *Advances in experimental social psychology* (v. 13), 1–37. New York: Academic Press.

De Rougemont, D. (1956). *Love in the Western world* (M. Belgion, trans.). New York: Pantheon.

Des Barres, P. (1987). *I'm with the band: Confessions of a groupie.* New York: Jove.

Dion, K.K., & Dion, K.L. (1975). Self-esteem and romantic love. *Journal of Personality, 43,* 39–57.

Douglas, J.D. (1967). *The social meanings of suicide.* Princeton, NJ: Princeton University Press.

Duck, S. (1982a) (Ed.). *Personal relationships 4: Dissolving personal relationships.* London: Academic Press.

Duck, S. (1982b). A topography of relationship disengagement and dissolution. In S. Duck (Ed.), *Personal relationships 4: Dissolving personal relationships* (pp. 1–30). London: Academic Press.

Festinger, L. (1957). *A theory of cognitive dissonance.* Stanford, CA: Stanford University Press.

Fincham, F.D., Beach, S.P., & Baucom, D.H. (1987). Attributional processes in distressed and nondistressed couples: 4. Self-partner attribution differences. *Journal of Personality and Social Psychology, 52,* 739–748.

Folkes, V.S. (1982). Communicating the reasons for social rejection. *Journal of Experimental Social Psychology, 18,* 235–252.

Freedman, J.L., & Fraser, S. (1966). Compliance without pressure: The foot-in-the-door technique. *Journal of Personality and Social Psychology, 4,* 195–202.

Frijda, N.H. (1986). *The emotions.* New York: Cambridge University Press.

Frijda, N.H., Kuipers, P., & ter Shure, E. (1989). Relations among emotion, appraisal, and emotional action readiness. *Journal of Personality and Social Psychology, 57,* 212–228.

Gergen, K.J., & Gergen, M. (1988). Narrative and the self as relationship. In L. Berkowitz (Ed.), *Advances in experimental social psychology* (Vol. 21, pp. 17–56). San Diego, CA: Academic Press.

Gonzales, M.H., Pederson, J.H., Manning, D.J., & Wetter, D.W. (1990). Pardon my gaffe: Effects of sex, status, and consequence severity on accounts. *Journal of Personality and Social Psychology, 58,* 610–621.

Greenberg, J., Pyszczynski, T., & Solomon, S. (1986). The causes and consequences of self-esteem: A terror management theory. In R. Baumeister (Ed.), *Public self and private self* (pp. 189–212). New York: Springer-Verlag.

Guttentag, M., & Secord, P.F. (1983). *Too many women? The sex ratio question.* Beverly Hills, CA: Sage.

Harvey, J.H., Flanary, R., & Morgan, M. (1988). Vivid memories of vivid loves gone by. *Journal of Social and Personal Relationships, 3,* 359–373.

Harvey, J.H., Weber, A.L., Galvin, K.S., Huszti, H.C., & Garnick, N.N. (1986). Attribution in the termination of close relationships: A special focus on the account. In R. Gilmour & S. Duck (Eds.), *The emerging field of personal relationships* (pp. 189–201). Hillsdale, NJ: Erlbaum.

Harvey, J.H., Weber, A.L., & Orbuch, T.L. (1990). *Interpersonal accounts: A social psychological perspective*. Oxford, England: Basil Blackwell.

Hatfield, E., & Sprecher, S. (1986). Measuring passionate love in intimate relationships. *Journal of Adolescence, 9*, 383–410.

Hazan, C., & Shaver, P. (1987). Romantic love conceptualized as an attachment process. *Journal of Personality and Social Psychology, 52*, 511–524.

Higgins, E.T. (1987). Self-discrepancy: A theory relating self and affect. *Psychological Review, 94*, 319–340.

Hill, C.T., Rubin, Z., & Peplau, L.A. (1976). Breakups before marriage: The end of 103 affairs. *Journal of Social Issues, 32*, 147–168.

Hogan, R. (1983). A socioanalytic theory of personality. In M. Page & R. Dienstbier (Eds.), *Nebraska Symposium on Motivation* (pp. 55–89). Lincoln, NE: University of Nebraska Press.

Hoffman, M.L. (1982). Development of prosocial motivation: Empathy and guilt. In N. Eisenberg (Ed.), *The development of prosocial behavior* (pp. 281–313). New York: Academic Press.

Holtzworth-Munroe, A., & Jacobson, N.S. (1985). Causal attributions of married couples: When do they search for causes? What do they conclude when they do? *Journal of Personality and Social Psychology, 48*, 1398–1412.

Janoff-Bulman, R. (1989). Assumptive worlds and the stress of traumatic events: Applications of the schema construct. *Social Cognition, 7*, 113–136.

Jensen, A. (1977). Genetic and behavioral effects of nonrandom mating. In C.E. Noble, R.T. Osborne, & N. Weyl (Eds.), *Human variation: Biogenetics of age, race, and sex*. New York: Academic Press.

Jones, E.E., Rock, L., Shaver, K.G., Goethals, G.R., & Ward, L.M. (1968). Pattern of performance and ability attribution. An unexpected primacy effect. *Journal of Personality and Social Psychology, 10*, 317–340.

Jones, E.E., & Wortman, C. (1973) *Ingratiation: An attributional approach*. Morristown, NJ: General Learning Press.

Katz, J. (1988). *Seductions of crime: The moral and sensual attractions of doing evil*. New York: Basic Books.

Kaufman, S.R. (1986). *The ageless self: Sources of meaning in late life*. New York: Meridian.

Kelley, H. H., & Thibaut, J. W. (1978). *Interpersonal relations: A theory of interdependence*. New York: Wiley.

Kenny, D.A., & Nasby, W. (1980). Splitting the reciprocity correlation. *Journal of Personality and Social Psychology, 38*, 249–256.

Kihlstrom, J.F., Cantor, N., Albright, J.S., Chew, B.R., Klein, S.B., & Niedenthal, P.M. (1988). Information processing and the study of the self. In L. Berkowitz (Ed.), *Advances in experimental social psychology* (Vol. 21, pp. 145–178). San Diego, CA: Academic Press.

Langer, E., Blank, A., & Chanowitz, B. (1979). The mindlessness of ostensibly thoughtful action: The role of "placebic" information in interpersonal interaction. *Journal of Personality and Social Psychology, 36*, 635–642.

Lerner, M.J., & Matthews, G. (1967). Reactions to suffering of others under conditions of indirect responsibility. *Journal of Personality and Social Psychology, 5*, 319–325.

Levenson, R.W., & Gottman, J.M. (1985). Physiological and affective predictors of change in relationship satisfaction. *Journal of Personality and Social Psychology,49*, 85–94.

Lewis, H. B. (1971). *Shame and guilt in neurosis.* New York: International Universities Press.

Macfarlane, A. (1986). *Marriage and love in England: Modes of reproduction 1300–1840.* Oxford, England: Basil Blackwell.

Maroldo, G.K. (1982). Shyness and love on a college campus. *Perceptual and Motor Skills, 55*, 819–824.

Maslow, A.H. (1968). *Toward a psychology of being.* New York: Van Nostrand.

Maugham, W.S. (1963). *Of human bondage.* New York: Viking Penguin. Originally published in 1915.

McAdams, D.P. (1985). *Power, intimacy and the life story: Personological inquiries into identity.* Homewood, IL: Dorsey.

McGraw, K.M. (1987). Guilt following transgression: An attribution of responsibility approach. *Journal of Personality and Social Psychology, 53*, 247–256.

Muehlenhard, C.L., & Hallabaugh, L.C. (1988). Do women sometimes say no when they mean yes? The prevalence and correlates of women's token resistance to sex. *Journal of Personality and Social Psychology, 54*, 872–879.

Murstein, B.I., & Christy, P. (1976). Physical attractiveness and marriage adjustment in middle-aged couples. *Journal of Personality and Social Psychology, 34*, 537–542.

Newman, K. S. (1988). *Falling from grace: The experience of downward mobility in the American middle class.* New York: Free Press.

Pines, M., & Aronson, E. (1983). Antecedents, correlates, and consequences of sexual jealousy. *Journal of Personality, 51*, 108–135.

Rodin, M.J. (1982). Non-engagement, failure to engage, and disengagement. In S. Duck (Ed.), *Personal relationships 4: Dissolving personal relationships* (pp. 31–49). London: Academic Press.

Rogers, C.R. (1959). A theory of therapy, personality, and interpersonal relationships, as developed in the client-centered framework. In S. Koch (Ed.), *Psychology: A study of a science* (Vol. 3, pp. 184–256). New York: McGraw-Hill.

Rook, K.S. (1987). Reciprocity of social exchange and social satisfaction among older women. *Journal of Personality and Social Psychology, 52,* 145–154.

Rosen, S., Johnson, R.D., Johnson, M.J., & Tesser, A. (1973). Interactive effects of news valence and attraction on communicator behavior. *Journal of Personality and Social Psychology, 28,* 298–300.

Rosenbaum, M.E. (1986). The repulsion hypothesis: On the nondevelopment of relationships. *Journal of Personality and Social Psychology, 51,*1156–1166.

Ross, M. (1988, August) *Memory in a social context.* Invited address, American Psychological Association, Athens, GA.

Ross, M., & Holmberg, D. (1990). Recounting the past: Gender differences in the recall of events in the history of a close relationship. In J.M. Olson & M.P. Zanna (Eds.), *Self-inference processes: The Ontario symposium, Vol 6.* Hillsdale, NJ: Erlbaum.

Rubin, Z. (1970). Measurement of romantic love. *Journal of Personality and Social Psychology, 16,* 265–273.

Rusbult, C.E. (1980). Commitment and satisfaction in romantic associations: A test of the investment model. *Journal of Experimental Social Psychology, 16,* 172–186.

Rusbult, C.E. (1983). A longitudinal test of the investment model: The development (and deterioration) of satisfaction and commitment in heterosexual involvements. *Journal of Personality and Social Psychology, 45,* 101–117.

Schlenker, B.R. (1982). Translating actions into attitudes: An identity-analytic explanation of social conduct. In L. Berkowitz (Ed.), *Advances in experimental social psychology* (Vol 15, pp. 193–247). New York: Academic Press.

Schönbach, P. (1990). *Account episodes: The management or escalation of conflict.* Cambridge, England: Cambridge University Press.

Shanteau, J., & Wagy, U. (1979). Probability of acceptance in dating choice. *Journal of Personality and Social Psychology, 37,* 522–533.

Shaver, P., Hazan, C., & Bradshaw, D. (1988). Love as attachment: The integration of three behavioral systems. In R. J. Sternberg & M. L. Barnes (Eds.), *The psychology of love.* (pp. 68–99). New Haven, CT: Yale University Press.

Sichrovsky, P. (1988). *Born guilty: Children of Nazi families* (J. Steinberg, trans.). New York: Basic Books.

Simpson, J.A. (1987). The dissolution of romantic relationships: Factors involved in relationship stability and emotional distress. *Journal of Personality and Social Psychology, 53,* 683–692.

Smith, D.F., & Hokland, M. (1988). Love and salutogenesis in late adolescence: A preliminary investigation. *Psychology: A Journal of Human Behavior, 25,* 44–49.

Snyder, M., & Simpson, J.A. (1984). Self-monitoring and dating relationships. *Journal of Personality and Social Psychology, 47,* 1281–1291.

Steck, L., Levitan, D., McLane, D., & Kelley, H.H. (1982). Care, need, and conceptions of love. *Journal of Personality and Social Psychology, 43,* 481–491.

Sternberg, R.J. (1986). A triangular theory of love. *Psychological Review, 93,* 119–135.

Stone, L. (1977) *The family, sex and marriage in England 1500–1800.* New York: Harper & Row.

Sullivan, H. S. (1953). *The interpersonal theory of psychiatry.* New York: W. W. Norton.

Tangney, J.P. (1991). Moral affect: The good, the bad, and the ugly. *Journal of Personality and Social Psychology, 61,* 598–607.

Tannahill, R. (1980). *Sex in history.* New York: Stein & Day.

Taylor, E. (1963). *The fall of the dynasties: The collapse of the old order 1905–1922.* New York: Dorset.

Taylor, S. E. (1983). Adjustment to threatening events: A theory of cognitive adaptation. *American Psychologist,38,* 1161–1173.

Taylor, S.E. (1989). *Positive illusions: Creative self-deception and the healthy mind.* New York: Basic Books.

Taylor, S.E., & Brown, J.D. (1988). Illusion and well-being: A social psychological perspective on mental health. *Psychological Bulletin, 103,* 193–210.

Tennov, D. (1979). *Love and limerence: The experience of being in love.* New York: Stein and Day.

Tesser, A. (1988). Toward a self-evaluation maintenance model of social behavior. In L. Berkowitz (Ed.), *Advances in experimental social psychology* (Vol. 21, pp. 181–277). New York: Academic Press.

Tesser, A., & Rosen, S. (1975). The reluctance to transmit bad news. In L. Berkowitz (Ed.), *Advances in experimental social psychology* (Vol. 8, pp. 193–232). New York: Academic Press.

Tyler, T.R., & Sears, D.O. (1977). Coming to like obnoxious people when we must live with them. *Journal of Personality and Social Psychology, 35,* 200–211.

Vaughan, D. (1986). *Uncoupling.* New York: Oxford University Press.

Walster, E., Aronson, V., Abrahams, D., & Rottman, L. (1966). Importance of physical attractiveness in dating behavior. *Journal of Personality and Social Psychology, 4,* 508–516.

Walster, E., Berscheid, E., and Walster, G.W. (1976). New directions in equity research. In L. Berkowitz (Ed.), *Advances in experimental social psychology* (Vol. 9, pp. 1–42). New York: Academic Press.

Weiss, J.M. (1971). Effects of punishing the coping response (conflict) on stress pathology in rats. *Journal of Comparative and Physiological Psychology,* 77, 14–21.

Zahn-Waxler, C., & Kochanska, G. (1990). The origins of guilt. In R.A. Thompson (Ed.), *The Nebraska symposium on motivation 1988: Socioemotional development.* (Vol. 36, pp. 182–258). Lincoln, NE: University of Nebraska Press.

Zuckerman, M. (1979). Attribution of success and failure revisited, or: The motivational bias is alive and well in attribution theory. *Journal of Personality,* 47, 245–287.

Index